What the Airlines Never Tell You

by Maureen Clarke

IDG Books Worldwide, Inc.
An International Data Group Company
Foster City, CA • Chicago, IL
Indianapolis, IN • New York, NY

ABOUT THE AUTHOR

Maureen Clarke is the editor-in-chief of *Lehigh Valley Magazine*. She has written for *The Village Voice*, *Aperture*, and the *Daily News*, among other publications. A former staff editor at *Artforum* and the Aperture Foundation, she also edits exhibition catalog text for the Guggenheim Museum.

IDG BOOKS WORLDWIDE, INC.

An International Data Group Company
919 E. Hillsdale Blvd.
Suite 400
Foster City, CA 94404

Find us online at **www.frommers.com**

ISBN 0-02-863594-9
ISSN 1524-1491

Editor: Kelly Regan
Production Editor: Donna Wright
Design by Amy Trombat
Page Creation by John Bitter, Eric Brinkman, and Kendra Span
Cover Illustration by George McKeon

Manufactured in the United States of America

5   4   3   2   1

CONTENTS

Acknowledgments

Special thanks to Paul Hudson, executive director of the Aviation Consumer Action Project; Ed Perkins, consumer advocate for the American Society of Travel Agents; and Mike Spring, publisher of the Frommer's Travel Guides.

My fullest gratitude goes to my editor, Kelly Regan, for her friendship, and deft editing; to my parents, Pat and Pat Clarke, for giving me safe harbor; and to George Magalios, for his patient support and good cheer.

An Invitation to the Reader

In researching this book, we discovered many useful tips and helpful resources—Web sites, hot lines, books, and more. We're sure you'll find others. Please tell us about them, so we can share the information with your fellow travelers in upcoming editions. If you were disappointed with a recommendation, we'd love to know that, too. Please write to:

> *Frommer's What the Airlines Never Tell You*
> Frommer's Travel Guides
> 1633 Broadway
> New York, NY 10019

An Additional Note

Please be advised that travel information is subject to change at any time—and this is especially true of prices. We therefore suggest that you write or call ahead for confirmation when making your travel plans. The author, editors, and publisher cannot be held responsible for the experiences of readers while traveling. Your safety is important to us, however, so we encourage you to stay alert and be aware of your surroundings. Keep a close eye on cameras, purses, and wallets, all favorite targets of thieves and pickpockets.

Find Frommer's Online

www.frommers.com offers up-to-the-minute listings on almost 200 cities around the globe—including the latest bargains and candid, personal articles updated daily by Arthur Frommer himself. No other Web site offers such comprehensive and timely coverage of the world of travel.

INTRODUCTION

FLIGHTMARE

SINCE DEREGULATION IN 1978, THE AIRLINE INDUSTRY HAS been moving up, up, and away from consumer concerns with renegade abandon—a gradual, but exponentially faster ascent toward greater profits and fewer responsibilities toward the public.

In 1998, customer complaints to the Department of Transportation rose 26% from the previous year. In February 1999, the University of Michigan surveyed 2,000 adults from across the nation regarding customer satisfaction with various industries. The airline business fell near the bottom of the heap, ranking 31 out of 34.

Passengerrights.com, a New Jersey–based Web site that files public complaints about airline service with the Department of Transportation, logged 72,000 hits from 3,100 users over a 2-day period in early 1999.

Although America's domestic airlines transported a record 611 million passengers in 1998 without a single fatality, planes are more crowded than ever: over one million passengers were bumped from overbooked flights in 1998. The hub system has made for fewer direct flights, longer segmented flights, and more last-minute reroutings and schedule changes. While airlines are cracking down on the permissible number of carry-on bags per passenger, nearly $2^{1}/_{2}$ million air travelers suffered lost or mishandled luggage in 1998; that's one incident of bungling for every 200 bags traveling through the system—an all-time high.

Fewer customer amenities are available on board major carriers. Southwest Airlines arrived in the market in 1971, and proudly eliminated meals in order to curtail operating costs and lower the price of flight. Other major carriers have followed suit—cutting meals on many domestic flights and charging extra for in-flight movies and alcohol—and yet fares have not dropped as recompense for diminished services.

In 1998 the U.S. Justice Department began an investigation into the major airlines' anticompetitive practices toward start-up budget airlines like Vanguard and Sun Jet; American, Continental, and Northwest will go on trial in October 2000. The safety and operating standards of some low-cost carriers have come into question in the wake of ValuJet's 1996 crash in the Florida Everglades; but their existence has served to make the marketplace more competitive, which helps to lower ticket prices.

Currently, the government regulates the airline industry only in regard to safety and smoking (see chapter 5, "Life Preservers"), oversold flights (see chapter 1, "Ticketing Pitfalls"), and lost or mishandled luggage (see chapter 3, "Lost in Space"). Otherwise, nothing comes between you and your carrier except the "conditions of carriage," which spells out the minimum services each airline agrees to provide in exchange for the fare you pay. This contract, however minimal its stipulations, is your one legal recourse should an airline fail to satisfy the terms of its own agreement.

Vice-President Al Gore and members of Congress have tried to intervene with passenger-rights proposals that would increase the airlines' responsibility toward consumers. The prospective legislation would double the maximum compensation due passengers who are bumped from scheduled flights. Also, tickets would be refundable for the first 48 hours after purchase.

Airlines would have to announce and provide an explanation for flight cancellations and delays when such scheduling problems were known in advance. They would have to disclose the number of seats available to frequent fliers on each flight. Airline reservationists would have to mention all available fares—including discounted tickets offered through e-mail programs and Web sites. Finally, carriers would have to hold ticket reservations for at least 24 hours, so consumers would have time to comparison shop.

The Air Transport Association, the main lobbying group for the airlines, drafted guidelines for its member carriers in August 1999, to attempt to improve the quality of service from within—and to stave off government intervention. The guidelines only dimly recall the passenger rights proposals pending in Congress, however, and they're not binding in the least. In fact, many industry experts consider them a joke. American Airlines even posted a new "customer service plan" on its Web site with this caveat: "The Customer Service Plan does not create contractual or legal rights.... We are not responsible for any ... instances in which we do not meet our service goals."

The bottom line is that the airline industry spent over $16 million on lobbying in 1998. Consumers spent next to nothing. Until the airlines are held responsible for their own policies, the onus is on you, the consumer, to protect yourself. Fortunately, you can avert a host of mishaps with the right information. This book will help you learn how to fly more efficiently, comfortably, and inexpensively.

Among other things, you will:

- Find out which airlines provide the best service in regard to promptness, luggage handling, and safety.

- Learn what to anticipate if your flight is oversold or canceled, if your bags are lost or stolen, or if you are flying with a disability.

- See how to use the Internet to snare rock-bottom fares, earn bonus frequent-flier miles, and land the best seat on the plane.

- Determine when you're most likely to be bumped and where you're apt to find the cheapest airfares.

- Discover where to find the best plane seats, the best cyberbargains, and the best mile-earning credit cards.

- Find out why some coach seats cost much more than others on the same flight, and why frequent-flier mileage is so easy to earn and so hard to use.

- Master how to pack, minimize jet lag, and beat the fear of flying.

- Learn how to complain effectively in case your best-laid travel plans are foiled—with detailed instructions on everything from registering a grievance with the proper party at each major airline to small claims court procedures.

Know your rights before your next flight. It's high time to take back the skies.

TICKETING PITFALLS: KNOW YOUR RIGHTS BEFORE THE FLIGHT

In 1998, a crowded flight was canceled on United Airlines. A single ticket agent was rebooking the entire line of irate, delayed passengers.

Suddenly, one especially furious man pushed his way up to the front of the queue. Slapping his ticket down on the counter, he said, "I have to be on this flight, and it has to be first class!"

The agent replied, "I'm sorry sir. I'll be happy to try to help you, but I've got to help these other customers first. Then I'm sure we'll be able to work something out."

Unimpressed, the passenger bellowed, so the entire line could hear, "Do you have any idea who I am?"

Without hesitation, the gate agent smiled and grabbed her public address microphone. With her voice resounding through the terminal, she said, "May I have your attention please? We have a passenger, here at the gate, who does not know who he is. If anyone can help him find his identity, please come to the gate, it would be most helpful!"

The fact that you paid top dollar for an airline ticket is no guarantee that you won't encounter problems—through little fault of your own—before reaching your destination. The flight may be oversold and you may be bumped and have to depart at a later time. The airline may suddenly delay or cancel your flight and reroute you through the carrier's hub, far from the direct route that would have delivered you swiftly to your home. You may even lose your fare altogether if you reach the check-in gate and discover that a travel agent sold you a stolen ticket. (This does happen, believe it or not.)

Problems such as these are enough to exasperate even the most experienced traveler. Should you run into problems regarding your ticket or reservation, you'll save yourself a great deal of time and hassle if you know your rights, as well as a few handy coping strategies.

1   READING THE FINE PRINT: THE CONDITIONS OF CARRIAGE

THE **CONDITIONS OF CARRIAGE** IS A CONTRACT THAT outlines an airline's minimal responsibilities to customers. You should make every effort to find out what those obligations are before you shell out money for a fare. The U.S. Department of Transportation (DOT) requires that airline tickets at least mention this contract; some actually bear an imprint of it. The DOT also mandates that tickets clearly state restrictions and penalties for changing flight dates.

You can obtain the complete conditions of carriage document from most airline ticket offices or customer relations departments or you can request a free copy by mail. (See chapter 9, "The Squeaky Wheel," for the customer relations numbers of major carriers.)

On international flights, different regulations apply, and the contract is referred to as the "tariff rules." Foreign carriers usually keep a copy of the tariff rules at city and airport ticket offices.

The Department of Transportation requires that all domestic airline ticket agents furnish any customer who asks with a "concise and immediate" description of its most important policies. Armed with the information laid out in this chapter, you can ask the right questions before purchasing your ticket to be sure you know what to do should a problem arise. (See "Questions to Ask Before You Book," below.)

Since deregulation, the federal government regulates only four aspects of air travel: safety, smoking, lost and mishandled baggage, and the compensation due passengers who are bumped from oversold flights. But as discussed elsewhere in this book, consumer complaints about airline service and performance are on the rise, and the government has begun to investigate the practices of the major carriers. According to the Aviation Consumer Action Project, a consumer watchdog group founded by Ralph Nader in 1971, buying an airline ticket is a lot like buying a car or a TV. Their advice? Ask a lot of questions, shop around, and make sure you're familiar and satisfied with the fine print.

2   CROWDS IN THE SKY: THE BUSINESS OF BUMPING

ACCORDING TO THE AIR TRANSPORT ASSOCIATION, 10% to 15% of ticketed airline passengers in the United States—many of them business travelers with expensive, refundable tickets—don't show up at the airport on the day of departure. Consequently, airlines have developed the habit of **overbooking,** or selling more tickets than they have available seats.

As you may know from first-hand experience, when too many passengers actually do line up with tickets in hand, domestic carriers solve the problem by asking passengers with flexible travel schedules to forfeit seats and wait for a later flight, often in exchange for a round-trip ticket elsewhere. According to the Department of Transportation, there were 1,081,204 such **"voluntary bumpings"** among the 10 major airlines in 1998, the highest level in 9 years.

VOLUNTARY BUMPINGS

It sounds like a great deal at first, and sometimes it truly is. You're scheduled to fly to Albuquerque in the morning to visit cousin Quentin before he moves to Queens. Your flight is overbooked, the airline offers a free round-trip ticket to volunteers, and you've got all day. Why not lounge around the airport a while, catch a later flight—then make a free visit to Uncle Howie in Maui another time?

You could visit a lot of long-lost relatives this way, booking flights that are likely to be oversold, then volunteering your seat. Or you could *become* a long-lost relative yourself, stranded in standby for hours, with friends and loved ones wondering what ever happened to you. This is especially true during holidays, when it may be next to impossible to book another flight.

So before you forfeit your reservation, ask a few simple questions to be sure you're getting a deal. (For bumping policies on international flights into the United States or flights between foreign cities, see "Denied Boarding Overseas," below.)

- **When is the next flight on which you can get a *confirmed seat?*** The Department of Transportation recommends that you ask for a confirmed seat before you give up your original. Don't end up on standby.

- **What strings are attached to your free ticket?** How long is it valid? Where can you travel and when? Are holidays included? Can you reserve a seat, or must you fly standby?

- **Will the airline take care of you until the next flight out?** You may be entitled to phone calls, meals, taxis, even a hotel room, for long waits.

- **Are there other volunteers?** Find out how many volunteers the carrier needs. If it's clear that you're the only one and the airline needs more, don't take the first offer. Wait until the gate agent ups the ante then use your vantage to bargain for extra perks like hotel stays, phone calls, and meals.

While the government regulates the minimum the airline must pay you if you're involuntarily bumped, there isn't a fixed minimum or maximum if you offer up your seat. The amount you receive will depend on how desperately the carrier needs your seat, how effectively you bargain, and the gate agent's receptiveness to your demands. Use the government's "denied boarding compensation" law as your guideline (see "Money-Back Guarantees," below) and see how many additional perks you can hold out for.

INVOLUNTARY BUMPINGS

In the absence of Good Samaritans, the situation gets a little hairier. The airline requires certain passengers to travel on a later flight, in a practice known as **"involuntary bumping."**

Typically, passengers who booked or checked in last are the first to get the shaft. You're also an easy target if you arrived at the airport without a seat reservation—so be sure to check in early if this is the case. If your reservation requires reconfirmation, don't skip this crucial step; your timely passage may be hanging on a simple phone call. Lately, airlines are even bumping passengers who refuse to check their carry-ons, so be sure you know how many bags your carrier allows on board and measure your bag carefully (wheels and handles included) to make sure its dimensions fall within limits. (See "Quit Your Carrying On," in chapter 3, "Lost in Space").

It's wise to take a morning flight if you're booking last-minute travel during a major holiday, when even the skies aren't immune from festive madness. If you are bumped, you'll have greater opportunity to fly later that day.

MONEY-BACK GUARANTEES: WHAT ARE YOU OWED?

If you do get bumped, the DOT requires airlines to remunerate you, with a few stringent stipulations: You must have a confirmed reservation; you must have purchased your ticket within the required amount of days since you made the reservation; and you must have met the check-in deadline. Check-in times vary according to both the carrier and the airport, so be sure to ask for specifics when you book. On domestic flights, the check-in deadline is usually an hour before departure; on international trips, it's 2 hours before takeoff (sometimes as many as 3).

Beware! If you check in with under 20 minutes to spare before takeoff, the airline has the right to revoke your reservation altogether—with no money back!

The Department of Transportation says that if the airline can get you where you're going within an hour of your scheduled departure, it owes you nothing more. You'll just have to wait empty-handed for the next flight—swearing of course that you'll check in promptly next time.

If the carrier can put you on a plane in 1 or 2 hours, it must compensate you for the cost of the one-way fare, up to $200. If the wait lasts longer than 2 hours (4 for international travel), you are entitled to twice the value of your one-way ticket, up to $400.

This is the minimum compensation required by the Department of Transportation. If the delay ends up, say, costing you a job or causing some other type of irreparable damage, you can turn down the airline's offers and demand more money from the complaint department. Remember, however, that once you've accepted an offer of money, you won't be able to go back and renegotiate for more. (See chapter 9, "The Squeaky Wheel.")

Once you've agreed to the airline's compensation, the airline must issue your free ticket, cash, or check immediately. If it doesn't, forget the deal and ask them to refund your original ticket on the spot.

AIRLINES' BOARDING GATE DEADLINES
(Before Departure)

CARRIER	DOMESTIC (IN MINUTES)	INTERNATIONAL (IN MINUTES)
Alaska	20	40
America West	30	30
American	15	30
Continental	20	45
Delta	20	45
Northwest	30	60
Southwest	10	N/A
TWA	10	45
United	15	15
US Airways	10	30

AIRLINES' SUGGESTED CHECK-IN TIMES
(Before Departure)

CARRIER	DOMESTIC (IN HOURS)	INTERNATIONAL (IN HOURS)
Alaska	1	$1^1/_2$
America West	1	$1^1/_2$
American	$1^1/_2$	2
Continental	1	2
Delta	1	$1^1/_2$
Northwest	$1^1/_2$	2
Southwest	1	N/A
TWA	1	2
United	1	1
US Airways	1	$1^1/_2$–2

Note: These policies, in effect at press time, are meant to provide an overview of current protocol. Be sure the same rules are still valid when you book your ticket.

Note: The Department of Transportation does not mandate compensation for bumped passengers on small plane flights (under 60 passengers) or travelers whose flights were rerouted onto a smaller aircraft for safety or operations reasons. (However, if you were booked on a large aircraft and were then "downsized" to a smaller plane that could not fit all of the passengers on your original flight, those passengers bumped would be compensated.) If you refuse the airline's offer to place you in another section of the aircraft at no extra charge, they owe you no compensation. Also, the DOT requires no compensation if you are bumped from charter flights, international flights returning to the United States, or flights from one foreign city to another (the DOT considers the latter two situations outside their jurisdiction).

The Department of Transportation requires that airlines provide bumped passengers with a written explanation of overbooking and involuntary bumping—including a summary of who gets bumped and who doesn't. Be sure to ask for this written explanation and read the fine print carefully to be sure you're getting your due.

In general, the busiest flight times are usually between 7:30 and 9:30am and 5:30 to 7:30pm, especially during the week. The sky is especially crowded on Monday mornings and Friday evenings. Air traffic and flights also tend to be congested during major holidays and the few days before

THE BUMP RAP: WHO BUMPED MOST IN 1998
(Denied Boardings)

AIRLINE	VOLUN-TARY	INVOLUN-TARY	NO. OF PASSEN-GERS	RATE/ PASSEN-GERS
TWA	50,005	6,039	23,132,879	2.61
Southwest	81,201	10,230	59,053,217	1.73
Alaska	24,530	1,822	13,028,998	1.40
Delta	233,732	13,449	102,405,802	1.31
America West	49,811	2,074	18,174,910	1.14
United	142,057	4,561	79,813,016	0.57
American	221,826	3,387	73,618,441	0.46
Northwest	120,045	1,394	46,025,183	0.30
US Airways	81,830	1,267	56,564,712	0.22

Source: U.S. Department of Transportation.

Note: Does not include canceled, delayed, or diverted flights.

Denied Boarding Overseas

The bumping policies of international carriers, especially in small or underdeveloped countries, are unpredictable. If you must take an international flight into the United States, or fly an international carrier between foreign cities, be sure you understand the airline's bumping policy before you book your ticket.

and after. Take extra care to check in early if you're flying at these times.

3   DEALING WITH DELAYS, CANCELLATIONS & LOST TICKETS

IN THE INSTANCE THAT YOUR FLIGHT IS DELAYED OR canceled, you'll be wishing that you *had* been "involuntarily bumped." Delays are fairly common, and airlines reserve the right to postpone or cancel flights at the last minute. They're also under no obligation to compensate you for lost time and inconvenience if you're stranded at the airport due to a cancellation or delay: no free food or phone calls, no complimentary hotels, no flight vouchers—especially if the scheduling problems are due to inclement weather.

However, if the flight is waylaid because of mechanical difficulties or staffing problems, the carrier may try to make it up to you—though again, it's under no obligation to do so. So if you happen to miss a business meeting that ends up costing you money, the carrier may try to remunerate you in good faith, but it is not required to by law.

INVOLUNTARY REROUTING

Most domestic airlines will attempt to place you on the next available flight with empty seats or give you a voucher to fly another airline. This is called **involuntary rerouting.**

Before you agree to the rescheduling, however, make sure no additional fees are involved. If you're flying on a discount fare or a "no frills" airline like Southwest, you might be offered a choice of seats on the next available flight or a refund.

Once you know a flight has been canceled, it's wise to **find a phone immediately and rebook the next flight that's available** (rather than waste time waiting in what's bound to be a long line of stranded, disgruntled travelers). Then stand in line to have your old ticket validated for departure at a later time or on another airline.

If you need to fly another carrier and hold a ticket you purchased at a discount, you'll not have the same priority as full-fare passengers. If it looks like you'll be stranded overnight, politely ask a front-desk ticket agent at the airport to arrange a "distressed passenger rate" for you at a local hotel. Be aware, however, that here too the carrier may be willing to help you but is under no legal obligation to do so. To secure assistance, you can only rely on tact, diplomacy, and the mercy of a particular airline agent. If you're a frequent flyer, be sure to mention this fact.

If you don't get anywhere with the airline, try calling the **American Society of Travel Agents' (ASTA)** 24-hour toll-free referral line (☎ **800/965-2782**). They can recommend a travel agent in the area where you're waylaid who may be able to tell you which local hotels offer "distressed passenger rates."

If you're unsure of an airline's policy regarding cancellations and delays, inquire when you book your ticket. You probably know this already, but it's also wise to fly in the day before an engagement that may make or break your bank account, career, or reputation.

MISSED CONNECTIONS

Should a delay cause you to miss a connecting flight on a different airline, the airline is not required to pay you a dime for your hardship. If you have to make a connecting flight, it's wise to allow yourself anywhere from 45 to 90 minutes to make your connection—depending on the size of the airport, the history of delays for that particular flight, and the amount of baggage you checked.

According to the Aviation Consumer Action Project, the airlines allow anywhere between 20 and 90 minutes turnaround time between segmented flights. Every minute spent on the ground costs a carrier money, so they keep profits high by scheduling quick turnaround times.

If your flight leaves late and you're concerned about missing a connection, ask an attendant if the airline would be willing to arrange for special transportation to your connecting gate. Peruse the in-flight magazine to make yourself familiar with the layout of the airport that you're going to have to navigate at breakneck speeds in order to catch your next plane. Remember that these magazines are meant to be taken home, so don't be shy about taking it with you—or at least tearing out the airport map.

SO WHAT DOES "ON TIME" REALLY MEAN?

When you book a flight, get in the habit of asking the reservationist what the **on-time arrival performance** is for the flight you're planning to take. On a reservationist's database, each flight is assigned a number between zero and nine. If a flight rates a six, this means it arrives on time 60% to 69% of the time. If it's especially important that your flight be prompt, look for one that rates at least an eight.

Note: Keep in mind that a flight is considered "on time" if it lands within 15 minutes of its scheduled arrival. Also know that it's common industry practice for an airline to pad its flight times to improve its promptness rating. If a flight takes 45 minutes, for instance, some carriers will say it takes up to 90 minutes—and then come out looking "on time" when it arrives an hour and 10 minutes after departure.

MAJOR AIRLINE PROMPTNESS RATINGS
(On-Time Arrivals for 1998)

AIRLINE	PERCENTAGE OF ON-TIME ARRIVALS
Southwest	80.8
American	80.1
Delta	79.6
US Airways	78.9
TWA	78.3
Continental	77.2
United	73.8
Alaska	72.0
Northwest	70.7
America West	68.5

Source: Department of Transportation.

Note: A flight is considered on time if it arrives within 15 minutes of schedule.

DOMESTIC AIRPORT PROMPTNESS REWARDS FOR 1998

AIRPORT	PERCENTAGE OF ON-TIME ARRIVALS
Dallas/Fort Worth	88.0
Miami	82.6
Pittsburgh	82.1
Houston	81.8
Denver	79.7
Minneapolis	76.6
St. Louis	76.5
Atlanta	76.4
Chicago O'Hare	76.0
Detroit	74.9
Los Angeles	72.1
Boston	65.3
Newark	64.9

Source: Department of Transportation.

Note: A flight is considered on time if it arrives within 15 minutes of schedule.

LOST TICKETS

If you lose your ticket, you'll be in a much better position to replace it if you **wrote down the ticket number when you first received it in the mail.** The airline will be able to process your refund more quickly if you make time for this little bit of documentation. At the same time, it's wise to make sure the name and other information on the ticket is accurate as well.

The most common fee for replacing a lost ticket is $75, but it may run higher than $100. While some airlines will replace your ticket as soon as you fill out the application and pay the fee, others may reimburse you later—sometimes as long as 2 to 6 months later—and require you to buy a new ticket for immediate travel at the going rate for that time period. If you're replacing the ticket on the day of departure, for instance, you may end up paying over three times the amount you paid for an APEX fare, if you purchased the lost ticket far in advance of your trip. If you tend to lose things, you may want to ask what you'll be charged to replace the ticket when you purchase it.

YOU CAN'T LOSE A TICKET IF YOU DON'T HAVE ONE

Or consider "ticketless travel" by booking an electronic ticket. You book your fare over the phone or on the computer, and the airline presents you with a confirmation number. Electronic ticketing saves the airline money on labor and postage, so the major carriers offer frequent flier bonuses for booking e-tickets online. (For details, see chapter 8, "Cheap Fares.")

Here as well, however, documentation is crucial: In order to claim your reservation at the airport, you may need to present this confirmation number along with your photo identification. It's also prudent to ask the airline to fax or mail you a copy of your ticket. If the computers are down when you check in at the airport, that hard copy will serve as proof of purchase.

HOT TICKETS

If you're not careful about choosing a reputable travel agent or consolidator, you could find yourself with a ticket that was stolen from someone else. While this happens rarely, it is possible, and you probably won't find out about it until you check in on the day of your flight. Only your airline representative will know for sure, and will most likely confiscate the hot property and force you to buy another if you want to fly that day—which means you could end up paying the full last-minute fare.

Should you find yourself a victim of ticket fraud, you do have legal recourse—though you still may have to lay out money for a new ticket before you're guaranteed a refund.

The Department of Transportation, for one, is on your side. They contend that consumers should not be held responsible for the misdeeds of fraudulent travel industry operators, and may lobby the airline for a refund on your behalf. While the airline is under no obligation to understand your plight, it's still a good idea to write to its customer affairs office immediately and explain what happened. Try as best you can to document the fact that you had no idea you were purchasing illegitimate tickets, and request a refund or voucher for future travel. (See chapter 9, "The Squeaky Wheel," for the customer relations numbers of the major carriers.)

At the same time, write to the **Department of Transportation (DOT),** Aviation Consumer Protection Division, U.S. Department of Transportation, C-75, 400 7th St. SW, Room 4107, Washington DC 20590 (☎ **202/ 366-2220**). Ask them to intervene on your behalf in requesting a refund. Be sure to mention prominently in your letter to the airline that you're approaching the DOT for help. In fact, send the airline a copy of the DOT letter and send a copy of the airline letter to the DOT. (For other tips on how to complain effectively, see chapter 9.)

Because such misfortune is possible, it's wise to purchase airline tickets with a credit card. This way you can also write to your credit card company, explain what happened, and dispute the charge with them. It's especially worth your while to pay by credit card, now that so many credit-card companies allow you to accrue frequent-flyer mileage with each purchase. (See chapter 7, "Sky Hounds.")

4 THE HUB HULLABALOO

BEFORE THE AIRLINE INDUSTRY WAS DEREGULATED IN 1978, commercial planes traveled according to the point-to-point system—from departure city to destination in pretty much a straight line, making stops along the way like a Greyhound bus. Planes usually left the ground 60% to 64% full. After deregulation, however, airlines established the **hub-and-spoke system** in order to operate fuller planes—and thereby secure greater profits.

HOW THE HUB SYSTEM WORKS

Rather than transport passengers directly from small airports to their destination cities or from large airports to smaller towns, "feeder planes" now deliver passengers first to the hub city, where the carrier may control as much as 80% of the business. From there, the carrier dispatches travelers to their destinations.

If you're traveling from a small city to a large one, you will most likely travel to the hub in a small jet and then to your destination in a much larger plane, along with passengers who came in from umpteen other places. For example, a typical flight from Chicago to New York gets its passengers from about 10 feeder planes. Rather than send 10 different half-empty flights (from 10 different points of origin) all to New York, the airline consolidates the flights at its Chicago hub. Conversely, if you're flying from a large city to a smaller one, you will most likely travel to the hub in a large, full jet and from there be dispatched to your small city on a smaller plane. This consolidation has allowed airlines to expand service dramatically, and move into many smaller markets.

HUBS: THE DOWNSIDE

Under this system, planes now carry 70% to 80% of their capacity, on average. Paul Hudson, executive director of the Aviation Consumer Action Project, says, "Mathematically, the hub-and-spoke system is more efficient for both the airlines and consumers—but only when the proper reserve capacities are in place." With such a highly interconnected network of very full planes, major carriers need: spare airports, in case one airport is out of commission; spare planes, in case a scheduled aircraft breaks down; and spare airline employees, in case pilots or flight attendants are sick.

Let's take, for example, that flight from Chicago to New York again, which gets its passengers from about 10 feeder planes coming in from mostly smaller airports. If eight of those feeders arrive on time and two are delayed, the airline is faced with a dilemma: Does it strand passengers on the late flights in order to depart on time, or does it wait for all 10 feeders to reach Chicago and depart late for New York? Either way, efficient operations are disrupted.

Hudson says that with the proper reserve capacities, the airline would have a second smaller plane waiting to pick up the late passengers. Although this strategy would save consumers time and make the whole system run more effectively, it also costs the airlines more money. So guess what usually happens to the passengers whose flights are delayed? Because the airlines would rather stretch their assets to the breaking point than "squander" profits on reserve facilities, delayed passengers are simply stranded and inconvenienced, with no legislation in place that would demand they receive compensation. Likewise, when technical difficulties occur, flights are often simply canceled. Without proper reserves, the system is so tightly wound that one little snafu produces a far-reaching ripple effect.

Hudson says this problem is aggravated by the fact that industry-wide, the airlines are now aiming to increase their flight capacity to 80% to 90%. Hudson says, "With planes running this full, one little blip in the system can throw off flight schedules from 1 to 3 days." Because the hub system's primary objective is fuller planes, it also makes for more overbookings, cancellations, delays, and reroutings.

THE MONOPOLY GAME

Under the hub-and-spoke system, each major airline focuses its resources on a handful of cities around the country, and controls most of the business in that particular market. For instance, American Airlines controls 70% of the business at its hub in Dallas/Fort Worth, with some 800 departures there daily. As a result, the top 20 airports control 55% of the nations flights; the top 60 control 94%. Small airports often can't send you anywhere but to the dominant airline's hub.

Since an airline supplies most of the business at its hub airports, it is able to demand higher prices there with little threat from outside competitors. Earlier this year, the U.S. Justice Department filed suit against American Airlines, charging that the carrier was monopolizing passenger service in Dallas–Fort Worth (DFW). The government contends that American repeatedly attempted to drive budget airlines out of the DFW airport by saturating their routes and lowering fares to match the budget carrier's. Once the small carrier went under, American would drastically raise prices again.

The government maintains that American attempted to drive out Vanguard, Sun Jet, and Western Pacific this way. After Vanguard folded, American raised its prices 50% with Vanguard out of the way. American contends that this is the way any business competes. This is true—but only in the sense that several other major airlines have used similar

WORLD'S TOP 50 AIRPORTS
(Ranked by Passenger Numbers January–December 1998)

AIRPORT	NO. OF PASSENGERS	PERCENT CHANGE FROM 1997
1. Atlanta Hartsfield (ATL)	73,474,298	7.7
2. Chicago O'Hare (ORD)	72,369,951	3.0
3. Los Angeles (LAX)	61,216,072	1.8
4. London Heathrow (LHR)	60,659,500	4.3
5. Dallas/Ft Worth (DFW)	60,482,700	N/A
6. Tokyo Haneda (HND)	51,240,704	3.9
7. Frankfurt (FRA)	42,734,178	6.1
8. San Francisco (SFO)	40,059,975	−1.1
9. Paris Chas. de Gaulle (CDG)	38,628,916	9.5
10. Denver (DEN)	36,817,520	5.3
11. Amsterdam Schiphol (AMS)	34,420,143	9.0
12. Miami (MIA)	33,935,491	−1.7
13. Newark (EWR)	32,445,000	5.0
14. Phoenix Sky Harbor (PHX)	31,771,762	3.6
15. Detroit Metro (DTW)	31,544,426	0.1
16. New York John F Kennedy (JFK)	31,295,000	−0.2
17. Houston (IAH)	31,025,726	8.1
18. Las Vegas McCarran (LAS)	30,217,665	−0.3
19. Seoul Kimpo (SEL)	29,429,044	−19.9
20. London Gatwick (LGW)	29,173,257	8.2
21. St Louis Lambert (STL)	28,640,345	3.5
22. Minneapolis/ St Paul (MSP)	28,532,487	−2.8
23. Hong Kong (HKG)	27,897,619	−3.8
24. Orlando (MCO)	27,748,571	1.6
25. Toronto Pearson (YYZ)	26,744,530	2.5

anticompetitive practices, and are now under government investigation for doing so.

TAKING THE SCENIC ROUTE

For consumers, the hub system also means fewer direct and nonstop flights and inefficient segmented flights. For

AIRPORT	NO. OF PASSENGERS	PERCENT CHANGE FROM 1997
26. Boston Logan (BOS)	26,415,593	5.1
27. Seattle-Tacoma (SEA)	25,825,688	4.4
28. Bangkok (BKK)	25,623,720	2.0
29. Rome Fiumicino (FCO)	25,254,520	1.0
30. Madrid Barajas (MAD)	25,254,338	7.0
31. Paris Orly (ORY)	24,951,984	−0.4
32. Tokyo Narita (NRT)	24,441,365	−4.8
33. Philadelphia (PHL)	24,230,967	8.0
34. Singapore (SIN)	23,803,180	−5.4
35. Charlotte (CLT)	22,947,613	0.7
36. Honolulu (HNL)	22,920,793	−3.9
37. New York La Guardia (LGA)	22,679,700	5.0
38. Sydney (SYD)	21,206,897	2.8
39. Cincinnati (CVG)	21,179,226	4.0
40. Pittsburgh (PIT)	20,556,075	−1.0
41. Salt Lake City (SLC)	20,252,339	−3.9
42. Munich (MUC)	19,321,355	8.0
43. Zurich (ZRH)	19,301,424	5.3
44. Osaka (KIX)	19,223,600	−2.7
45. Mexico City (MEX)	18,946,440	6.2
46. Brussels (BRU)	18,481,897	16.0
47. Palma de Mallorca(PMI)	17,660,402	6.7
48. Manchester (MAN)	17,507,635	8.3
49. Beijing (PEK)	17,318,999	2.4
50. Copenhagen (CPH)	16,670,511	−1.0

Source: Airport Council International via @airwise.com.

instance, if you found a cheap flight on Northwest from New York to San Francisco, it's very likely you'd have to change planes in Memphis, one of Northwest's principle hubs—but far from the most direct route to the Bay Area.

I happened to be on a recent Delta flight from San Francisco to Pittsburgh that was rerouted to pass through

Delta's hub in Atlanta. A red-eye, the flight was originally due to stop in Delta's other hub in Cincinnati, which would have made for a much straighter path. That flight, however, wasn't full enough; neither was the red-eye out of San Francisco to Atlanta. So Delta canceled the flight to Cincinnati at the last minute and crammed everybody onto the later flight to Atlanta.

Just before daybreak, I reached Atlanta with only moments to make my connection—only to discover the small flight to Pittsburgh was overbooked! They managed to squeeze me onto the first flight out, but we sat in miserably cramped conditions in the wee hours of the morning. The flight that I originally reserved had been due into Pittsburgh at 8am. Cranky and restless from sleep deprivation, we didn't land in Pittsburgh until 11am—3 hours later than planned.

LEARN TO LOVE YOUR HUB

The system that means fuller planes and greater profits for the airlines means greater inconvenience for air travelers. What's a consumer to do? You can try to book nonstop or direct flights whenever possible. Or, you can console yourself by focusing on the fact that connecting flights are typically cheaper than direct routes. You can fly a discount airline, which may also make out-of-the-way stops but will cost much less. Or, you can take advantage of overbooking to try to score free tickets. (For more on ways to use the hub system to your advantage, see chapter 8, "Cheap Fares.")

You can also complain. While the airline industry is in no way ready to revert to a more consumer-friendly routing system (though so-called "budget" carriers like Southwest, Sun Country, and Vanguard still use the point-to-point system), you can seek compensation for hassles you suffer because of the present mode of operations. (See the end of this chapter and chapter 9, "The Squeaky Wheel," for suggestions on how to complain effectively.)

HOME IS WHERE THE HUB IS

CARRIER	HUB CITY
Alaska	Seattle
American	Dallas–Fort Worth, JFK, Miami, Chicago O'Hare
America West	Phoenix, Las Vegas, Columbus (Ohio)
Continental	Houston, Cleveland, Newark
Delta	Atlanta, Cincinnati, Dallas, Orlando, JFK, Salt Lake City, LAX
Midwest	Milwaukee, Omaha
Northwest	Minneapolis, Memphis, Detroit
Southwest	Phoenix, New Orleans
TWA	St. Louis, JFK
United	Chicago O'Hare, Denver, Washington D.C. Dulles, San Diego, LAX
US Airways	Pittsburgh, Charlotte (North Carolina), Philadelphia, Baltimore, Washington D.C. Dulles

5 ALLIED FORCES: CODE SHARING & PARTNER PROGRAMS

MAJOR AIRLINE ALLIANCES ARE ANOTHER RECENT industry trend that probably hurts consumers in the long run. The U.S. Justice Department is currently investigating a proposed alliance between Continental and Northwest Airlines that verges on a full-fledged merger. American Airlines/US Airways and United Airlines/Delta were considering similar arrangements—though at press time, labor unions are holding up these partnerships as well.

Each major domestic carrier is already allied with several foreign and regional carriers as well. The airlines contend that these partnerships increase route options and expand frequent-flier benefits (see chapter 7, "Sky Hounds," for details on frequent-flier reciprocity). Several consumer watchdog groups and the U.S. Justice Department, however, contend that these affiliations will ultimately serve to jack up prices.

CODE SHARING

The most prominent feature of alliances is their **code-sharing** policies. Code sharing is when an airline sells seats under its own name on a flight operated by another carrier. If you leave the country on a domestic aircraft and change planes outside the United States, you could end up covering the second leg of your trip on a foreign code-share partner's aircraft. Reservationists are supposed to tell you this when you book your ticket, but more often than not they don't. So, say you have chosen one airline for the last 5 years because of its safety record; you may be disappointed to end up flying, without warning, on a carrier with a less pristine performance record.

A HIDDEN BIAS?

Consumer Reports Travel Letter warns against another hidden snare of code sharing, known as **"CRS (computer reservation system) bias"**—when travel agents' databases favor code-share alliance flights by listing them before other segmented flights.

Travel agents' computer reservations systems always list **nonstop flights** first because consumers prefer them. **Direct flights** (flights that proceed directly to your destination but may have a stop or two along the way) are listed next, followed by **on-line connections,** flights with a plane change on the same airline. **Interline connections,** connecting flights on different airlines, come last because they are the least desirable commercially.

Although code-share connections between alliance partners are *technically* interline flights that should come last, they are *listed* like online connections higher up on the list, and receive higher billing than other, possibly cheaper, connections. The code-share flight will also probably be listed twice, making it far more likely to be the flight your travel agent books, even if the price is higher, because it seems to be a connection on the same airline.

According to *Consumer Reports Travel Letter,* this is just the latest twist on an old trick. In the 1980s, some of the most popular computer reservations systems used by travel agents were actually subsidiaries of major airlines. The Sabre system, for instance, was owned by American Airlines and gave American higher billing than other carriers. Now that the Department of Transportation prohibits CRSs from ranking flights by airline name, the industry has hit upon this subtle technique for thwarting government regulation against anticompetitive practices.

WHAT THIS MEANS FOR THE BUDGET GUYS

In 1998, the U.S. Justice Department investigated the alliances and ruled that the partnerships indeed could stifle competition and therefore needed to be monitored closely. On the same grounds, *Consumer Reports Travel Letter* has also come down strongly against these quasi-mergers.

It's that much harder now for a small, budget airline like Tower to get off the ground when it's up against bigger, stronger competitors allied in pairs. Flying a low-cost carrier can mean savings of up to 50%. The Department of Transportation determined in 1996 that budget airlines were saving consumers $6.3 million a year.

Budget carriers not only tend to be much cheaper than major carriers, but their very presence at an airport tends to lower prices all around, even on major airlines. Their demise would surely put a higher price on flight.

AN ALLOYED DEFENSE: WHAT YOU CAN DO

You can defend yourself against these allied forces. *Consumer Reports Travel Letter* makes several recommendations.

- **Shop online.** You'll be able to see flight information directly and know if the cheapest fare on your route involves a code-share.

WHO'S IN CAHOOTS
(Airline Partnerships at Press Time)

PRIMARY AIRLINES	PARTNER AIRLINES
Alaska Air	American Airlines, American Eagle, British Airways, Canadian Airlines, Continental Airlines, Horizon Air, KLM, Northwest Airlines, Qantas Airways, TWA
America West/ America West Express	British Airways, Continental Airlines, Northwest Airlines, Virgin Atlantic
American Airlines/ American Eagle	Aer Lingus, Aerolineas Argentinas, Air Pacific, Alaska Airlines, Asiana Airlines, British Airways, British Midland Airways, Canadian Airlines International, Cathay Pacific, Crossair, El Al, Finnair, Grupo Taca, Hawaiian Airlines, Iberia, Japan Airlines, LanChile Airlines, Midway Airlines, Qantas Airways, Sabena, Swissair, TAM Airlines, Turkish Airlines, US Airways
Continental/ Continental Express	Aces Airlines, Air France, Alaska Airlines, Alitalia, America West, Avant Airlines, British Midland, BWIA, China Airlines, COPA, CSA Czech Airlines, EVA, Frontier, Hawaiian Airlines, Horizon Air, Northwest, Quantas Airways
Delta/Delta Connection	Aeromexico, Air France, Air Jamaica, China Southern, Finnair, Korean Air, Malaysia Airlines,

- **Ask about code-shares.** If you must use a travel agent or book from an airline directly by phone, ask if your itinerary includes a code-share flight. If so, ask if there are any cheaper "interline" connections on nonallied airlines.

- **Call the code-share partner directly.** If you're ready to book a flight that involves a code-share, call the secondary airline directly and ask them for

PRIMARY AIRLINES	PARTNER AIRLINES
Delta/Delta Connection (cont.)	Singapore Airlines, South African Airways, TAP Air Portugal, United Airlines
Northwest Airlines	Air China, Alaska Airlines, Aloha Airlines, America West Airlines, Big Sky Airlines, Braathens, Business Express Airlines, Continental, Eurowings, Garuda, Hawaiian Airlines, Japan Air System, Jet Airways, Kenya Airways, KLM Royal Dutch Airlines, Malaysia Airways, Midwest Express, Pacific Island Aviation
Southwest	No Partner Airlines
TWA	Air India, Alaska Airlines, Horizon Air, Iceland Air, Royal Jordanian Airlines, Trans World Express
United/ United Express	Aeromar, Air ALM, Aloha Airlines, British Midland, Cayman Airways, Delta Airlines, LAPA, Mexicana, Saudi Arabian Airlines, Singapore Airlines
US Airway/ USAir Express	Alitalia, American Airlines, American Eagle, ANA (All Nippon Airways), Austrian Airlines, LatinPass (includes Aces, Avianca, Aeropostal, Aviateca, Copa, Lasca, Nica, Saeta, and Taca), Mexicana, Metrojet, Northwest, Quantas, Sabena, Swissair

the cheapest fare available on your route. You may find a better bargain.

- **Complain.** The Department of Justice is already watching alliance partnerships vigilantly. Write to them and complain if limited competition at your local airport has sent fares skyrocketing. (See chapter 9, "The Squeaky Wheel," for advice on how to complain effectively.)

Department of Justice
Antitrust Division
601 D St., NW
Washington, DC 20530
☎ **202/514-2008**

6 QUESTIONS TO ASK BEFORE YOU BOOK

YOU CAN AVOID WASTING TIME AND MONEY IF YOU ASK
a few key questions before you book your fare.

- **Confirmation and reconfirmation.** Must I reconfirm my reservation? How far in advance must I
  check in? Will my reservation be canceled if I fail to
  reconfirm or check in on time?

- **Delays and cancellations.** What does the airline
  owe me if my flight is canceled? Will I be guaranteed a spot on the next available flight at no additional charge? Will I be placed on another carrier if
  necessary at no extra cost? How much, if at all, will
  the airline pay for hotels, meals, and phone calls in
  the meantime?

- **Fares.** What are the penalties if I cancel? Am I able
  to get a refund if necessary? If so, what are the
  terms and conditions? How much extra will it cost
  if I lose or return my ticket, or if my ticket must be
  rewritten?

- **Baggage.** What are the rules regarding carry-on
  baggage and lost or mishandled luggage, beyond
  the federal guidelines for lost or mishandled luggage? (See chapter 3, "Lost in Space.") Will the airline be responsible for fragile checked items, such as
  skis or golf clubs?

- **Code Sharing.** Will I fly any portions of my flight
  on a code-share partner's aircraft? If so, how will

that affect the principle airline's responsibility
regarding confirmation and reconfirmation, cancellations and delays, fares, and lost or mishandled
baggage? (For a discussion of code sharing and airline alliances, see "Allied Forces," above.)

7 GESTURES OF REFORM?

THE AIR TRANSPORT ASSOCIATION (ATA) DRAFTED NEW
guidelines for the airline industry in June 1999. These new
guidelines outline such customer service reforms as
prompter handling of complaints; greater disclosure regarding fares, delays, and frequent-flyer rules; and more consis-
tent bumping policies. At press time, the 10 major carriers
are in the process of revising their own guidelines to adhere
to the ATA's recommendations. Member airlines have agreed
to post their revised customer service plans on their Web
sites sometime in 2000. While the guidelines are a start,
some proposals are far more substantive than others—and
none are legally binding. With airlines continuing to crowd
planes, cut corners, and milk record profits, it's still important that you be wary of pitfalls and know how to sidestep
them before you purchase a ticket to ride.

2

THE HOT SEAT: HOW TO PICK THE BEST SPOT ON THE PLANE

A crowded flight with Muhammad Ali on board was preparing for takeoff. The flight attendant noticed Ali's "Fasten Seat Belt" light was on—and Ali was reclining in his seat like a Roman emperor, the picture of comfortable privilege.

The flight attendant approached him and politely said, "Mr. Ali, it's time to buckle up now. We're ready for takeoff."

Ali looked up and said, "Miss, Superman don't need no seatbelt."

The flight attendant looked down and replied, "Champ, Superman don't need no plane."

Even if you're not one of the greatest athletes of the 20th century, when it comes to reserving an airline seat, the old real estate bromide really does hold true: location, location, location. With a general trend toward smaller seats in coach, overbooked flights, and diminished customer service, a good perspective is everything. From an aisle seat you're almost guaranteed happier passage than you'd experience squeezed between a colicky baby and a chunky chatterbox in a row of five.

You can almost always beat the crowd to the best seats by booking early and reserving a seat number in advance (see "Seat Assignment Policies of the Major Domestic Airlines," below). Reservationists are supposed to ask your preference, but often they don't and you'll have to speak up for yourself if you want to fly in comfort. Sometimes the prime spot can depend on the plane model. While reservationists won't volunteer particulars on this front either, they do work with a seating chart and at your request will use it to walk you through the cabin in search of a comfy perch. If you'd rather scope out the lay of the land yourself, check the airline's Web site: At press time, Delta, Northwest, TWA, and US Airways post the seating arrangements of each plane model in the fleet. (See "Surfing for Sales," in chapter 8, for airline Web site addresses.)

Remember that you won't receive your boarding card with the printed seat assignment until you get to the airport. So be sure to write down your seating assignment when you get it and bring the numbers with you the day of your flight, to make sure you get the spot you requested.

1 SITTING PRETTY: ADVICE FOR CHOOSING YOUR SPOT

WHETHER YOU'RE FLYING A PROP OR THE CONCORD, a few rules of thumb may help keep your flight from becoming a long day's journey into night.

ARE YOU LOOKING FOR LEGROOM?

- Check in early and ask to sit on the aisle in an **emergency-exit row,** which has extra leg room and sometimes one fewer seat per row in coach. These are assigned at the airport, usually on a first-come, first-serve basis—unless you're an elite frequent flier, in which case you may be able to reserve an emergency-exit row seat when you book your ticket. The drawback to this position: In the unlikely event of an emergency, you may be called upon to help the flight crew with evacuation procedures.

In order to sit in an emergency-exit row seat, you must be able to see clearly, understand and effectively communicate instructions in English, have sufficient dexterity and strength to open the door quickly, and assist other passengers through the door or off the emergency-exit slide. Children under the age of 15 are not allowed to occupy these seats.

Your responsibilities may include: determining if the emergency exit is safe for passage (free of smoke, fire, and debris); opening the door; helping to stabilize the escape slide and assist others as they get off the slide; and removing obstructions weighing 25 to 55 pounds from the exit row and door area.

- You'll find extra legroom in a **bulkhead seat** in the front row of the coach cabin. Be aware, however, that this option is fretted with a few minor drawbacks. You'll have to stash your carry-ons in the overhead bin (so check in early before the bin nearest you fills up). You may get a crick in your neck during the in-flight movie (so bring a gripping novel as backup). Finally, you may end up with wee screamy neighbors, as families often sit in the bulkhead. (Earplugs are often a must if you choose to sit here.)

- Try to score an **aisle seat** if you want more room and aren't overly concerned about the view. To boot, you won't have to climb over fellow passengers to move about the cabin, and you'll have to contend with only one next-door neighbor. Better yet, try for an aisle seat in a three-seat row. You're far more likely to end up with the row to yourself or with just one neighbor two seats away.

DO YOU CHOOSE TO SNOOZE?

- If you're flying coach and want to snooze, a **window seat** will offer the broadest headrest and the least disruption from passengers leaving and returning to their seats. Book a window seat in a three-seat row, and you're more likely either to have the row to yourself or have an empty seat separating you from the nearest neighbor.

- Be sure to get a **fully reclining seat.** If your chair won't tilt back—which is usually the case if you're sitting right in front of an emergency-exit door or in the last row of a section—you'll end up losing up to 20%, or 5 inches, of precious horizontal space. As many as 10% of a coach cabin's seats remain locked in the upright position, and most reservationists will not volunteer this information unless you ask. It's up to you to make sure you don't get stuck in a straight-backed chair.

Skirting the Issue

On a recent El Al flight, a woman in a miniskirt and sleeveless blouse was assigned to a three-seat row with only one other occupant—an Orthodox Jewish man, whose faith required him to avert his eyes from strange women.

In order to deflect temptation, he requested a seat change, and she got to rest her head against the window and stretch her bare legs out across two adjacent seats!

(This is strictly a seating trick mind you, not a fashion tip. As you know, under most circumstances her outfit would more likely attract row mates than rid her of them! Furthermore, bare limbs may compromise your safety in the event of an emergency. See chapter 5, "Life Preservers.")

IS SPACE A PRIORITY?

- If you're traveling with a friend in coach, ask for the **window and aisle seats in a three-seat row,** as the middle seat often remains empty—and even if the flight sells out, no one in his right mind would refuse a switch to an aisle or window so you can sit next to your companion.

- On wide-bodied planes, try for **an aisle seat in a center section toward the back of coach,** as these seats are often assigned last, and you're more likely to score two for the price of one.

- Arrive early and scope out **empty adjacent seats** while passengers board, then hightail it to the nearest pair the second the plane door closes.

MAPPING A STRATEGY

- One way to ruin a plum aisle seat is to sit near a **lavatory or galley** on a crowded flight. You're sure to be jostled and bumped for the duration of your journey. Try to land a spot at least four rows away. If you're flying with children, however, you may save yourself a lot of legwork by sitting near the rest rooms. Even then, you don't want to be too close. These areas are bustling, and your children are far more likely to be hurt by oblivious passersby.

- Reserve a seat toward the **front of the plane,** especially if you need to make a connecting flight.

Know the Lingo

In the airline industry, "pitch" is the distance in inches between one seat back and the back of the seat in front of it. So the larger the pitch, the more legroom you have.

You'll be the first to disembark, once the gangway is in place.

- If turbulence unnerves you, ask for a **wing seat,** where the ride will feel less bumpy.

AIM HIGH: WHO KNOWS?

- If you're an elite frequent flier or a base frequent flier with a full-fare coach ticket, ask for an **upgrade.** Although airlines are getting strict about their upgrade policies, you still may be able to move into business class if seats are available there and your luck is good. (See "The Politics of Upgrading," in chapter 7, "Sky Hounds.")

2 SEAT ASSIGNMENT POLICIES FOR THE MAJOR DOMESTIC AIRLINES

American

- **At booking:** Anyone can make a seat reservation; only elite members and base frequent fliers paying full coach fares may reserve seats in the front of the coach cabin, in an emergency-exit row, or in bulkhead.

- **At check-in** (up to 4 hours before departure): Anyone can reserve an emergency-exit row or bulkhead seat, if available.

Continental

- **At booking:** Anyone can reserve a seat; only elite members, the elderly, and disabled passengers can reserve emergency-exit row seats, bulkhead seats, and seats in the front of the coach cabin.

- **24 hours before departure:** Basic frequent fliers can move into priority coach, if seats are available.

- **At check-in, 4 hours before departure:** Frequent fliers may upgrade to priority coach or even first class, if seats are available; anyone may upgrade into seats in emergency-exit rows or bulkhead.

Delta

- **At booking:** Anyone can reserve a seat, including emergency-exit row spots, if the passenger is qualified to assist other passengers in the event of an emergency; only elites can reserve seats in the front of the coach cabin.

- **At check-in (up to 4 hours before departure):** Frequent fliers may upgrade into priority coach seats, if available.

Northwest

- **Ninety days before departure:** Anyone can reserve a seat 90 days in advance of travel; only elites may reserve seats in the first 10 rows of coach, emergency-exit rows, and bulkhead.

- **At check-in (up to 4 hours before departure):** Anyone may upgrade into priority coach seats, if available.

TWA

- **Ninety days before departure:** Anyone can reserve a seat assignment 90 days in advance of travel; only elites paying full coach fares may reserve priority seating in the first 10 rows of coach.

- **At check-in (up to 4 hours before departure):** Frequent fliers can reserve front-of-coach seats, if available; anyone may reserve seats in bulkhead and emergency-exit rows.

United
- **At booking:** Anyone can make a seat reservation; only elites can reserve seats in the front of coach.
- **At check-in (4 hours before departure):** Frequent fliers may upgrade to front of coach, if seats are available; anyone can reserve seats in emergency-exit rows or bulkhead.

US Airways
- **At booking:** Anyone may make a seat reservation, even in bulkhead, 11 months in advance; only elite members and frequent fliers on full-fare coach tickets may reserve seats in the first 10 rows of coach; only the highest elite members may reserve emergency-exit rows.
- **At check-in (4 hours in advance):** Frequent fliers may upgrade into the front of the coach cabin; anyone may reserve a seat in emergency-exit rows; on rare occasions, frequent fliers may be able to move to first class, if coach is completely full.

3 THE CLASS STRUGGLE

AS YOU PROBABLY KNOW ALL TOO WELL, NOT ALL airline seats are created equal. For the most part, where comfort in the air is concerned, you get what you pay for. Upgrading is no longer as easy as it once was, as airlines have reduced the number of seats available for award travel and prevented basic frequent fliers from qualifying for complimentary upgrades. (See "The Politics of Upgrading," in chapter 7.) Unless you're an elite flier or you're traveling on Continental—which still has a fairly generous policy toward basic frequent fliers—the cost of upgrading is prohibitive for most economy passengers.

WHO HAS PRIORITY?

Priority coach seats—the first 10 rows of the cabin, the emergency-exit row, and the bulkhead row—are usually reserved first for elite frequent fliers and disabled passengers, then for basic frequent fliers who paid full coach fare (though disabled passengers aren't qualified to sit in the emergency-exit rows). Other travelers may not reserve one of these spots until check-in time on the day of departure (typically 4 hours before flight time).

Basic frequent-flier status boosts your shot at priority coach only on Continental—which allows its basic frequent fliers to reserve a prime seat 24 hours before departure. (At check-in, Continental's basic frequent fliers may even upgrade to first class, if the seats are still available.) (See chapter 7 for each major airline's frequent-flier program.)

Even if you're flying on a discounted coach ticket, you don't have to fly in cattle-car conditions if you have a reliable travel agent. Ed Perkins, consumer advocate for the American Society of Travel Agents, says, "Good agents can get into the computer and assign their customers prime seats even when an airline's reservationists say certain seats are unavailable on discounted fares." (See "Working with a Travel Agent," in chapter 8, "Cheap Fares.")

COACH: THE CINDERELLA CLASS

Though economy class passengers still populate the vast majority of seats on most flights, the airlines hesitate to invest too much energy in their comfort, knowing full well that if budget travelers need to cross the ocean their paramount concern will be a low fare—even if it means riding like dominoes, with a mere 31-inch pitch between seat backs and 18 inches between armrests.

Even within the same coach cabin, passengers pay vastly different prices for the same crowded quarters, the same bad food—a product with no significant qualitative difference. One recent search turned up round-trip fares on

LEGROOM IN COACH ON DOMESTIC AIRLINES

AIRLINE	PITCH IN INCHES (SPECIFIC AIRPLANE MODEL)
Alaska	N/A
America West	32" (737)
	32 (757)
	32–33 (Airbus 319)
	32–33 (Airbus 320)
American	31 (all other models)
	32 (767, 757, 737, Airbus, and some DC-10s)
	34 (MD11)
Continental	31
Delta	31 (757, MD80)
	32 (727, 737, L-1011)
	33 (767)
Midwest Express	33–34 on all planes
Northwest	30 (DC9)
	30–32 (757)
	31–32 (Airbus, DC10, 727)
	31–33 (747)
Southwest	31 (737-200)
	32–33 (737-300, 737-500)
TWA	N/A
United	31 (737, 767, 777)
	31–32 (Airbus)
	31–34 (747)
	31–36 (757)
	32 (737-200, 727)
	36 (DC10)
US Airways	N/A

Source: Consumer Reports Travel Letter.

the same flight that ranged from $102 to $651 for a short hop of less than 500 miles; $378 to $2,072 for a cross-country flight; and $328 to $1,686 for a transatlantic trip.

In the past, frequent fliers were able to upgrade to first or business class, on even a discounted coach ticket. Now even this refuge is no longer an option for most basic frequent fliers, unless they paid full coach fares.

SO WHAT'S THE SILVER LINING?

Several carriers are taking pity on the poor pedestrians in coach. While no one's turning pumpkins into glass carriages just yet, several airlines have made attempts to make flights a wee bit more sufferable for the airlines' underclass.

A Coach Overhaul

At press time, the Brits lead the way in economy service. For years, **Virgin Atlantic** has worked hard to ensure comfortable passage for its bread and butter customers in coach. Coach seats feature footrests and individual seat-back screens with more than 28 channels and 10 Nintendo games for kids to choose from. Premium Economy perches have adjustable headrests as well.

Not to be outdone by its arch rival, **British Airways** is also upgrading comfort features in coach. On extended flights, British Airways will offer a World Traveller Economy Class and install cushier seats on its 747s and 777s over the next 2 years. Seats will have footrests, an extra inch of knee space, contour in the lower back area to ensure extra lumbar support, and headrest wings to make it less likely that your noggin will flop around if you nod off. Economy seats will also feature double-decker meal trays, and seat-back videos with 12 video channels and six movies to choose from, many of them custom selected for children.

Only a few American carriers will follow suit. In August 1998, **United Airlines** decided to remove a row of seats from 450 of its jets (the Boeing 777s, Boeing 737-500s, Airbus A320s, and A319s), and reconfigure the first 6 to 11 rows of coach as an Economy Plus section. The changes will make for an extra 5 inches of legroom for each passenger (which amounts to 35 to 36 inches between seat backs). The jets were expected to be refurbished by mid-2000. Of course, elite frequent fliers and full-fare coach passengers will have first dibs on these roomier seats.

Delta is considering a similar reconfiguration in coach. As this book went to press, however, the airline had not made a definite decision or plan.

On international flights, **United** is also offering an "S"-back coach seat contoured for extra lower-back support and adjustable wings on its headrests so you can nap more comfortably.

American is removing rows from the coach section of every aircraft in its fleet. On international flights, it will redesign coach seats to equip each one with a headrest. To boot, eight American 737s flying from New York and Boston to London also feature individual seat-back videos.

But even with all this good news for coach passengers, there is still a price to be paid. Fewer seats in coach means more over crowding on flights and more intense competition for what many see as a dwindling number of low-cost fares. (United, for one, plans to charge Economy Plus passengers more than standard coach fare.) Another consequence of this less-is-more approach to coach is there will be fewer seats available for frequent-flyer awards.

Wider Is Better: The 777

Several carriers are snapping up the new, wide-body Boeing 777s, which allow coach travelers to breathe a little easier. The planes are nearly 20 feet wide and feature individual viewing screens for every seat (even in coach) and larger overhead bins. The seats afford only an extra inch between the back of each seat and the one in front of it. Beyond actual square footage, however, the cabin feels more spacious and airy, with its curved ceiling and nearly vertical walls.

Of the domestic airlines, American, Continental, Delta, and United have added a number of 777s to their fleets. They're used mainly for long-haul flights departing from an airline's hub and traveling as far as Europe, Japan, or South America. Among the popular 777 routes are United's flights from New York JFK to Buenos Aires and Miami to Rio de Janeiro; Continental's flights from Newark to Tel Aviv and Houston to Paris; American's flights from Dallas–Fort Worth to Tokyo and Chicago to London Heathrow; and Delta's flights from Cincinnati to London Gatwick and Atlanta to Frankfurt.

BUSINESS CLASS: THE TOP BANANAS

Despite the premium price paid by first-class customers, the airlines don't depend on their fares the way they rely on business-class travelers—the real darlings of the industry. According to *Consumer Reports Travel Letter,* an airline can break even on a transatlantic flight if it fills only 40% of its business-class seats. So guess which travelers are the usual beneficiaries of any innovations in flying comfort?

Consumer Reports Travel Letter rated the best business-class carriers as Aerolineas Argentinas, Air Canada, Alitalia, Ansett Australian, Continental, TWA, US Airways, and Virgin. Most aircraft models on these lines give the business-class traveler **54 inches of leg room**—compared to the standard 31 inches in coach. These airlines even furnish business travelers with fully reclining sleeper seats.

Delta recently combined its first-class and business sections with a new BusinessElite class, which will feature the best of both worlds. Though seats won't recline fully, like in first, they will come equipped with lots of legroom, data ports, and power outlets.

Aer Lingus, Air Canada, Alitalia, Canadian, Continental, Sabena, SAS, and TWA no longer offer intercontinental first-class service but have chosen to pamper business-class passengers instead.

Virgin Atlantic—which has never had an official first class, just an enhanced business class—plans to go for broke and rig its high-fare section on the new Airbus A340-600 with private quarters equipped with double beds, a bar and lounge area, showers, and exercise rooms. Virgin's highest paying customers already enjoy the services of the Virgin LimoBike, a chauffeured motorcycle shuttle from London to Heathrow, and the Virgin LimoBoat, which transports

LEGROOM IN BUSINESS CLASS

AIRLINE/AIRCRAFT	SEAT CONFIGURATION[A]	PITCH IN INCHES
Air Canada		
A319	2-2	38
A320	2-2	38
A340	2-2-2	58–60
B747	2-2-2	55
B767-200	2-2-1	55
B767-200[b]	2-2-2	45
B767-300	2-2-1	55
DC9[b]	2-2	38
American		
A300	2-2-2	50
B767-200	2-2-2	50
B767-300	2-2-2	48
MD11[c]	2-3-2	51
MD11[d]	2-3-2	55
British Airways		
B747-100	2-3-2	40
B747-200	2-3-2	40
B747-400	2-3-2	50
B757-200	2-2	50
B767	2-2-2	40
B777	2-3-2	50
DC10	2-3-2	50
Continental		
B747	2-2	55
B757	2-2	55
B777	2-2-2	55
DC10	2-2-2	55

passengers to the airport via the Thames, with several sight-seeing stops at places like Westminster and the Millennium dome.

Though business class costs less than first-class service, the price is still nothing to sneeze at. Business fares can

AIRLINE/AIRCRAFT	SEAT CONFIGURATION[A]	PITCH IN INCHES
Delta		
B767	2-2-2	50
L1011	2-3-2	50
MD11	2-3-2	50
Northwest		
B747-100	2-2	48–50
B747-200	2-2/2-3-2	48
B747-400	2-2/2-3-2	47–50
DC10	2-2-2	47
TWA		
B757	2-2	57
B767	2-2-2	57
United		
B747-200	2-3-2	40
B747-200	2-3-2	48–50
B747-400	2-3-2	48–50
B767-200	2-2-2	40
B767-300	2-2-2	48
B777	2-3-2	49
US Airways		
B767	2-2-2	55
Virgin Atlantic		
A340	2-2-2	55
B747	2-2	55

Reprinted in part from Consumer Reports Travel Newsletter, July 1998

(a) Where indicated, 2-2 seating on 747s is in upper-deck cabin or front cabin.
(b) Used mainly on short-haul flights.
(c) On Pacific flights.
(d) On Atlantic flights.

cost as much as $550 to $800 for domestic hops under 500 miles; $1,100 to $2,000 for cross-country domestic trips; and a whopping $5,000 to $6,000 for transatlantic travel. Yet business-class features vary widely from carrier to carrier. It's good to know what you're paying for before settling into a cramped pricey seat to cross the Atlantic. Here's how business class compares, in carriers around the world.

NO-NONSENSE ADVICE FOR FLYING IN COMFORT

- **Dress sensibly.** Wear layers of comfortable clothes in natural fabrics. The climate in airplane cabins is unpredictable. You'll be glad to have a sweater or jacket to put on or take off as the on-board temperature dictates. Natural fabrics, as you probably know, breathe better than synthetics, and will help you adapt more readily to shifts in temperature. You'll also be better off in the case of an emergency: Synthetics may melt and stick to the skin in the case of a cabin fire. (See chapter 5, "Life Preservers," for more on safety precautions.)

- **Choose comfy shoes.** For maximum comfort, you'll probably want to kick off your shoes before takeoff. Nevertheless, it's wise to wear comfortable footwear, since your legs and feet are bound to swell during air travel. If you have to squeeze back into stiletto pumps, surely you'll be pining for your Hush Puppies. (See "Deep-Vein Thrombosis," in chapter 5.)

- **Moisturize, brush, and lubricate.** Airplane cabins are notoriously dry places—with less humidity than air in the Sahara. Take a travel-size bottle of moisturizer or lotion to refresh your face and hands at the end of the flight. If you're taking an overnight flight (the red-eye), don't forget to pack a toothbrush. If you wear contact lenses, take them out before you get on board and wear glasses instead. Or at least bring eyedrops.

FIRST CLASS: FIRST IN COMFORT

A first-class ticket on average costs 10 times more than an APEX economy fare. That said, the first-class seat is usually

---

- **Brown-bag it.** If you know your plane will still be airborne come mealtime, pack some food in your carry-on bag. You may cause a bidding war on the plane for your home-made sandwich and some truly fresh fruit—but many travelers would rather fight than digest airline food. If your preflight schedule won't allow you time for food preparation, leave yourself at least enough time to buy a sandwich at the airport.

- **Drink up.** Bring bottled water on board and drink plenty of it before, during, and after your flight. When you're on a plane—one of the driest places on earth—your skin evaporates as much as 8 ounces of water per hour. (For more information see "Dehydration," in chapter 5.)

- **Keep your blood flowing.** Circulation slows when you sit for extended periods of time. Get up and walk around as often as you can while you're in the air. Try some stretching exercises near the lavatory, if there isn't a line. Also check out some of the neat little exercises you can perform inconspicuously from your seat. (See "Deep Vein Thrombosis," in chapter 5.)

- **Try to catch some z's.** See "Snooze Boosters & Other Tools of the Flying Trade," in chapter 6, "Beat the Clock," for pillows, eyeshades, and other paraphernalia that will help you to relax during your flight.

22 inches wide (4 inches larger than the seats you have to squeeze into in coach), with a full 60 inches of legroom between your seat and the one in front of you (compared to the paltry 31 inches you get with an economy fare). Your seat will recline as fully as a La-Z-Boy lounge chair, and you'll probably be able to extend your legs fully on a leg rest. You'll most likely enjoy a seat-back viewing screen, and your neck of the cabin will be cordoned off, like a private lounge club. While first-class meals are prepared in advance and reheated just like the forgettable food in coach, first-class food is prepared by premium chefs, and the wine list is far superior.

TWA is enlarging its first-class sections from 12 to 20 seats on 170 jets, mostly the MD-80s, in order to enable more frequent fliers to upgrade to first class. For the same reason, American Airlines has expanded its first-class sections from 12 seats to 20 seats on most of its MD-80s and its new Boeing 737-800s.

United and American Airlines are purchasing new Boeing 777s, with newfangled, nearly 180° sleeper seats in first class that allow you to stretch out fully prone and catch some maximum z's. Qantas, Lufthansa, and Singapore Airlines also plan to install sleeper seats in their first-class sections. Japan Airlines furnishes first-class passengers with movie-screen goggles that simulate a 62-inch screen, so the viewer can lie flat out, don the goggles, and view a movie.

More and more carriers—such as Aer Lingus, Air Canada, Alitalia, Canadian, Continental, KLM, Northwest, Sabena, SAS, and TWA—are abandoning their first-class service on intercontinental flights in order to lavish more luxury on their business travelers. Delta is merging its first-class and business-class services into one new BusinessElite section. (The hidden pitfall here is that frequent fliers will receive only the standard 25% bonus for flying business class, rather than the more generous 50% bonus for flying first class.)

3

LOST IN SPACE: HOW TO COPE WITH BAGGAGE SNAFUS

A man checks his bags at the airport and says, "I'd like the blue one to go to Chicago, the red one to go to Los Angeles, and the brown one to go to Washington, D.C."

"Why sir," says the clerk, "that's simply impossible."

"Impossible?" the man asks. "But you managed to do it last week."

We all know someone who has experienced a lost luggage nightmare: A businessman traveling to Tokyo for a conference the following morning ends up having to buy a new suit there, at three times the price of the original. A Catholic nun traveling to Dublin finds out her suitcase was waylaid to Belfast. A student flies home to Wisconsin for Mother's Day, but her carefully wrapped gift packages find their way to Hawaii.

1 BAGGAGE KNOW-HOW: HOW TO PREPARE YOURSELF

ACCORDING TO THE DEPARTMENT OF TRANSPORTATION, airline travelers reported 2,484,841 cases of lost or mishandled luggage in 1998—a rate of 5.16 instances for every 1,000 passengers, which translates to one lost bag for every 200 travelers! With this alarmingly high level of mishap, it's imperative that you take a few precautions if you want your belongings to reach your destination when you do.

- **Double-check your luggage tags** to make certain the flight number and airport code are correct. Make sure the stub you're given is accurate.

- In case your bags are lost, you'll increase your chances of recovering them quickly if you **mark them clearly with your name, address, and phone number** before you check them. (You might even want to include a clearly labeled forwarding number at your destination.)

- Get in the habit of **removing old tags** as soon you return from a trip, so your next destination is perfectly clear to frenzied luggage handlers.

- Confusion is all too likely in a crowded baggage-claim area. Avoid losing your goods in the shuffle by buying **brightly colored tags,** especially if your luggage is black—or better yet, opt for **brightly colored bags**—so you can identify your suitcases immediately and reduce the chance of a stranger walking off with them.

- Call the airline the day of departure to find out if your flight is overbooked or crowded; if it isn't, **pack as much as you can in two carry-on bags.** (But first make sure your airline allows you two carry-ons; see "Quit Your Carrying On," below.) Bin space fills up more quickly than ever these days, so you want to give yourself the greatest possible advantage by arriving early. Stake out a seat near the gate so the minute the gate agent calls

LOSERS & ABUSERS
(Lost & Mishandled Luggage by Carrier 1998)

AIRLINE	TOTAL INCIDENTS	INCIDENTS PER PASSENGER
United	595,874	7.79
Alaska	84,727	7.27
Northwest	278,733	6.63
TWA	123,020	5.39
Southwest	267,689	4.53
American	282,085	4.40
Delta	412,811	4.27
US Airways	230,062	4.09
Continental	142,233	4.06
America West	67,607	3.88

Source: U.S. Department of Transportation Air Travel Consumer Report for 1998.

your row you'll be first to board. If bins are crowded near your seat, look for space in sections that haven't been boarded yet.

- Be sure your **carry-ons are durable and secure,** in case the flight is crowded and you're required to check one of them. (The airlines are cracking down on the number of carry-on bags permitted per passenger (see "Quit Your Carrying On," below).

- If you're a frequent flier traveling in coach on a crowded flight, **try to get an upgrade** (see "The Politics of Upgrading," in chapter 7, "Sky Hounds"). Premium-class passengers are usually allowed to carry more bags on board than coach travelers.

- **Pack items you absolutely need** for the first 24 hours of your trip **in a regulation-size carry-on bag,** in case your checked luggage disappears.

2 The Bottom Line: What Do the Airlines Owe You?

IF AN AIRLINE DOES HAPPEN TO LOSE YOUR LUGGAGE, federal and international laws require the carrier to reimburse you. Unfortunately, the maximum it must pay may fall well below the value of your belongings. On domestic flights, the airline is responsible for the depreciated value of the lost goods, up to only $2,500 per person. If you're traveling overseas, the rules for reimbursement are even stingier. Foreign carriers owe you a mere $9.07 per pound, up to $640, for lost goods. (The international rate is dictated by the Warsaw Convention, which, for the record, dates from 1929. Imagine trying to buy a replacement business suit for the same price you would have paid over 70 years ago!)

If your bags are delayed or routed incorrectly, the airline may reimburse you for reasonable expenses and deliver your bags, once found, to your door. The law does not require them to do this, however, and airlines do not have specific policies regarding delayed baggage. If the airline does offer compensation, the amount may depend on everything from the nature of your trip, the mood of the customer relations agent, the length of the delay, whether your luggage was lost away from home, and perhaps most of all, your own powers of persuasion. If your bags are only a few hours late, for instance, they may pay you nothing at all. If you are traveling to attend a special awards ceremony, they may agree to pay for the rental of formal wear. If your bags are missing in action for weeks, they may reimburse the purchase of a limited amount of new clothes.

WHAT ARE THE LIABILITY LOOPHOLES?

Mishandled luggage is one of the few aspects of the airline industry subject to government regulations, but you can be sure that carriers will try to get away with paying you as little as possible. As mentioned earlier, airlines pay only the depreciated value of your possessions. Lost luggage forms require detailed information about the contents of your bags, and some airlines may even ask you to document the value of your possessions with receipts.

Most airlines impose a 21-day deadline on lost-luggage claims and can deny your reimbursement if you're late to report missing goods. If your bags are lost, it's imperative that you ask to speak with your airline's customer service representative or a floor manager, and file a lost baggage report *immediately*—before you leave the airport, if possible. Once you've filed a report, be persistent about your refund. A claims department may take months to respond. In the worst cases, they may wait up to 6 months in order to deem the bag lost and only then send a check to reimburse you. (See chapter 9, "The Squeaky Wheel," for tips on how to complain effectively, if you've waited for 2 months and still haven't received compensation for lost luggage.)

If you are flying in segments on two different airlines, the final carrier is responsible for lost or damaged luggage— even when they can prove the first airline is to blame. If your luggage is lost or damaged on international flights with a domestic segment, however, you will receive only the lower international reimbursement. When you're booking a segmented flight, allow yourself at least an hour between connections. Your bags, like you, will be more likely to reach their destination at the scheduled time.

By all means, stash heirloom rubies and the like in your handbag or a carry-on that meets the new size restrictions (see "Quit Your Carrying On," below). Likewise, carry your computer on board with you in a regulation-size bag. If you plan to travel with expensive gifts, ship them instead. Airlines will refuse liability for valuables such as jewelry, electronic equipment, or documentation, even if they lost your luggage.

Likewise, the airlines are not held responsible for theft of individual items in checked luggage, even if you can prove that your bag was pilfered while in the carrier's keep. If you're packing your favorite designer cocktail dress, don't leave home without buying a good luggage lock. **Magellans Travel Supplies** (☎ **800/962-4943** or 214/792-4000; www. magellans.com) sells an exceptionally strong and reliable combination lock by Prestolock, for $9.85.

LAST RECOURSES

If all this has you ready to make your next trip with nothing but the shirt on your back, take heart. Paul Hudson, executive director of the Aviation Consumer Action Project, recommends a somewhat extreme precaution if you're traveling with clothes that are worth more than the airlines' liability: Insure your bags before you travel. Hudson says that a scant few airlines have effective systems to monitor the security of checked luggage. He claims that many of the bags that are reported lost have actually been stolen by airport and airline employees. Hudson says, "If you really want compensation as a passenger, file a police report the minute you realize your bags are missing, to ensure full compensation from your insurer."

If you've purchased homeowner's or renter's insurance, you're probably already covered for the cost of goods lost or stolen during travel. Check your policy carefully before you make your next trip and by all means purchase a rider for your existing policy if you travel a lot and aren't covered for lost or stolen bags.

If you don't hold homeowner's or renter's insurance, it's best to purchase insurance from a travel agent, according to Ed Perkins, consumer advocate for the American Society of Travel Agents (ASTA) and former editor of *Consumer Reports Travel Newsletter.* Baggage coverage used to be commonly available at airport insurance counters, but these are becoming increasingly concerned with accident insurance, and when they do sell excess valuation, it's expensive.

Perkins says, "Some airlines still make excess valuation insurance available at the check-in counter, but most don't. In a crowded check-in line, the last thing an airline employee is going to want to do is sell you travel insurance. It's much more convenient to buy in advance from a good travel agent."

Baggage insurance usually comes bundled with other types of travel insurance, such as trip-cancellation or emergency-evacuation coverage. Typically you purchase coverage for each trip. According to ASTA, the following insurance companies are the largest providers, all of them reputable: **CSA** (☎ **800/348-9505** or 214/792-4000); **Travel Guard** (☎ **800/826-1300** or 214/792-4000); and **Access America** (☎ **800/284-8300** or 214/792-4000). For rates, see "Travel Insurance Demystified," in chapter 5.

DAMAGED LUGGAGE

If your alligator suitcase gets banged up a bit in passage, airlines are not required to reimburse you for damage resulting from "normal wear and tear." This policy is obviously subject to broad interpretation. Nicks and scratches happen, however, so you're best off buying sturdy, practical luggage. (Expensive bags also signal a pricey stash inside, and will make you a juicier target for theft.) Carefully inspect your baggage before you check it. You should by all means seek reimbursement for broken zippers, wheels, or handles. Even with this evidence of mishandling, however, you may have to make a case for yourself. Contact an airline official before you leave the airport and try to file for reimbursement.

3   WHAT MAKES FOR STURDY LUGGAGE?

- You'll reduce the risk of damage to your luggage if you look for bags with **cushioned handles,** reinforced with **metal and double rivets.** Avoid handles attached with single rivets.

- Avoid bags with loose stitching. The **tighter the stitches,** the more durable the bag.

- Look for luggage with **recessed wheels,** as these are least likely to snag or break.

- **Check the bindings.** If the space between the seam and the binding is narrow, it will be less likely to hold.

- **Zippers** that are **large and far from the edge** are less likely to break.

- While leather bags are beautiful, they're also weighty—not to mention expensive looking, and more likely to be stolen. A **good, sturdy nylon** is much stronger. Look for nylons with 430 denier or

TOP 10 LARGE, WHEELED, SOFT-SIDED SUITCASES

MODEL NAME	PRICE
1. Andiamo Valorosa VJ25	$495
2. Impuls Targa 3692-26	$230
3. Pathfinder by Paragon 8002-B	$190
4. Ricardo Beverly Hills, Big Sur 1825	$160
5. Briggs & Riley U-26WG	$350
6. American Tourister 500 Series/ Cadence 2712411163	$230
7. TravelPro Crew Series Plus 7693-1	$260
8. Samsonite 550 Series/ Ultralite 3 353111163	$200
9. Lark 750 Series 935111181	$300
10. Skyway Freeport Sky Track 89872C	$200

Source: Consumer Reports, *December 1998.*

* *Denotes a* Consumer Reports *Best Buy*

Note: Consumer Reports *performed a series of trials to test each bag. Each was loaded to 50 pounds and pulled, by eight staff members of varying heights, through an ersatz airport up and down ramps, and over ridges, a simulated curb, carpeting, tiles, and an obstacle course. Each bag, loaded with books wrapped in towels, was also placed inside a tumbler and knocked around to simulate years of serious abuse by baggage handlers. On the weakest bag—not listed above—zippers* more, such as **bomb cloth, Cordura,** and **Ballistic Nylon.** Cheaper nylons or polyester are more likely to tear.

- If you want a shoulder bag, be sure to find one with a **wide, padded strap** for comfortable handling.

- If you're looking for a carry-on with wheels, look for a **long handle.** Drag the bag around the store before you buy it, to make sure you can manage it comfortably. Place some things inside and turn a few corners to test maneuverability and balance.

FEATURES & EASE OF USE	CONSTRUCTION	DURABILITY
very good	very good	excellent
very good	excellent	very good
excellent	excellent	fair
very good	excellent	good
excellent	very good	fair
excellent	good	good
very good	very good	good
excellent	fair	good
very good	very good	fair
very good	good	good

and seams tore, plastic feet popped off, and protective plastic piping wore through to expose the wire beneath. Finally, features were scrutinized and rated highly for the presence of internal and external pockets, a pull-handle that locks in both extended and retracted positions, internal dividers to keep contents in bag from shifting, and skids near the wheels to make it easier to drag the bag up stairs.

- A **piggyback strap** on a wheeled bag will let you yoke your attaché or large purse to your suitcase and wheel it along.

- **Pockets,** both inside and outside, almost always come in handy. *Consumer Reports* especially recommends a wet pouch for soggy bathing suits.

4 QUIT YOUR CARRYING ON

LAST JULY, THE FAA REQUESTED THAT DOMESTIC AIRlines clarify their restrictions regarding carry-on luggage. As a result, every airline but Northwest now limits each passenger to two bags on board. Northwest's policy is stricter—one carry-on per passenger—but several other airlines reserve the right to impose the dreaded one-carry-on maximum on crowded flights. Permissible dimensions vary, but the strictest airlines say carry-ons must measure no more than 22 by 14 by 9 inches, including wheels and handles, and weigh no more than 40 pounds. (Only America West's weight limit is tighter: 26 pounds.)

United has gone so far as to furnish X-ray machines at more than 40 airports with templates that literally block any carry-on bigger than 22 by 14 by 9 inches. The dim bright side of United's new policy is that flight delays caused by gate-checked cargo at United's hub in Chicago dropped 72% over the Thanksgiving holiday in 1998, with the newly installed templates in operation. Southwest, TWA, and Delta plan to mount the bandwagon as well and install templates of their own—though all three of these carriers are a bit more generous, allowing bags that measure under 24 by 16 by 10 inches.

WHY ALL THE FUSS?

Because mishandled luggage rates have reached an all-time high, consumers are trying to divert disaster by bringing as many of their possessions as they can on board. Planes are also more crowded than ever, however. On an overbooked flight, as you well know, cabin space in coach is all too finite. Under these circumstances, it's not surprising that up to 4,500 travelers are injured each year by carry-ons, according to the Association of Flight Attendants, which issued the most vehement calls for onboard-luggage caps. Heavy bags drop onto passengers while their owners are trying to stash them overhead or when the bins are overstuffed or loaded sloppily. During emergency landings or even when a plane hits turbulence, the bins sometimes pop open, and bags drop onto people. Continental is the only carrier that plans to side with consumers on this issue and actually create more storage space in coach. By the end of 2000, the entire Continental fleet will feature 130 planes with bigger overhead bins for carry-on storage.

The Association of Flight Attendants is still not entirely happy with the new guidelines and wants the FAA to step in and impose a federal limit on carry-ons. In fact, a bill is underway in Congress right now that would limit travelers to one bag on board—across the board, consumer-friendly Continental included.

WHAT'S A CARRY-ON?

The definition of a carry-on varies according to the airline's policy, the airline gate agent's discretion, and the capacity of the flight in question. For instance, purses are carry-ons according to the official policies of all the major airlines except Continental, America West, and Delta. Even these three carriers, however, allow gate agents to deem large handbags as carry-ons if space is tight. On especially crowded flights, any purse that's bigger than a loaf of bread may be considered a carry-on bag. Briefcases and laptop computers, if toted separately, classify as carry-ons with every carrier but Continental; so you may want to consider stashing your laptop inside another bag before you board. Unchecked child seats and strollers are classified as carry-ons by almost half

Made to Fit

Luggage manufacturers immediately jumped to the aid of consumers and designed carry-ons that meet the new size restrictions. The first to fit the bill were the **Samsonite Cabin Carry-On,** which comes in a number of styles ($129 to $175), **Tumi's 20-inch Wheel-a-Way Carry-On 2265** ($475), and **Andiamo's J22SX** ($475 to $525), **J19-S** ($399 to $450), and **J-19-DSX** expandable ($450 to $499). Each bag was designed to fit through even the tightest templates and holds roughly 2 or 3 days' worth of formal business attire.

---

the major carriers. (See "Traveling with Children," in chapter 5, "Life Preservers," for details.)

Industry-wide, exempt items include coats, umbrellas, reading material, cameras, and assistive devices for travelers with disabilities.

Although coach passengers will be the first to have to forfeit a bag, even elite frequent fliers and first-class passengers may be forced to check a carry-on if the flight is full. However, Alaska, Continental, Delta, Northwest, and TWA allow crew members to make exceptions to the guidelines—although this can work for or against consumers, depending on everything from space constraints to the mood swings of the crew.

If you plan to bring more than one bag aboard a crowded flight, be sure your medications, documents, and valuables are consolidated in one bag in case you are forced to check the second one.

5 THE WELL-PACKED BAG

CAREFUL WARDROBE PLANNING IS THE FOUNDATION of an efficiently packed bag. You'll get the most mileage from your selections if you stick to solid, neutral colors that you can mix and match. Keep prints and offbeat colors to a minimum.

You may want to leave your linen at home—unless you don't mind sacrificing trip time to the task of ironing. Obviously, it's best to stick to fabrics that won't wrinkle.

If your luggage barely holds the clothes you think you'll need, you may want to consider wearing your bulkiest shoes and clothes, so you won't have to squeeze them into your luggage. Carry your umbrella, coat, camera, and reading material outside your luggage. The airlines don't count these items as carry-ons, so you can tote them without forfeiting luggage space. Some carry-on bags, such as the Travelpro Rollaboard, feature a metal hook for items like these.

A PECK OF PACKING TIPS

- Pack your bags on a **hard surface.** This will help you to fill corners and distribute the weight of your belongings evenly throughout the bag.

- If your suitcase isn't very full, consider **stuffing in a few towels** to fill up space and prevent contents from shifting.

- Pack **heavy items in** whichever part of the bag will serve as the **"bottom"** during transit, and lighter, fragile items in whichever part of the bag will travel on top.

- Save **plastic dry-cleaning bags** and use them for packing. The plastic reduces friction. If you use it to separate garments, they won't wrinkle. Tissue paper prevents wrinkles equally well.

- If you don't have plastic or tissue paper, **fold your clothes in overlapping layers,** so they cushion each other. For instance, lay pants on the bottom of the suitcase. Place the top half of a sweater over the top of the pants. Fold the bottom half of the pants over the sweater, and the bottom half of the sweater over the pants.

- **To avoid knee creases,** pack the top half of pants on the bottom of the suitcase. Lay down plastic or tissue, then place sweaters and shirts on top, with each layer separated by plastic. Fold the bottom half of the pants over the stack, add plastic, then place one more sweater or shirt on top, to hold the pile in place.

- **Fold shirts below the waist.** If they crease in transit, you can tuck the wrinkles away.

- **Pack lingerie, socks, and stockings last.** Squeeze them inside shoes and into the spaces between clothing, especially along the edges of the suitcase.

- **Turn jackets or blazers inside out** before you pack them.

- If you can live with a few minor wrinkles, **roll your clothes.** You'll be able to pack them much tighter, and they will not crease.

- **Seal toiletries in resealable plastic bags.** Don't fill liquid bottles to capacity, or they'll be more likely to leak. Fill them partially and squeeze out the excess air before you close them, which will create a vacuum seal.

- If you run out of space, zip your suitcase and **drop it on the floor.** Repeat this until the contents settle and free up space.

- If you absolutely must have neatly pressed clothing for your trip, consider purchasing **a travel iron. Travel Smart** makes a $1^{1}/_{2}$-pound model with a retractable handle that folds flat and packs easily. It's available from Magellans for $36.85 (☎ **800/ 962-4943** or 214/792-4000; www.magellans.com).

WHAT'S CONSIDERED CONTRABAND?

Research into the infamous ValuJet crash in the Everglades in 1996 revealed that the plane was brought down by a fire caused by oxygen generators that hadn't been properly labeled and deactivated.

Many common household items that you use safely every day at home or in the office—such as paint, adhesives, bleach, and cigarette lighters—become much more potentially dangerous in an airplane cabin. In flight, shifts in air pressure and temperature may cause these items to leak, generate toxic fumes, or ignite.

Airline policies differ slightly regarding hazardous materials, but violations may result in civil penalties of up to $25,000 or even criminal punishments. In general, you may be prohibited from carrying on board the following substances: fireworks, including signal flares, sparklers, and other explosives; fuel; cigarette lighters with a flammable liquid reservoir and lighter refills; household cleaners such as polishes, waxes, drain cleaners, bleach; solvents; insecticides and pesticides; matches; lighter fluid; poisons; flammable gases, liquids, or solids such as paint, paint thinners, lighter fluid, and adhesives; explosives; corrosives such as wet-cell batteries and acids; oxidizing materials; radioactive materials such as uninstalled pacemakers; mercury, including thermometers; briefcases with installed alarm devices; magnetic materials; or pressurized containers such as tear gas, oxygen, scuba tanks, aerosol spray cans, butane fuel, CO_2 cartridges, self-inflating rafts, propane tanks; mace; gun powder and ammunition; pepper spray; dry ice; camping equipment with fuel; gasoline powered tools such as chain saws or lawn mowers.

Sporting guns may be allowed, but they must be declared in accordance with international regulations. They also must be unloaded and packed in hard-sided containers or a crush-proof case manufactured especially for shipment by air. Containers with handguns must be locked.

6 WHEN YOUR BAGGAGE HAS A PULSE: TRAVELING WITH YOUR PET

THE SAFEST WAY TO FLY WITH PETS IS TO BRING THEM on board with you in a suitable carry-on enclosure. Domesticated dogs, birds, and cats are allowed on flights within the United States, provided that you make an advance reservation for them. Be sure to ask the deadline when you book. In order to qualify for the cabin, animals must be at least 8 weeks old, fully weaned, under 20 pounds, and healthy. The airline will usually ask you to furnish a clean bill of health from a veterinarian, prepared within 10 days of your departure. On some airlines, you may be asked to present certification that your pet is vaccinated against rabies.

The airlines also ask you not to feed your animal solid food within 6 hours before flight time. You are also expected to exercise and provide water for the pet before you stow it in the carrier.

Some airlines forbid pets to ride on board transoceanic flights and in first or business class. Each carrier has different restrictions regarding carrier size and the number and types of animals allowed. Pets that assist disabled passengers are usually able to accompany their owners in the cabin free of charge. Be sure to investigate your airline's policy when you book your ticket.

PETS IN THE CABIN

The animal must ride in a crate that fits under the seat in front of you. Animals are not allowed to ride in the overhead bin. Airline regulations allow both soft-sided pet carriers and hard-sided kennels. While the soft carriers will usually fit under the seat more easily, the American Humane Society recommends hard-sided kennels for safety, as they offer your animal greater protection.

Animals must remain in their kennels for the duration of the flight. Usually they must stay crated in boarding areas

FUR ALLERGIES

Though animals rarely end up flying with their owners in an airplane cabin, it does happen, and can pose a problem to neighboring passengers with allergies to dog and cat hair. Unfortunately, pet owners who reserved a spot for Spot in advance are under no obligation to move or otherwise accommodate fellow travelers with allergies.

If you suffer from allergies and end up sharing cabin space with a furry animal, persuasive diplomacy is your only hope. Unfortunately, the airlines owe you nothing, no matter how badly you suffer in the presence of furry creatures. It's up to you to convince someone to switch seats with you, or to persuade a member of the flight crew to lobby on your behalf with passengers seated farther away, to entreat them to switch positions with you.

If your allergies are severe, get in the habit of asking the gate agent, before you board, if any pets will be traveling on your flight. The gate agent has the power to switch your seat—but likewise bears no obligation to do so. Put on your most sympathetic smile and be prepared to plead your case as plaintively as possible.

It also doesn't hurt to prepare for the worst. Pack some antihistamines, tissues, and an inhaler in your carry-on bag.

---

and airport lounges as well, so it's best to book a nonstop flight where possible. The ASPCA recommends that you line the bottom of the crate with shredded paper or towels to absorb accidents. You might also want to avoid traveling with your pets in excessively hot or cold weather. If you must travel in the heat, it's best to book a night flight.

Pets usually count as one piece of carry-on luggage, but you still must reserve a spot for your animal when you book your own flight. On most carriers, two carry-on pets are permitted in coach class per person, and only one per person in first class on airlines that allow pets in first class. You may have to pay a small fee—usually around $50—to bring your pet on board. Once you've made the reservation, your pet will enjoy the same rights as any other paying passenger: If your next-door neighbor, for instance, is allergic to animal fur, the onus to move will fall on him or her. You and your pet have every right to remain in the seat assigned to you.

PETS AS CARGO

If for whatever reason you need to check your pet, the animal will ride with cargo in the belly of the plane. You should use a USDA-approved, hard-sided kennel in this case. The crate should be large enough that your pet can stand, sit, and change position comfortably. You can purchase these from many pet-supply stores and sometimes from the airline itself.

The ASPCA recommends that you write the words LIVE ANIMAL in letters at least 1 inch high, on top of the crate and on at least one side of the enclosure. Show the upright side of the kennel with prominent arrow indicators.

You should also write the name, address, and telephone number of the your pet's destination on the crate—even if you are riding on board the same flight. This information should be easy to read and secured on top of the carrier. Your pet should also be wearing identification tags on a collar. Cat collars should be elastic.

The ASPCA also recommends that checked pet crates be rigged with separate compartments for food and water. Some airlines require this. These compartments may also have to allow airline personnel access without their having to open the door where the pet is stowed. The ASPCA recommends that you freeze the pet's water so that it doesn't splash out during loading but will melt by the time your pet is thirsty.

The ASPCA warns against tranquilizing dogs before a flight, especially if the animal is traveling in cargo. Dogs control their body temperature by panting, not sweating. When tranquilized, dogs may be unable to pant, which leaves them

ANIMAL RIGHTS: THE ASPCA SPEAKS

According to Peter Paris, the ASPCA's vice president of public affairs, pet owners should think twice about checking their pets as baggage, even if they're traveling on the same flight. Conditions in the cargo hold are far from ideal: Temperatures may vary, or the pilot may forget to turn on the air exchange. Paris says it's not uncommon for pets to die or suffer injury in cargo. Unfortunately, these mishaps are recorded as incidents of lost or mishandled luggage, and bereaved owners are due no more than the maximum compensation for a lost suitcase.

Paris says, "If your animal is worth more than $2,500 to you, think twice about sending it by air. If you can easily transport the animal by car, leave it with a friend or relatives, or place it in a kennel while you're away, don't risk putting it on a plane for your own convenience."

If you must transport your pet by air, Paris says you should make your best effort to travel on the same flight. Publicize the fact that you are traveling with an animal. Paris says that concerned pet owners should go so far as to poke their heads in the cockpit when boarding to let the pilot know there's an animal in cargo, so he's sure to turn on the air exchange.

Congress is currently considering a bill that would improve travel conditions for pets in the cargo hold and record incidents of pet injury or death. In the meantime, it's up to you to be vigilant. If you have a complaint about the way an airline employee treated a pet, write to the **U.S. Department of Agriculture,** Animal Care Staff, APHIS-REAC-AC, 4700 Riverdale Rd., Riverdale, MD 20737 (☎ **214/792-4000** or 301/734-7833).

no defense against temperature irregularities in the cargo hold, which obviously is not monitored like the airplane cabin on the same flight.

For trips that last longer than 12 hours, you should attach a plastic bag with dry food on top of the carrier with feeding instructions for airline staff.

The ASPCA also suggests that you acquaint your pet with the crate the day before the trip. You may want to place its food and water inside, for instance, so it gets used to eating there.

Be sure that the crate is closed securely, but do not lock it. Airline staff needs to be able to open the crate in case of an emergency.

In the unlikely event that your pet is lost—which is a rare misfortune, but one that does occur from time to time—airlines will usually remunerate you according to the same rates used for lost luggage compensation.

Individual airline policies may differ, but in general animals that exceed 100 pounds must be checked in the airport freight area, rather than the baggage check area.

4

White Knuckle Combat: How to Conquer the Fear of Flying

If you are looking for perfect safety, you will do well to sit on a fence and watch the birds.

—Wilbur Wright

Despite the well-documented fact that air travel is the safest form of transportation in the United States, fear of flying—also known as **aviophobia**—is second only to fear of public speaking in the pantheon of top American phobias, according to the National Institute of Mental Health. In 1980, the Boeing Aircraft Corporation conducted a study that determined that 25 million Americans fear plane flight, and one in six Americans is at the very least uncomfortable stepping on a plane.

Yet the facts say that you're far more at risk when you hop in your car to fetch a stick of butter from the supermarket. Most people don't think twice about settling into their cars, betting on the fact that they will be transported safely from point A to point B. Yet car accidents account for more than 90% of transportation fatalities and are the leading cause of death for people aged 6 to 27, according to the U.S. Department of Transportation.

According to the National Transportation Safety Board, your chances of dying in an automobile are 1 in 5,000; on a train, the probability diminishes to 1 in 367,000; on a plane, the likelihood of death dwindles to a mere 1 in 10 million chance.

1   PROFILE OF AN AVIOPHOBE

IF YOU SUFFER FROM AVIOPHOBIA, TAKE CONSOLATION in the fact that you're in good company: Despite the fact that Stanley Kubrick's most brilliant pictures feature obsessively recurrent flight imagery—the fighter plane in *Dr. Strangelove,* the space ship in *2001: A Space Odyssey*—the late director was deathly afraid to fly. Aretha Franklin turns down concerts that require air travel. The notoriously phobic Danish director Lars Von Trier is so acutely fearful of flying that he refused to travel to Cannes when his 1996 film *Breaking the Waves* was nominated for the Palm D'Or.

According to statistics from the National Institute of Mental Health, aviophobes tend to be successful, perfectionist, and intelligent—certainly smart enough to know that flying is safer than driving, but nonetheless unable to conquer the irrational fear. Some frequent flyers spend half their lives on planes for years on end and suddenly find themselves overcome with aviophobia, out of the blue, so to speak.

WHAT CAUSES THE FEAR?

Fear of flying may stem from a variety of influences. Some aviophobes—perhaps the most justified of all—suffer from post-traumatic stress disorder when they set foot on an aircraft because they actually survived a plane crash. Other aviophobes fear flying as an extension of phobic disorders such as claustrophobia (fear of enclosed spaces), acrophobia

THE GREATEST AVIOPHOBE: MUHAMMAD ALI

The fear of flying afflicts the biggest and the best of us. In 1960, before Cassius Clay became Muhammad Ali and the world heavyweight boxing champion, his biggest fight to date was slated for the Summer Olympics that year in Rome. As the U.S. heavyweight contender for the gold medal, Clay was his characteristically hyperconfident self—until he learned that the only way to get to Italy was to board a plane and fly across the Atlantic.

With all his terrible force of will, Clay refused to set foot on an aircraft. He had never ridden a plane before; previously, he had traveled to faraway matches by rail and by station wagon. His first trainer, Joe Martin, had to reason with him for 4 hours to convince him that he could not get to Europe by train and that his only alternative to flying was to stay home—and forfeit his shot at an Olympic gold medal.

Clay finally succumbed, but he went straightaway to the army-and-navy store and bought himself a parachute. He wore it on the plane and ended up on the floor in the aisle, praying, when the plane hit turbulence.

Then, of course, he went on to win the gold medal for his legendary fearlessness in the boxing ring.

(fear of heights), the fear of losing control, panic attacks—even guilt. The tendency to suffer from these fears is often inherited.

Fear of flying may also stem from a general distrust of people in life. Victims of childhood violence or sexual abuse often distrust others, understandably, and may extend their apprehension toward pilots, airplane mechanics, and other strangers responsible for their safety in the air. Children of overprotective parents may also grow to look proactively for danger in their environment, and may perceive flying as a potential risk to safety.

THE WRIGHT ATTITUDE

Even Orville and Wilbur Wright, the earliest pioneers of aviation and perhaps the bravest air travelers of all, were not without trepidation on December 17, 1903, near Kitty Hawk, North Carolina, when they made the first successful human flight in a motorized airplane, despite a bitter temperature and 27 mile-per-hour winds.

The flight lasted all of 12 seconds and covered a mere 120 feet of ground. Yet when Wilbur Wright saw his brother Orville off in the airplane, as Wilbur himself held onto the wing for balance and ran alongside the craft, he looked by all accounts like a man whose own reflection had just fled from him in the mirror.

Together, the Wright brothers had unwittingly begun to invent the airplane as youngsters when they abandoned all other toys for the little bamboo hand glider their father brought home from a trip abroad. As young boys, they graduated to kites— which they continued to fly as grown men (to the neighbors' amusement and disdain) and modeled their first plane on these primitive man-made birds.

As it turned out, the flight was successful. The brothers took turns making three more that same afternoon, despite the freezing cold and whipping winds—which the brothers, with 10 years of 20/20 hindsight, admitted were perilous for their earliest, most naive flying machine. Nevertheless, Orville later wrote, "With all the knowledge and skill acquired in thousands of flights in the last 10 years, I would hardly think today of making my first flight on a strange machine in a 27 mile-per-hour wind, even if I knew that the machine had already been flown and was safe."

People who suffer from severe phobias unconsciously use their fear as a sieve for perceiving information. Aviophobes believe so firmly that they will die by setting foot on a plane that they are far more likely to remember information that supports their belief and discard information that refutes it—namely, say, the well known fact that air travel is safe in comparison to other forms of modern transportation.

Many aviophobes who tremble at the mere thought of airplanes are fearless in the face of bigger threats to their health and safety. For instance, many people who refuse to set foot on a plane don't hesitate to drive in treacherous, icy conditions, with no more fear than the healthy amount that inspires caution. Many an aviophobe puts his life at risk by smoking two packs of cigarettes a day, without giving more than passing thought to the certifiably lethal threat of lung cancer.

SYMPTOMS OF AVIOPHOBIA

As you probably know, when you perceive danger, the brain responds by signaling the hypothalamus gland to prepare for action, to kick into the "fight-or-flight" response and allow you to escape from the perceived threat. This instinctive defense mechanism may be fueled by a real fear—say, a stranger in the window with a gun and a stocking over his head—or an imagined danger. Fear of air travel is not entirely imagined; planes occasionally do go down and when they do, the results are often catastrophic and thoroughly, spectacularly documented by the news media. It's fair to say, however, that most cases of aviophobia are largely fabricated or at least exaggerated in the imagination of the victim.

Once a severe phobia develops, even a person's physiology chimes in to make that fear harder to beat. The fight-or-flight response releases hormones into the bloodstream that inspire a range of physiological symptoms, many of which serve to magnify the fear.

In aviophobes, the response to air travel—even the very idea of flying on a plane—ranges from sweaty palms to severe hysteria. Mild aviophobes can sometimes manage to psych themselves through a plane ride with nothing more than a case of hives, but in severe cases aviophobes must either refrain from air travel or undergo therapy.

As with any irrational fear, aviophobia usually manifests first as a siege of racing, irrational thoughts regarding the fear. The mere mention of air travel can unleash a parade of worst-case scenarios to fly past the mind's eye. In response to the perceived danger, brain activity actually shifts from the cerebrum, the center of conscious thought, to the brain stem, a very primitive part of the brain that hosts mental activity when a person is in "survival mode." Consequently, your access to information stored in the cerebrum may be cut off entirely. Memory is severely impaired. Concentration may become next to impossible. Dizziness may set in and make it difficult to walk or even speak.

The victim's heart will also respond to the fear. In the face of a threat, a person's heart rate escalates from 72 beats per minute, the average resting pace, to more than 140 beats per minute. The heartbeat may become irregular, and palpitations may occur. Blood vessels constrict, and blood pressure skyrockets. Sensing danger, the body responds by releasing blood sugars into the bloodstream. This usually serves to intensify fear and convinces many victims that they are having a heart attack.

In the face of fear, the body also requires more oxygen in order to escape from the perceived danger. Normally a person takes 6 to 15 breaths per minute, but when someone is intensely scared, that rate may increase to 20 or 30 or more breaths per minute.

A frightened person will also breathe from the thorax, the upper part of the chest, which allows the body to consume oxygen and dispel carbon dioxide much more quickly than when breath is taken in from the diaphragm—the healthy, relaxed way to breathe, which fills the lungs to capacity from the bottom up. When a person breathes too much oxygen, the pupils may dilate and cause vision to blur. Dizziness may set in from the shortage of carbon dioxide. If someone gasps for shallow breath from the upper part of the chest for a long enough time, that person may start to feel a sort of choking sensation and eventually will pass out. This is how the body manages to overcome fear and ensure that a healthy level of carbon dioxide is restored to the respiratory system.

The stomach also responds to fear by secreting more acid. Someone who is very scared may also draw more than the normal level of oxygen into the stomach. These two effects, solo or combined, may cause stomach upset or diarrhea or both.

Fear of flying usually also makes for sweaty palms. The victim's lips, hands, and feet tingle and go cold. The face flushes. Hands may tremble and make it impossible to hold a glass.

Muscles tense up in response to flight fright, especially in the lower jaw, shoulders, lower back, calves, and legs. If leg muscles tense for an extended period of time, the legs may begin to tremble conspicuously or even give out. A person may have trouble standing up if the fear is severe enough. In the worst instances, aviophobes experience such great muscle tension that they may feel the urge to attack a flight attendant or fling open the emergency exit doors— which, by the way, is impossible while the plane is in flight.

2 So What Can Be Done About It?

DR. DUANE BROWN, WHO TEACHES COUNSELING AND counseling psychology at the University of North Carolina, Chapel Hill, and leads American Airlines' fear of flying program, offers a fairly simple, drug-free program for coping with the fear of flying. It attends to both the psychological and the physiological aspects of aviophobia. His book *Flying Without Fear* (New Harbinger Publications: Oakland, 1996) is very user-friendly and offers a host of techniques you can try on your own, without any formal workshop or seminar training.

The program teaches you how to curb the irrational, involuntary thoughts that make your heart pound and your teeth chatter. It also shows you how to curb these physiological symptoms of fear, which undeniably aggravate the phobia and make it harder to overcome. The program also emphasizes the importance of reeducation and offers a new information base about the safety of air travel. These facts are sometimes at odds with the media's terrifying treatment of airplane disasters. They also challenge the somewhat natural human fear of the unknown, which allows so many aviophobes to tremble in the sky yet feel entirely comfortable racing along the freeway at killer speeds.

CURBING THE INVOLUNTARY "FIGHT-OR-FLIGHT" MECHANISM

To some extent, the fear of flying is an involuntary response. You cannot control the thoughts that enter your mind, and once the idea of a plane crash enters an aviophobe's head, a series of physiological responses is triggered, which usually serves only to intensify the fear. In *Flying Without Fear,* Dr. Brown suggests that you can actually curb your initial fear and reduce or eliminate the more advanced stages of flight fright.

The first step is to **identify your fear** and decide you don't want to live with it anymore. Brown recommends that you actually wear a thick rubber band over the palm of your hand on the day of your flight. The minute you have second thoughts about flying or you start to imagine a crash scene, a cabin fire, or your funeral, he recommends that you snap the rubber band. It will hurt, but not as greatly as the pain you'll experience if you panic and your imagination goes into overdrive. Next, he recommends that you actually command your fear to go away. You must not be hard on yourself as you command your fear to flee; keep your anger trained on the fear itself.

The shortness of breath and heart palpitations that usually accompany scary thoughts about air travel may set in within a fraction of a second after you first entertain the fear.

This response is involuntary, so even if you snap the rubber band and try to quell your anxiety, your body will have already started secreting fight-or-flight hormones, your heart will have already started pounding in your chest, and your breathing will quicken and become shallow. You can take action, however, to retard these somewhat automatic responses even after they've set in.

CONTROL YOUR BREATH

The minute after you snap your rubber band, you should **focus on your breathing.** Make an enormous effort to breathe slowly and deeply from your diaphragm. Place your hand on your stomach and take a deep breath. If your belly compresses when you inhale, you are breathing correctly, diaphragmatically. If not, you are probably breathing from the chest, which will intensify your response to the terror.

Keeping your hand on your belly, **practice slow, deliberate inhalation,** sucking your belly in as you fill your lungs with air. After several long, deep breaths, you will begin to perceive an overwhelming sense of calm. As you probably know, deep, diaphragmatic breathing is the cornerstone of ancient relaxation strategies like yoga. Think of your breath as an instrument of healing that will help to cure you of your fear.

If you are still feeling lightheaded after breathing deeply, your chest muscles are probably too worked up to relax entirely. In this case, Dr. Brown recommends that you **grab a plastic bag**—if you're already on the plane, use the air sickness bag in the pocket behind the seat in front of you. Cover your nose and mouth with the bag, pressed against your face so that no air escapes, and breathe normally. Eventually, the air you're breathing will become pure carbon dioxide, which will curb your dizziness once it is restored to its normal levels. Be sure, however, that you remove the bag as soon as your symptoms disappear. Also be sure not to seal the bag over your nose and mouth; just hold it there. Children should not try this.

CONTROL YOUR HEART RATE

You can also slow a pounding heart with a technique called the **Valsalva Maneuver.** Please be aware, however, that only people with healthy cardiovascular systems should try this exercise, as it can altogether stop the heart of someone who has suffered a heart attack or stroke. If you have even slight doubts about the healthiness of your cardiovascular system, consult a doctor before trying this procedure.

If you're convinced your ticker is strong and healthy, try the following steps the minute you can feel your heartbeat speed up and intensify. Sit up straight in your seat. Breathe slowly and deeply from your diaphragm. As you are filling your lungs, pull in your stomach. When your lungs feel full, hold your breath. Use your stomach muscles to push down on your lower intestines, as you would if you were suffering from constipation. As you are bearing down, count 5 seconds: one one-thousand, two one-thousand, and so on. Exhale and release the tension. Your heart rate should slacken by about 20 beats per minute. Repeat the process three or four times, until your heart is beating at a normal pace.

Now, focus all your attention on your breathing, drawing in long, deep breaths from the diaphragm and exhaling slowly. This will keep your heart beating at a normal, relaxed rate.

RELAX TENSE MUSCLES

You will also need to work on relaxing your muscles, focusing on those that are most susceptible to stress: the trapezius, which are the large shoulder muscles that support the neck; the jaw muscles; and the leg muscles.

To eliminate stress in the shoulders, try an exercise called **the turtle.** Sit up straight in your seat. Shrug your shoulders at the same time that you pull in your neck, as though you were a turtle. Aim to touch your ears with your shoulders. Hold the position and count out 5 seconds as you rotate your head to massage the muscles in your shoulders. At the count of five, release the tension. Let your shoulders relax completely, and then repeat this exercise three to five times.

To eliminate stress in the jaw, try **the piranha.** Stick out your lower jaw as far as you can. Try to extend it beyond the teeth in your upper jaw. Hold the position as you count out 5 seconds. Release and allow your jaw to slacken. Repeat three to five times.

To eliminate stress in the legs and prevent them from trembling, try **the ballerina.** Slide your feet as far under the seat in front of you as you can. (This exercise works best in coach, where you won't have much room for your legs.) Lift one foot off the floor, arch your foot, and point it toward the front of the plane. Count out 5 seconds. Then rotate your foot so your toe is pointing toward you. Try to point your foot toward your chin and count out 5 seconds. Drop your foot to the floor and relax. Repeat this exercise three to five times with each leg. You can also try walking to the back of the plane, where you'll have more room to stretch your legs. The walk will also do you good.

REEDUCATE YOURSELF: AERODYNAMICS 101

In order to overcome a fear of flying, it's crucial to replace your old belief—that air travel is life-threatening—with a new set of facts that support the safety of flight, relative to other modes of modern transportation.

The mass media makes this reeducation considerably difficult. However tragic and uncommon, airplane disasters are attention-getters. They strike a chord of sympathy among a wide range of news consumers, they're spectacular fodder for TV broadcasts, and they make for riveting headlines. For every plane crash that makes the front page for 3 days straight, however, 2,000 auto crashes go entirely unreported. The fact that they don't happen all that often makes the media feed on them with greater frenzy when they do. So it's hard to shake the popular notion that air travel is a high-risk mode of transportation because empirical evidence seems to support that idea.

It's one thing to have somebody tell you to replace your fear of flight with the knowledge that air travel is, in fact, a safest way to travel. It's another thing to be able to witness, firsthand, the principles of aerodynamics—the natural forces that work against gravity and wind drag to keep a plane off the ground, once it's in the air.

Lift

The most basic principle of aerodynamics is called **lift,** and it's provided primarily by the plane's wings. When a wing pushes through the air fast enough, at a certain angle, it creates a pressure wave—a column of condensed air that travels with the plane, between the plane and the ground. As the plane accelerates, the pressure wave grows taller and taller and lifts the aircraft higher and higher.

How does this work? The top surface of the wing has a higher curve than the bottom surface. Like a bike passing over a ramp, the air that passes over the peaked top surface of an airplane wing travels farther than the air that passes underneath it. Although the same quantity of air is passing above and below, the air above the wing is more diffuse, less pressurized, because it's traveling farther and stretching over more ground; the air below the wing is denser and more pressurized—so much so that it defies the force of gravity and lifts the plane.

If you're having doubts about this, try a simple trick you probably tried 1,000 times before as a kid. The next time you're traveling on a highway by car, roll down the window, stick out your arm, and hold it out parallel to the blacktop with your hand stretched flat and your palm facing down toward the highway. (If you're the passenger, that is. You shouldn't try this stunt if you're the one behind the wheel.) Now cup your hand and slowly turn your palm to face forward. Voilà! Your arm should fly toward the roof of the car, demonstrating the principle of lift.

The speed of the plane and the angle of the wing increase lift: The faster the speed and the greater the angle, the higher the plane will rise. Aircraft manufacturers design wings with devices known as "flaps" and "slats," which further expand the size and angle of the wing so the plane can alight at the relatively low speed of 150 miles per hour. Even from inside the cabin, you've probably seen these flaps opening and closing on the back edge of the wing, and the slats opening and closing on the front edge of the wing.

Once the plane is aloft, the pilot can retract the flaps and slats, because it's safe to increase velocity enough to keep the plane ascending. When a pilot reaches cruising altitude, he slows down the aircraft in order to level off the flight path. When it's time for descent, the pilot decreases speed even further in order to diminish lift and bring the plane down from the sky. When the pilot is ready to land, he opens the flaps and slats again—this time to create drag, or wind resistance, in order to touch down on land again.

Thrust

Thrust is the principle of aerodynamics that sends the plane forward into space. On large jets, thrust is provided by the engine; on smaller planes (often called "props planes,") propellers do the job.

Jet engines create thrust by taking in air from the front of the engine, compressing it, heating it so the air molecules expand, then expelling the diffused air from the back of the plane.

Like lift, you can easily demonstrate thrust at home with a trick you probably tried many times before as a child. Inflate a balloon. Rather than tie the neck, release your hold on it. The balloon will hurtle forward, with a flatulent racket that kids just love.

3 EASE YOUR ANGST: UNDERSTANDING GOVERNMENT SAFETY ENFORCEMENTS

DR. BROWN BELIEVES THAT ANOTHER WAY TO EASE angst about the perceived precariousness of air travel is to become familiar with the government's monitoring of safety standards. The U.S. government regulates domestic air travel far more rigorously than car travel. The Federal Aviation Administration monitors every aspect of airline safety, from mechanical inspections to pilot training to air traffic control to airport management. (For a discussion of safety standards on foreign carriers, see chapter 5, "Life Preservers.")

Under FAA regulations, each and every commercial plane in the United States is subject to two preflight inspections before it can legally get off the ground. First, an in-service mechanic thoroughly scrutinizes both the exterior of the plane and the cockpit, cross-checking his own observations and findings against the information recorded in the aircraft's log book, also required by the FAA. Each time an airline disaster introduces a safety glitch that goes unaddressed by the current guidelines, the FAA revises its standards and requires mechanics to look out for the problem in the future.

Before they are hired, airline mechanics undergo rigorous, FAA-approved training. Throughout their careers, they are subject to annual retraining and random drug tests.

Often, the preflight mechanic has few corrections to make, since planes and their engines are also subject to strict, routine maintenance overhauls. Also, the minute pilots or crew members detect a mechanical problem, they dispatch a report before the plane even lands. This way, if new parts are needed, mechanics can see to it that they're ready the minute a plane lands. If mechanics make a repair, they indicate that the aircraft is fixed and ready to fly by signing and recording an employee number in the plane's log book. A supervisor then checks the repair and also signs the log book with an employee number.

After the mechanic signs off on an aircraft, indicating that the plane has passed preflight inspection, the pilot and copilot conduct a second inspection of more than 100 items both inside and outside the plane. During the inspection process, baggage is unloaded; gas, food, and drinking water are replenished; and waste is expelled in preparation for the next flight.

Bye-Bye Birdie

In the past, a significant hazard to flight safety was—believe it or not—birds. Planes could suffer serious engine damage if they happened to crash into a flock of birds or even a single bird, if it was large enough.

Now, however, engines are designed to ingest birds after a tangle, so they can continue functioning normally after the encounter. In fact, airplane mechanics test new engines by firing dead chickens into them. In order to pass FAA inspection regulations, an engine must be able to sustain the impact of an eight-pound bird.

Of course it would be naive to assume that aircraft inspectors and mechanics adhere perfectly to every aspect of their job descriptions. Because one small goof can lead to catastrophe, however, the government levies strict fines against airline employees who get sloppy on the job. If a repair proves to be faulty, both the mechanic and the supervisor who signed off on the work are held responsible. Each may be fined as much as $5,000 out of pocket—with no help from the airline.

(For a more detailed discussion of airline safety, both domestic and international, see chapter 5, "Life Preservers.")

HOW FLIGHT PLANS ARE PREPARED

Two hours before a scheduled departure, an airline's dispatchers, who are licensed by the FAA, prepare a flight plan. In light of weather conditions, temperature, and wind velocity, they evaluate the plane's route and determine optimal cruising altitude (typically 35,000 feet) and speed (typically 500 miles per hour at cruising altitude). They determine how much fuel to load by weighing the fastest possible flight time with the most economical amount of fuel. Every

Heavy Traffic

The FAA estimates that 10 million flights take off and land each year in the United States. One and one-half million flights depart and return to Canada annually.

commercial plane that leaves the ground carries enough fuel to transport the plane to its destination, surplus fuel for expected delays and reroutings, 1 or 2 hour's worth of "hold fuel" for unexpected delays, and a minimum of 45 minutes' worth of "reserve fuel," required by the FAA.

HOW AIR TRAFFIC IS CONTROLLED

Once the dispatchers establish the flight plan, they run it by air traffic control. The plan is not official until the FAA's central computer in Washington approves it, and then it is filed electronically and available to every air traffic control tower responsible for a plane along its route.

From their glassed-in towers at the airport, controllers command the skies, monitoring both the sky above their own airport and landing conditions at the destination terminal. If they anticipate congestion when the plane is scheduled to

Air Traffic Violation

The next time you're about to complain about a $150 speeding ticket, be glad you're not a pilot. Commercial pilots have a steep incentive to listen to air traffic controllers, the traffic cops of plane travel. Planes flying at an altitude below 10,000 feet are not allowed to exceed 281 miles per hour. If a plane exceeds the speed limit, the captain can be fined $10,000. If a pilot deviates from the minimum distance allowed between planes, he may receive a fine of up to $10,000.

In both these instances, the pilots themselves are responsible for coming up with this cash; the airline doesn't bail them out.

NEAR MISSES: SO CLOSE & YET SO FAR

For commercial aircraft flying at altitudes under 29,000 feet, air traffic controllers space planes 1,000 feet apart vertically and 3 to 20 miles apart horizontally. For commercial aircraft flying above 29,000 feet, air traffic controllers space planes 2,000 feet apart vertically and 10 miles or more apart horizontally. Near misses are registered every time a plane deviates from this minimum space allowance. Certainly, from 10 to 20 miles away, you are in no danger of a midair collision, just because a flight was called a near miss.

In fact, only three midair collisions have occurred on commercial air carriers between 1982 and mid-1995, resulting in 103 fatalities. While any loss of life is too much, more people die every day in car accidents on U.S. highways than the total number that died in midair collisions.

---

land, controllers at the departure airport have the power to postpone the flight.

Via computerized video screens, each controller monitors a tier of the airspace around an airport. Throughout a flight—on average every 3 to 4 seconds—air traffic controllers maintain direct communication with a plane's pilot via headphones. Each plane appears as a blip as it travels over a variety of digital maps on screens.

The pilot first makes contact with a controller 15 minutes before takeoff. The plane is transferred from one controller to another as it moves from the gate to the runway to the air. Once the plane leaves a control tower's jurisdiction, it is transferred to controllers at other towers en route.

HOW PILOTS ARE TRAINED

Every commercial American airline flight has three pilots in the cockpit: a captain, a first officer, and a second officer.

Pilots must have 2,000 hours of experience in the air and pass a rigorous series of tests before commercial airlines will consider hiring them.

Pilots usually receive their training from either a military service academy (such as the Air Force Academy), an undergraduate military ROTC (Reserve Officers Training Corp) program, or a college or university program that focuses on airline technology. Pilots receive a variety of flying licenses en route to earning their commercial pilot's license.

Once hired, a pilot undergoes another battery of strenuous training; both written and oral testing; flight simulation; and at least 25 hours of flight time, supervised by the FAA, on the type of aircraft he will be flying. A pilot is retrained each time he switches aircraft. New pilots must demonstrate that they know how to perform every aspect of their job before they're allowed to fly. New hires also hold probationary status for 1 year and undergo monthly evaluations by fellow crew members. Captains, flight engineers, and first officers are retrained every year. If they cannot perform satisfactorily with each retraining, they are dismissed.

The FAA also appoints doctors who examine captains twice a year and first officers and flight engineers once a year. Pilots over 40 must receive an EKG. On each flight, the captain and first officer are served different meals, in the "off" chance that the airline food is bad and causes food poisoning. Pilots also undergo random drug testing throughout their careers, and no-notice checks at the hands of FAA officers and airline supervisors.

DO INTERNATIONAL GUIDELINES EXIST?

International carriers are not subject to the FAA's safety requirements, but in order to land and take off on American soil, they must meet the guidelines established by the United Nation's International Civil Aviation Organization,

FLYING BLIND

A flight from San Francisco to Los Angeles was delayed for 45 minutes after passengers had already boarded the aircraft. Needless to say, nearly everybody on board was feeling irritable by the time the flight departed. To make matters worse, the plane had to make an emergency stop in Sacramento. With no further explanation, the flight attendant announced that there would be another 45-minute delay there. As minor consolation, she added that passengers could disembark, provided that they returned in 30 minutes.

Everybody got off the plane except one gentleman who was blind. It seemed pretty clear that he had flown before. His Seeing Eye dog lay quietly underneath the seats in front of him throughout the entire flight, as though he had done so many times before. The pilot approached the man as though he were no stranger, and finally even called him by his first name. He said, "Keith, we're in Sacramento for almost an hour. Would you like to get off and stretch your legs?"

Keith replied, "No thanks, but maybe my dog would like to stretch his legs."

Picture this: All the disgruntled passengers were hanging around the gate area when the pilot—who also happened to be wearing dark sunglasses—walked off the plane with the Seeing Eye dog. First the passengers, en masse, froze. Then they started scattering! Not only did many of them try to change planes; some tried to change airlines!

---

headquartered in Montreal. The FAA itself inspects each foreign carrier and oversees its adherence to ICAO standards. This does not mean that all foreign carriers are as safe as American aircraft—although some are safer. The ICAO

SAFETY BY THE BOOK

The following air travel safety ordinances are still on record in various cities and states around the U.S.

- Lingerie can't be hung on a clothesline at the airport unless the undies are carefully hidden from prying eyes by a "suitable screen" (Kidderville, New Hampshire).

- It is a violation of local law for any pilot or passenger to carry an ice cream cone in his pocket while either flying or waiting to board a plane (Lowes Crossroads, Delaware).

- Pilots and passengers are prohibited from eating onions between the hours of 7am and 7pm (Bluff, Utah).

- No turtle races shall be held at the airport (Bourbon, Mississippi).

---

has failed certain foreign airlines. For a detailed description of ICAO rules and how foreign carriers rate for safety, see chapter 5, "Life Preservers."

4 KNOW YOUR METEOROLOGY: WEATHER DANGERS DEMYSTIFIED

FEARFUL FLIERS TEND TO SUFFER NEEDLESSLY IN THE face of weather patterns in the air that seem to herald danger but, in fact, pose little threat to air travelers. Some weather events certainly do make for hazardous flight conditions, but the FAA prohibits takeoff under these circumstances. Again, here Dr. Brown recommends educating yourself about some of the most commonly feared weather phenomena, and the actual threat they pose to air safety.

- Gargling is prohibited while flying (Hackberry, Arizona).

- Loud burping while walking around the airport is prohibited (Halsted, Kansas).

- It is against the law to sneeze in an airplane (Lynch Heights, Delaware).

- No flying instructor can place his arm around a woman without a good and lawful reason (Rock Springs, Wyoming).

- Juggling in front of an airplane is illegal (Wellsboro, Pennsylvania).

- Roosters may crow, only if it is done at least 300 feet from the airport (Stugis, Michigan).

TURBULENCE

Turbulence, one of the scariest aspects of flight, happens to be relatively innocuous. The biggest threat posed by turbulence is injury inside the cabin if you happen to be standing or sitting without a seat belt when the plane encounters especially rough turbulence, which does jostle the plane a bit. Turbulence is essentially streams of air in motion. Picture what happens when you insert a running hose into a pool of water: The hose water runs as a current, moving faster than the rest of the water and displacing it, sending the displaced water elsewhere. The air moves similarly. When a stream of cold wind, say, encounters warmer air, it runs right through it, cold air being more highly pressurized than warm air, and causes the warm air to rise and go elsewhere. These crashing streams of air are obstacles for airplanes, which manage to fly right through them, but not without some resistance. Air travelers experience this resistance as turbulence. Flying through turbulence is comparable to, and no more dangerous than, driving over gravel in a truck.

A common misnomer for severe turbulence is "air pockets." Air pockets are sort of like the Loch Ness monster of air travel—no more real and no more of a threat, despite their mythic proportions in the aviophobe's mind. The misleading term was coined during World War I by a journalist who was merely trying to describe turbulence. Contrary to popular myth, air pockets cannot cause planes to drop out of the sky or fall hundreds of feet. They are nothing more than a severe form of turbulence.

Turbulence is hard to predict, but it tends to occur near thunderstorms, over mountain ranges, and over very warm areas like Florida. The most dangerous type of turbulence is called clear-air turbulence. As its name suggests, it occurs unexpectedly in otherwise calm, clear skies. Clear-air turbulence poses a mild threat only because the plane will encounter it unexpectedly. If you happen to be walking about the cabin at that moment, you may fall or bang into something. If you're traveling on a smooth flight, and the pilot turns on the "fasten seat belts" light, it is usually because he is expecting some clear-air turbulence. When this happens, follow the flight crew's instructions. You might want to stop drinking hot beverages until the light goes off. It's also wise to wait a minute if you were planning to use the rest room or pull belongings down from the overhead bin.

Flight attendants are actually at greatest risk when the plane encounters turbulence, since they move about the most during a flight. When a pilot asks the flight attendants to sit, it is usually not because the plane is in grave danger, but because the flight path is passing through choppy skies.

Pilots will often try to escape turbulence by ascending or descending to another altitude, where the air may be less agitated. This too does not mean the plane is endangered, but rather that the pilot is simply trying to give his passengers a smoother ride. Neither are they struggling to maintain control of the plane, another popular misperception of turbulence. In fact, many captains navigate rough skies on auto pilot, which is better able to anticipate shifts in temperature and air pressure.

THUNDERSTORMS

Thunderstorms do pose a danger to air travel. Flight plans are devised to help pilots avoid them, and the FAA prohibits planes from flying in the perilous core of a storm. Commercial aircraft must remain 20 miles away from this turbulent center of high winds, hail, and heavy rain. When a plane does enter a windy, rainy part of the sky, it must stay within the storm's outer reaches—where the biggest threat is turbulence. Most pilots try to avoid thunderstorms altogether, however, to provide their passengers with a smoother ride.

Even lightning, contrary to popular belief, cannot "strike" an airplane and electrocute passengers, because the plane is not grounded. Lightning hits planes almost every day and does no damage to the aircraft or to travelers, because it passes right through the plane. If lightning hits your plane, the worst you'll suffer is a ringing in your ears from the subsequent thunderclap.

WIND SHEAR

Wind shear is essentially a sudden change in wind speed or direction within a short distance. When it occurs, it usually accompanies a thunderstorm. The most severe form of wind shear is called a "microburst," which starts off as a strong head wind followed by a tail wind, torrential rain, and a fierce down draft that can literally run a plane into the ground if it is flying at low altitudes.

Although wind shear poses no threat at high altitudes, it can be dangerous to planes flying at lower levels. In the entire history of flight, however, only two planes have crashed because of it. Since the most recent incident, in 1994, pilots have been required to receive special training in flight simulators to detect wind shear and avoid it. After the initial training, pilots must take refresher courses every 6 months. Several newfangled wind-shear detection devices have also been invented since then. Most airports are equipped with mechanisms that measure wind speed and alert air-traffic control when wind shear is detected. Doppler radar is also able to detect wind shear in advance.

FOG

If fog happens to cloud the runway when a plane is scheduled to depart, air traffic control will delay the flight until visibility improves. Controllers don't always have the leisure, however, to postpone a plane's landing indefinitely. Because of this, planes are required to travel with enough fuel to allow them to postpone landing if visibility is poor.

Under certain conditions pilots are allowed to land, with help from electronics and computers, in even 0/0

THROUGH RAIN & SNOW & DARK OF NIGHT

When ValuJet crashed in the Everglades, it became public knowledge that ValuJet pilots were paid by the flight. If inclement weather forced the airline to cancel a departure, the scheduled pilot would be out of luck.

ValuJet pilots, however, had enormous say over whether their flight would be grounded in poor weather. In practice, this meant that many ValuJet flights got off the ground under hazardous weather conditions that would have prompted any major carrier to cancel the flight without question, because pilots didn't want to lose money. This practice helped ValuJet to earn its reputation as one of the least safe American airlines on record.

Air travelers will be relieved to know that most airlines pay pilots by the minute. If a hailstorm forces an airline to delay a flight, the pilots make more money, not less.

---

visibility. The term "0/0 visibility" means that the plane has no ceiling—it's under 300 feet above the ground—and the pilot can't see farther than 600 feet ahead. If the runway has an instrument called an "electronic glide slope" the pilot can use instruments to "see" ahead and land safely. Likewise, some planes are equipped with devices to make a safe 0/0 landing possible. Newer pilots, however, are sometimes prohibited from landing until visibility improves.

ICE

In freezing weather, airport runways are systematically inspected for ice and closed the minute ice is detected. Planes are also equipped with antilock and antiskid brakes as further protection against icy conditions.

The planes themselves are thoroughly deiced almost immediately before a flight and coated with a substance that prevents ice from forming. Once a plane is airborne, ice cannot develop on jets, because the engine, which is naturally very hot, distributes hot air to areas of the plane that may develop ice.

5 OTHER WAYS TO TREAT AVIOPHOBIA

SEVERAL PROFESSIONAL AVIOPHOBIA TREATMENTS are available and effective—though they may be more elaborate, less user friendly, and costlier than Dr. Duane Brown's program. They are all rooted in exposure therapy, which requires patients to confront their fear head-on.

EXPOSURE THERAPY

Exposure therapy is used to treat a number of anxiety disorders. Clients subject themselves to anxiety-producing situations—first minor, then moderate, and eventually severe. The objective is to recondition the client into experiencing a relaxed feeling when faced with an anxiety-producing situation. This often involves "homework" assignments, which require patients to research common myths about air travel in order to strengthen the cognitive foundation for a new, fearless attitude toward flying. For instance, patients might have to research the number of actual crashes at the local airport versus the instances of turbulence that felt life-threatening but were anything but.

Sometimes patients learn deep-relaxation techniques before they begin the systematic exposure. The exposure therapists at **Boston University's Center for Anxiety and Related Disorders** (☎ 617/353-9610), however, view even relaxation techniques as avoidance tactics that prevent the patient from really grappling head-on with their fears.

The client begins the process in an office setting, but the final stages of treatment take place where the patient experiences the greatest anxiety—first the airport, then the cabin of a grounded plane, and eventually aboard a short but very real flight from, say, Boston to New York.

The hottest version of exposure therapy at press time is **virtual reconditioning,** a high-tech way to systematically confront phobias. With the help of a software program called Virtually Better, clients ready themselves for flight without ever setting foot on a plane. Clients don head-phones and find themselves in a model airplane cabin, replete with ugly carpeting, newspapers, and cramped quarters. They experience ear popping, that implosive magnified vacuum sound you hear during takeoff, and even turbulence and thunderstorms, simulated through jarring seat vibration and earth-shaking sound effects. Eventually, the patient is escorted on a real flight. The therapy is very new, so it's difficult to gauge its long-term effectiveness, but since treatment, many recent clients have successfully ridden planes alone for extended time periods.

The following five research centers are currently testing the software: the **Center for Anxiety and Related Disorders** at Boston University (☎ 617/353-9610); **Virtually Better,** in Atlanta, where the software was developed (☎ 404/873-4404); the **Center for Advanced Multimedia Psychotherapy** in San Diego (☎ 619/623-2777, ext. 704); the **Phobia Clinic at Hillside Hospital** in Glen Oaks,

NY (☎ **718/470-8120**); and the **Phobia Center** in Cleveland (☎ **216/464-4101**).

FLOODING

Flooding, a more intensive variation on exposure therapy, is another popular treatment for fear of flying. Not for the faint of heart, flooding forces clients to face their fears all at once, in an airport or on an airplane. Clearly it's a faster way to deal with, and perhaps overcome, the fear of flying; in fact, the approach seems tailored to the kind of people who dive head-first into ice-cold water rather than wade in slowly. But while many clients do manage to confront their fears at first, existing data regarding the long-term benefits of flooding are still inconclusive.

6 SIMPLE REMEDIES FOR MINOR AVIOPHOBIA

IF YOU'RE LEAVING ON A JET PLANE TOMORROW, OR for some other reason don't have time to embark on an intensive treatment program, there are simple safeguards you can take to curb anxiety before you board a plane.

- **Eat a nutritious meal before boarding.** If you go too long without food, your body will try to compensate for your low blood sugar level by releasing adrenaline. This chemical reaction will make you feel stressed and anxious.

- **Avoid refined sugars** (candy bars and other junk foods), **caffeine** (a stimulant), and **alcohol.** While doctors sometimes prescribe one-time doses of anti-anxiety drugs like Xanax for aviophobia, the side effects can be a problem (drowsiness, withdrawal symptoms). Ultimately, it's a band-aid solution that doesn't get at the root cause of the phobia.

- Try to **get to the airport early.** The last thing you want to be when you step on a plane is nervous and anxious.

- **Avoid reports of air disasters.** If you suffer from untended aviophobia, you will tend to seek out information that supports your fear. Plane crashes make for great news stories. While they don't occur very often, they are mighty spectacular when they do, so the press tends to give them disproportionately extensive coverage.

- **Sit over a wing,** rather than in back, for a smoother ride. While turbulence is for the most part harmless—provided that you're seated and wearing a safety belt at the time it occurs—it is jarring and can easily fuel your fear if you're not in full control of your phobia.

- **Splurge on a first-class or business-class ticket** if your fear of flying stems from claustrophobia; it will guarantee you more space. If you must fly coach, try to book a bulkhead seat or check in early and reserve an emergency exit row seat (see chapter 2, "The Mercy Seat"). Either way, you'll have a little more room to stretch out.

- **Avoid sitting in a window seat** if your fear of flying stems from acrophobia, or fear of heights, where you will be able to look down and see how high you're flying.

- Finally, **take charge of your situation.** The safety of flying is not foolproof—despite the fact that evidence indisputably supports the safety of flying over travel by car or by train. Still, you can take a more active role in flight safety. Some seats, for instance, are safer than others, some airlines are safer than others, some airports are safer than others, some countries hold to more rigorous standards of safety than others. See chapter 5, "Life Preservers," for a full discussion of safe-flying strategies.

5

LIFE PRESERVERS: HEALTH & SAFETY IN THE AIR

Prepared for takeoff on a flight to Chicago, a very full, very popular budget carrier pulled away from the gate and taxied down the runway—business as usual. Suddenly, the pilot shut down the engines, turned around, and returned to the gate. The front door opened, and passengers and crew waited a full hour before the flight finally took off.

Once the plane reached cruising altitude and passengers were free to move about the cabin, a businessman asked a flight attendant what happened. "Oh, it was nothing," she said. "The pilot heard a noise in the engine—so they went back and got a new pilot."

As airlines cut corners in obvious ways—delaying half-empty planes in order to fill them up, routinely overselling flights, and eliminating onboard amenities—it's hard not to suspect they're cutting corners behind the scenes as well, in ways that could seriously jeopardize passenger health and safety. Head colds are extremely common to air travelers because airlines, as a cost-saving measure, pump recycled air into the cabin. The infamous ValuJet crash in the Everglades took place because mechanics rushing through a preflight check loaded 144 chemical oxygen generators—into the forward cargo hold, where no fire or smoke detection system could have alerted the cockpit of the fire that caused the explosion.

Short of wearing an oxygen mask and overseeing the preflight inspection, you can never be entirely sure you'll land as safe and as healthy as you were at takeoff. With the proper precautions, however, you can significantly increase the chances of arriving in one piece—without so much as a case of the sniffles.

1 TRAVELING SAFELY IN THE AIR

DESPITE THE SAFETY OF AIR TRAVEL, RELATIVE TO other mechanized forms of transportation, the fact remains that accidents do happen. You may find it surprising that the majority of airplane crashes happen during takeoff and landing. Your best safeguards in these situations are your seatbelt and your ability to make a fast exit to escape fumes before they incapacitate you—which can happen in as little as 90 seconds. Preparedness could end up saving your life.

SAFETY STRATEGIES

- **Keep your seatbelt fastened snugly around the hips**—not the waist—even after the captain turns off the "fasten seatbelt" lights. According to the FAA, the most common flying injuries result from turbulence that occurs suddenly and throws passengers from their seats. If you suddenly hit turbulence, you'll be safe even if you happened to fall asleep.

- **Sit near an exit.** Most plane crash fatalities result from smoke inhalation. The faster you can escape in the event of a disaster, the safer you'll be. Before takeoff, count the number of seats to the exit so you can feel your way there in case smoke makes it impossible to see.

- **Don't drink and fly.** Alcohol will affect you much more rapidly at high altitudes and make it much more difficult to escape quickly, in the event of an emergency.

- **Don't smoke in the rest rooms.** This can cause a fire even if the plane is in perfect working order.

- **Don't store heavy or pointed objects in the overhead bins.** These can become projectiles in a crash or even during severe turbulence.

- **Wear flat shoes on the plane.** You'll be able to evacuate the aircraft more quickly, in case of an emergency, and you won't risk puncturing the emergency slide.

- **Wear natural fabrics when you fly.** Synthetics can melt and adhere to the skin in a fire. (You'll also be more comfortable in natural fabrics, as they breathe better and will adjust more readily to shifting cabin temperatures.)

- **Listen carefully to the flight attendant's safety briefing** and read the safety card in your seat pocket. You will learn where emergency exits are and how to open them. You will also learn how to operate any other emergency equipment on the aircraft, such as oxygen masks and flotation devices. After you've digested the safety information, mentally rehearse your escape while the plane is still on the ground.

- **Count the seats to two of the nearest exits** before you take off. If the cabin begins to darken with smoke, you won't have to rely on sight to make your escape. If one of the doors is blocked or overcrowded, you'll be ready to escape through another.

- **Choose to fly only in aircraft with more than 30 seats.** These are held to the strictest safety regulations.

- **Fly nonstop when you can.** The fewer takeoffs and landings per flight, the lower the accident risk.

WHEN ACCIDENTS DO HAPPEN: WHAT YOU CAN DO

According to the National Transportation Safety Board, 60% of passengers involved in plane crashes end up surviving. Between 1978 and 1995, there were 164 accidents with at least one passenger fatality. In 37 cases more than 90% of all passengers survived. While it's obviously best not to dwell on the prospect of an emergency situation, it's wise to give it some consideration—to the same extent that you would rehearse a fire drill in school or in the workplace.

- If the flight crew instructs you to **adopt a brace position,** make sure your seat belt is low and tight across your hips. Bend from the waist and bring your chest as close to your knees as you can. Your head should touch the seat in front of you. Place your hands on top of your head, one on top of the other, and protect your face with your forearms. Pull your feet back slightly behind your knees.

- The minute you detect smoke, **cover your nose and mouth with a cloth,** preferably a damp one. If you know where the smoke or fire is coming from, move away as quickly as possible. Listen carefully for directions from the flight crew, as they may know more than you do about the source of the smoke or fire.

- As you evacuate the cabin, **stay as low to the cabin floor as possible.** Do not attempt to salvage any of your possessions.

- **Check for fire outside the emergency exit
  door** before you open it. If you find a fire, use
  another exit. This is why it's important to
  rehearse your evacuation, while you're still on the
  ground, through more than one nearby emergency
  exit.

- **If you're wearing high heels, take them off**
  before you evacuate via the emergency slide. They
  can puncture the slide and jeopardize you and
  passengers behind you.

- Once outside the plane, **move away as quickly as
  possible.** Help those who need assistance if you
  can, but never step back inside or return to a burn-
  ing aircraft.

Magellans (☎ **800/962-4943;** www.magellans.com) sells
an emergency escape hood that protects your eyes and lungs
from heat, smoke, and soot for up to 20 minutes. **Evac-U8**
($69, two for $125) will make you look like a Martian
when you slip its Teflon-coated hood over your head, but it
could save your life as it protects your face from up to 800°
temperatures.

2   THE VERDICT ON AIR SAFETY

IN 1997, SAFETY EXPERTS FROM THE AIRLINE INDUSTRY,
government aviation agencies, and academia assembled in
Washington for the International Conference on Aviation
Safety and Security in the 21st century, sponsored by the
White House and the George Washington University.
There, they concluded that U.S. air travel is among the
world's safest, with only four deaths per 10 million departures since 1980. The experts also shared the opinion, however, that several aspects of commercial flight were in need
of reform.

THE NEED FOR REFORM

Experts agreed that about two-thirds of air crash fatalities in the last ten years occurred because of a flight-crew error. Panelists asserted that more rigorous training and evaluation would significantly reduce this particular cause of problems. Experts also agreed that the industry needs to develop better navigational equipment and information about landing conditions around the world, to further curtail the number of accidents caused by flight crews.

The two areas most in need of reform, however, are **fire safeguards** and **emergency evacuation procedures.** As mentioned, many airlines now equip cargo areas with fire extinguishers, and many safety experts would like to abolish the environmental ban on halon-based fire retardant systems, which contain chlorofluorocarbons but remain unrivaled in the prevention of fire. Safety experts argue that they are so seldom used that their usefulness far outweighs the environmental risk associated with their use.

Finally, experts contend that evacuation procedures influence the gravity of plane crashes. Evidence suggests that more crash victims survive when they are assisted by more than the minimum number of flight attendants required by the FAA. Evidence also suggests that full-size emergency exit doors prevent more fatalities than the smaller exit doors found over the wing of a plane. One expert contended that high-density seating on planes slows down evacuation procedures, which could suggest that you're safer in spacious business or first class than you are when you're crammed into coach. While federal regulations require emergency-exit row aisles to be at least 20 inches wide, the FAA has issued waivers to most domestic carriers to narrow these aisles to 14 inches. Imagine running for your life in a smoke-filled aircraft through a space only 14 inches wide!

To boot, although the accident rate has remained relatively low for ten years, the volume of air traffic is increasing steadily. According to the findings of the International Conference on Aviation Safety and Security in the 21st century, air-travel volume is expected to double over the next decade—which means that a fatal crash will occur every 2 to 3 weeks by the year 2009. This level of frequency is unacceptable, by any standards. So, the experts are rallying to find ways to make the system better still.

The problem is that when crashes occur in the industrialized world, they are for the most part random events. When a catastrophic event occurs, government safety officials study it rigorously to root out the causes and prevent them from bringing down another aircraft. When ValuJet (now AirTran) crashed in the Florida Everglades, for instance, investigators discovered that fire brought down the aircraft after oxygen tanks, inadequately labeled and stowed onboard, ignited. In response, airlines began installing smoke detectors in their cargo areas to prevent the same type of tragedy from happening again.

INTERPRETING THE SAFETY DATA

Many consumers would be thrilled to see the FAA rate individual airlines for safety, but so far the government is reluctant to make this type of ranking public. FAA officials argue that it's nearly impossible to predict when a plane is going to crash because all the major carriers need to meet rigorous safety regulations in order to operate at all. They argue that past crashes don't help predict the cause of future accidents either, because lightning seldom strikes twice in the same place: As mentioned, crash causes are quickly detected and corrected. The experts say that even an analysis of minor safety infringements or snafus does not necessarily help predict major ones; some even argue that an inverse relationship exists between major and minor problems in the air. Furthermore, some of the information used to rate the airlines would have to come from the airline itself, and safety inspectors could be inclined to doctor data.

The FAA does publish safety data on its Web site (**www.faa.gov**), which includes the National Transportation Safety Board's Incident/Accident Database, organized by carrier. The FAA warns, however, that the definition of an aviation accident is very broad. If a flight attendant breaks his leg in the aisle, this qualifies as an accident—as does a CFIT, or "controlled flight into terrain," when a normally functioning plane that has passed inspection crashes, usually due to a flight-crew error. So the raw data can be misleading. It's nearly impossible for the general public to extrapolate any type of safety ranking from the statistics from the FAA site.

Ralph Nader's Aviation Consumer Action Project, is working with industry experts to evaluate the FAA data and rank the top 20 carriers according to their safety records. The information should be available in the summer of 2000. Keep your eyes open for this important document, which could serve to breathe new life into safety standards by making each carrier and crew member more accountable for safety on each and every flight.

SO WHAT DOES THIS MEAN FOR YOU, THE PASSENGER?

Mary Schiavo, former inspector general of the U.S. Department of Transportation, published a whistle-blowing expose called *Flying Blind, Flying Safe* (Avon: New York, 1997). Her tenure in the FAA convinced her that airline and FAA employees were cutting corners on safety and placing the flying public at greater risk than necessary. According to Schiavo, there is ample evidence—much of which she made public for the first time—to support that some airlines are safer than others, some airports are safer than others, some countries are safer than others, and some continents are safer than others. She makes the following recommendations:

1. Do not fly on airlines that the FAA has grounded or seriously disciplined in recent years. (See "Airlines Grounded & Disciplined by the FAA, 1995 to 1997," below.)

2. Do not fly on start-up budget carriers in their second or third year of operation, since their accident

rate is usually twice that of major carriers. New large carriers have an even worse safety record.

3. Do not fly on foreign carriers that fail FAA checks or receive only conditional approval (see "How Safe Are International Carriers?" below)

4. Do not fly on planes built in the former Soviet Union or on airlines operating from China. The crash rate is extremely high and may not even include the total number of accidents, since it's nearly impossible to obtain accurate data.

5. If you're flying to Africa or Latin America, use a domestic airline.

6. Purchase your ticket with a charge card in the United States, even if you're flying on a foreign aircraft. You will have far more rights as a passenger if something goes wrong.

7. Avoid commuter airlines and "prop" planes if possible. They are far more vulnerable in bad weather, and they are far more subject to turbulence created by the wake of larger jets.

8. When you choose a carrier, pay attention to its overall performance. Overall performance does not necessarily correlate with the safety of an airline. But common sense suggests that if a carrier is consistently late, if it loses or mishandles a relatively high amount of baggage per passenger, and if it receives a proportionately large number of complaints, chances are it's cutting corners on safety standards as well. (See data relating to on-time arrival ratings, in chapter 1, "Ticketing Pitfalls"; incidents of lost or mishandled luggage per carrier, in chapter 3, "Lost in Space"; and number of complaints lodged per passenger, in chapter 9, "The Squeaky Wheel.")

AIRPORTS PILOTS DO NOT LIKE—AND WHY

Boston Logan   Poor airport management; poor snow removal; salt used on runways and taxiways (which is not permitted); poor landing rules; hazards at the end of runways.

Cleveland   Runways and/or taxiways intersect; city neighborhoods hem in the airport; facilities are small, old, and inadequate relative to passenger load.

Detroit   Runways and/or taxiways intersect; city neighborhoods hem in the airport; facilities are small, old, and inadequate relative to passenger load; poor markings.

Juneau   Airport surrounded by glaciers and mountain peaks; ice, fog, and wind shear are very severe.

Los Angeles   Very high congestion.

New York La Guardia   Runways and/or taxiways intersect; city neighborhoods hem in the airport; facilities are small, old, and inadequate relative to passenger load.

San Diego   Runways and/or taxiways intersect; city neighborhoods hem in the airport; facilities are small, old, and inadequate relative to passenger load.

San Francisco   Very narrow parallel runways; poor visibility due to fog; inadequate equipment.

Sun Valley (Idaho)   Airport hemmed in very tightly by mountains.

Washington D.C. (Reagan National)   Runways and/or taxiways intersect; city neighborhoods hem in the airport; facilities are small, old, and inadequate relative to passenger load.

Source: Mary Schiavo, Flying Blind, Flying Safe, *1997*

AIRLINES GROUNDED & DISCIPLINED BY THE FAA, 1995 TO 1997

(Source: Mary Schiavo, *Flying Blind, Flying Safe,* 1997)

Alaska   Improperly modified main landing gear of a Boeing 737 and flew it that way on 9,000 passenger flights.

Air Tran (formerly ValuJet)   As Air Tran, committed serious safety violations—falsified documents, improper maintenance, faulty repairs, and failure to supervise contractors. As ValuJet, the airline was grounded in 1996 for gross safety violations and the fatal crash in the Everglades.

Arrow Air   This cargo hauler and charter was grounded for safety violations in 1995. They surrendered their certificate, and the name was taken over by AvAtlantic (see below).

AvAtlantic   This charter airline was grounded in 1997 for safety violations. Now operating out of Clearwater, Florida as Arrow Charter.

Delta   Charged with poor overall maintenance, operating old planes, and uncontained engine failure in 1997 (where the engine explodes and pieces fly through the plane). Experienced a 1997 enforcement action for flying with a closet door sealed shut; the closet had emergency equipment and fire extinguishers locked inside.

Great American Airways   FAA charged this airline with falsifying documents regarding training, flight, duty time, and load record.

Great Lakes Aviation   This company, which operates United Express and Midway Express flights, was voluntarily suspended after the FAA discovered it flew "unairworthy planes."

Markair   Shut down by the FAA in 1995 for maintenance violations.

Mesa   Fined by the FAA in 1996 and 1997 for safety violations.

PanAm   This familiar face was "reborn" in 1996 with old, unsafe Eastern Airlines planes; acquired Carnival (ruled very unsafe) in 1997. *Note:* In 1998, Pan Am ceased operations, then was acquired under a Chapter 11 Plan of Reorganization, and resumed service in October 1999 with a limited schedule.

Rich International   This charter airline was fined $2.6 million and grounded for stocking bogus parts in its maintenance bays.

Skyway Airlines   Now operates with Mesa under a code-share; in 1997, the former head of maintenance was fined and jailed for using bogus parts, lying to FAA inspectors, and submitting fake warranty claims as a cover-up.

Tower Airlines   This carrier's accident/incident rate is six times higher than the grounded ValuJet; it has the highest near-miss rate in the FAA's entire study of budget carriers.

ValuJet (now Air Tran)   See Air Tran, above.

VIP Air Charter   FAA revoked this air carrier certificate in 1997 for falsifying pilot training records, using unqualified pilots, and operating unairworthy or unauthorized aircraft.

World Airways   This carrier was fined $610,000 in 1997 for security violations.

3 HOW SAFE ARE INTERNATIONAL CARRIERS?

INTERNATIONAL CARRIERS ARE NOT SUBJECT TO THE FAA's safety requirements, but in order to land and take off on American soil, they must meet the guidelines established by the United Nation's International Civil Aviation Organization, headquartered in Montreal. The FAA itself inspects each foreign carrier and oversees its adherence to ICAO standards. This does not mean that all foreign carriers are as safe as American aircraft—although some are safer. The ICAO has failed certain foreign airlines.

ICAO RATINGS OF AIR TRAVEL BY COUNTRY

(Updated by the ICAO January 10, 1998)
Category I: Does comply with ICAO standards.
Category II: Failed to meet certain ICAO standards but is negotiating with FAA to correct the failures.

Category III: Does not comply with ICAO standards.

Country	*Category*
Argentina	I
Aruba	I
Australia	I
The Bahamas	I
Bangladesh	I
Belize	III (no current operators)
Bermuda	I
Bolivia	II
Brazil	I
Brunei	I
Bulgaria	I
Canada	I
Cayman Island	I
Chile	I
Colombia	II
Congo	no current operators
Costa Rica	I
Cote D'Ivoire	II
Czech Republic	I
Dominican Republic	III (no current operators)
Ecuador	II
Egypt	I
El Salvador	I

Country	Category
Fiji	I
France	I
Gambia	III
Germany	I
Ghana	I
Guatemala	II
Guyana	I
Haiti	III
Honduras	III (no current operators)
Hong Kong	I
Hungary	I
India	I
Indonesia	I
Israel	I
Jamaica	I
Jordan	I
Kiribati	II
Kuwait	II
Malaysia	I
Malta	III
Marshall Islands	I
Mexico	I
Morocco	I
Nauru	I

Country	Category
Netherlands	I
Netherlands Antilles	I (Curaçao, St. Martin, Bonaire, Saba, St. Eustatius)
New Zealand	I
Nicaragua	III (no current operators)
Oman	I
Organization of Eastern Caribbean States (Anguilla, Antigua and Barbuda, Dominica, Grenada, Montserrat, St. Lucia, St. Vincent and the Grenadines, St. Kitts, and Nevis)	II
Pakistan	II
Panama	I
Paraguay	III (no current operators)
Peru	I
Philippines	I
Poland	I
Romania	I
Saudi Arabia	I
Singapore	I
South Africa	I
South Korea	I

Country	Category
Suriname	III
Swaziland	III (no current operators)
Taiwan	I
Thailand	I
Trinidad and Tobago	I
Turkey	I
Turks and Caicos	II
Ukraine	I
United Kingdom	I
Uruguay	III
Uzbekistan	I
Venezuela	II
Western Samoa	I
Yugoslavia	I (Serbia and Montenegro)
Zimbabwe	III (no current operators)

SAFEST COUNTRIES & REGIONS TO FLY IN (AS OF 1997)

Source: Mary Schiavo, *Flying Blind, Flying Safe,* 1997

Canada Extremely safe; no fatal accidents by major carriers in 10 years

Caribbean Extremely safe; no fatal crashes by major carriers in 10 years (though Trinidad and Tobago ranked conditional in ICAO standards).

Central America   Among the world's riskiest; the worst: Aviateca from Guatemala, COPA from Panama.

South America   Avoid the airlines of Bolivia, Colombia, Venezuela, and Peru (and specifically the airlines ACES, Aero Peru, Aeropublica, AeroSur, Americana de Aviacion, Aserca, Austral, AVENSA, Avianca, Faucett, Intercontinental Colombia, LAN Chile, LAV, Lloyd Aero Boliviano, SAM Colombia, SATENA, SAM, Servivensas, TAM, and VIASA).

Western Europe   All airlines earned top marks except Air France, British Midland, Lauda, Martinair Holland, and THY Turkish Airlines.

Eastern Europe   Avoid carriers from countries of former Soviet Union; the worst: Aeroflot, Tarom (Romania).

Africa   Among the worst; in particular, steer clear of: ADC Airlines (Nigeria), Air Mauritanie (Mauritania), Ethiopian Airlines, Libyan Arab Airlines, Nigeria Airways, and Okada Air (Nigeria). Nigeria is the least safe place on earth to fly.

Middle East   Fairly safe, with the exception of Iran Air.

India   Air India is very risky; Pakistan International Airways passed ICAO standards conditionally.

Australia, New Zealand, South Pacific   Among the safest airlines in the world; safer than the United States.

Southern Asia   Fairly unsafe, with the exception of Singapore Airlines, which is extremely safe; the worst: Garuda Indonesia, Merpati Nusantara Airlines, Philippine Airlines, Thai International, and Vietnam Airlines.

Japan   Among the world's safest; no fatal accidents in the last ten years.

Northern Asia (except Japan)   Extremely unsafe, with exception of Cathay Pacific and Dragonair, which are very safe. The worst: Korean Airlines, Taiwan's China Airlines, China Eastern Airlines, China Northern Airlines, China Northwest Airlines, China Southern Airlines, and Xiamen Airlines.

4 HEALTH IN THE AIR: COMMON PROBLEMS & AILMENTS

THE BEST-LAID VACATION PLANS CAN BE FOILED BEFORE the fun even begins, if you manage to get sick on the plane ride there. Planes are like illness incubators, cramping and dessicating passengers, encapsulating germs, and exacerbating the symptoms of certain medical conditions. Healthy travel is happy travel, and well worth the price of advance preparation and know-how. Here's a rundown of the most common "bio-pitfalls" associated with flying, and ways to counteract them that will keep you flying in good health.

"SICK-AIRPLANE SYNDROME"

Even if you're a low-maintenance globetrotter, needing only the air that you breathe to feel content and alive, you may find yourself feeling cruddy and in need of some pampering soon after you board an airplane.

Many travelers experience flulike symptoms on planes that persist through the duration of a flight. Mistakenly, they attribute their temporary unwellness to jet lag, when in fact they may be suffering from a variation of "sick building syndrome" or experiencing the effects of dehydration.

If you work in a poorly ventilated, highly populated office space, you are probably familiar with the occupational hazard known as sick building syndrome. Fewer public places are as prone to this condition as an airplane cabin—where strangers are packed, elbow to elbow, with no access to fresh air, for extended periods of time.

Cabin air on almost every domestic aircraft is now recycled, which exacerbates the problem. For years, airlines pumped fresh air into their aircraft cabins from outside. At cruising altitude, air temperature is about 65°F, so the fresh air was pumped through the aircraft's jet engine compressors, which heated it to about 400°F, then chilled to comfortable temperatures by air conditioners and heat exchangers.

In recent years, however, airline executives discovered that they could curtail fuel expenses and boost profits by mixing 50% fresh air with 50% filtered, recycled cabin air. In fresh air, the oxygen you inhale contains under 1% carbon dioxide. The air you exhale, on the other hand, contains 4% carbon dioxide. When many people share a poorly ventilated, enclosed space for extended periods of time, the carbon dioxide level rises. Carbon dioxide, as you may know if you work in a poorly ventilated office space, is the primary culprit in sick building syndrome.

The more time you spend in an enclosed, highly populated space like an airplane cabin, the more likely you are to experience headaches, sluggishness, sore throats, coughing, and dry or watery eyes. To boot, the air at high altitudes is dryer than the atmosphere above the Sahara Desert—no kidding—so you may find your symptoms compounded by the effects of dehydration if you're not consuming copious amounts of water.

Furthermore, evidence suggests that more travelers develop colds in airplane cabins than in other enclosed, highly populated public spaces. This is due in part to the fact that dehydration diminishes the immune system; but it's also because, as mentioned, few other public spaces keep people in such close quarters for such an extended period of time.

Fortunately, sick building syndrome symptoms tend to vanish soon after you take leave of the offending space. Unfortunately, there's not too much you can do to prevent symptoms altogether. A few well-practiced tricks can make you feel a little bit better in the air.

- If your budget allows, **fly in first or business class,** where fewer people share air space.

- Don't leave home without your inhaler if you have asthma.

- Where possible, try to **avoid flying with a cold** (see "Flying with a Cold," below).

- If you're on a connecting flight, **try to get as much fresh air** as you can between connections.

- Clear your head with a **steaming hot shower** when you land.

- **Avoid smoke-filled bars** when you reach your destination or while you wait for a connecting flight.

Magellans travel supplier (☎ **800/962-4943;** www.magellans.com) sells an air purifier you can wear around your neck. **Air Supply** ($99) sucks up contaminated air, destroys impurities, and releases clean, fresh air to your mouth, nose, and eyes. Air Supply will run on one nine-volt battery for 30 to 35 hours. If you wear a pacemaker, however, you should not use this device.

DEHYDRATION

While the earth's desert regions have a 20% to 25% humidity level, the cabin of a plane flying at cruising altitude (35,000 feet) has a mere 15% humidity content. In this arid environment, your skin evaporates as much as 8 ounces of water per hour. This is why your eyes burn, your lips dry out, your head hurts, and you feel generally sluggish, lightheaded, and cranky while you're on a plane.

It's absolutely imperative that you drink lots of water before, during, and after your flight to maintain your body's fluid reserves. Not only will you feel much better, you'll help ward off a host of other maladies. The effects of dehydration compromise the immune system, so you're far more likely to catch the complimentary cold that comes with air travel if you don't drink enough water. Dehydration will also aggravate the symptoms of jet lag.

Even if you don't feel thirsty, drink up. Thirst doesn't necessarily precede the symptoms of dehydration, which can set in without warning. Experts recommend that you drink at least two 8-ounce glasses just before departure and 1 liter for every hour you spend in the air—in addition to the beverages you drink with meals.

Pack a travel-size bottle of skin lotion to replenish moisture in your face and hands during air travel. If you're taking an overnight flight, don't forget to pack a toothbrush, which will help you at least to *feel* fresher and less dry. Before you prepare to land, visit the lavatory and wash your face and hands, rinsing with cold water.

If you don't want your morning flight to feel like the red-eye, trade your contact lenses for glasses before you board, to keep your eyes from drying out, itching, and turning red. If nothing comes between you and your lenses, you should at least pack some rewetting drops in your carry-on bag.

FLYING WITH A COLD

Next to jet lag, the most ordinary health problem to worry about when you travel by plane is the common cold or flu. During takeoff and landing, even the healthiest travelers experience slight ear discomfort as pressure in the inner ear adapts to rapidly shifting air pressure in the plane cabin. When your mucous membranes are swollen from a cold, the eustachian tube, which connects the sinus cavity to the inner ear, is congested. There's very little room for air to reach the inner ear soon enough to avert severe discomfort—or worse. In the worst instances, you may suffer permanent damage to your eardrums if inner ear pressure can't match cabin pressure at a healthy clip.

If your cold is severe, you should consider postponing your flight. If you simply must fly, however, use a decongestant or nasal spray before takeoff and landing to minimize pressure buildup. Read the label of your decongestant carefully and time your preflight dose so that you'll be able to take another about 1 hour before you're scheduled to land, as sinus and inner-ear pain tend to be most severe during descent.

When you start to feel pressure build in your ears, you can make them pop with a "modified Valsalva maneuver." It's very simple: Pinch your nostrils closed and breathe in deeply. Then breathe out through the nose, as though you

---

Kids with Colds

It's even more difficult for kids to make their ears pop during takeoff and landing. The eustachian tube is especially narrow in children; the passage is even tighter when mucous membranes are swollen. This can make ascent and descent especially painful—even dangerous—for a child with congested sinuses. If your little one is suffering from a cold or the flu, it's best to keep him grounded until he recuperates, if that's an option. (If you simply must travel with your child as scheduled, see "Easing Travel with the Tots in Tow," below, for additional ways to help your kids clear their ears on the plane.)

---

were trying to blow your fingers off your nostrils. Blow out in short, firm bursts until you feel your ears "pop." Yawning, drinking liquids, or chewing gum also help to minimize pressure buildup during takeoff and landing.

Antihistamines are even more effective than decongestants, but they will also cause drowsiness. If you're driving yourself from the airport to your destination, it's best to avoid them.

DEEP-VEIN THROMBOSIS

Most air travelers experience some swelling in the feet, ankles, and legs after a long flight. Body fluids tend to settle and blood circulation slows down as a normal, though uncomfortable, side effect of protracted inactivity. When circulation is impaired for a long period of time, blood can also stagnate in the veins and become more likely to clot— a potentially dangerous condition known as deep-vein thrombosis (DVT). These clots will become hazardous if they dislodge and move to the lungs, where they can cause a pulmonary embolus and impede blood flow to the rest of the body. Elderly, pregnant, or obese passengers are especially susceptible to DVT.

If one of your feet, ankles, or legs swells or aches for longer than 24 hours after you board a plane, seek medical help immediately—from an emergency room, if necessary. The standard treatment for DVT is an injection of Heparin followed by an oral anticoagulant. This remedy thins the blood and will dissipate the clot—and possibly save your life.

To avoid such extreme measures, try to get up and walk around the cabin as often as you can, to rev up blood circulation in your legs. Try to keep your legs elevated during your trip. Aspirin also helps to thin the blood. Drink plenty of water and avoid caffeine and alcohol.

You can also stimulate blood flow with these tidy exercises, which you can perform from your seat without disrupting other passengers.

- **Flex and point.** From a sitting position, raise your feet slightly off the floor in front of your seat. Flex your left foot while you point your right. Then switch: point the left and flex the right. Try to perform 10 to 25 repetitions every hour.

- **Round the clock.** With your legs still elevated slightly, rotate both your feet outward in a full circle from the ankle—as though they were hands on a clock, one moving clockwise the other moving counterclockwise. Then switch: rotate them inward. Try to perform 10 to 25 repetitions every hour.

- **Stair master.** With your left foot on the floor, raise your right leg a few inches off the floor. Lower it, then raise your left leg to the same height. Repeat this motion, as though you were climbing a flight of very low steps. Try to perform 10 to 25 repetitions every hour.

- **Seated knee lifts.** With your left leg on the floor, raise your right knee as close to your body as you can comfortably manage. Return your right foot to the floor and raise your left knee the same way.

Return your left foot to the floor. Try to perform 10 to 25 repetitions every hour.

Magellans travel suppliers (☎ **800/962-4943**; www. magellans.com) sells an **Exercise and Support Cushion** ($9.85) that stimulates leg and foot joints and improves circulation when inflated. From a sitting position, you can use your feet to force air through special passages and chambers to relieve the restless sensation you experience when your legs are squeezed in the confines of most airline seats, particularly in coach.

5 Obtaining Medical Assistance While Airborne

WOE TO THE TRAVELER WHO HAPPENS TO FALL SERIously ill while in an airplane cabin. The airlines are under no obligation to provide medical assistance to passengers. In the absence of federal guidelines, most airlines simply hope there's a doctor in the house if a passenger suddenly needs medical attention.

Unfortunately, this default strategy is hardly foolproof. For fear of malpractice suits, many doctors are reluctant to provide assistance to strangers in the event of an emergency. Only one airline, Air Canada, provides full legal protection to doctors who come to the aid of passengers in need.

Doctors are especially afraid to get involved in in-flight emergencies when traveling to or from countries in the Middle East. Under Islamic law, an individual who is deemed responsible for a Muslim's death must pay blood money to the spouse of the deceased.

One doctor recently pressed charges against American Airlines after he intervened in a midair emergency. According to *Condé Nast Traveller,* Dr. John Stevens, a British psychiatrist aboard an American Airlines flight in early 1999, assisted a fellow passenger who suffered from a blood clot on the plane midflight. While he may have saved the passenger's life, he apparently found the experience less than fulfilling and ended up suing the airlines for $900—on the grounds that his vacation had been interrupted.

GROUNDING CONDITIONS: WHEN ARE YOU TOO UNHEALTHY TO FLY?

Because medical facilities on board most aircraft are limited, the American Medical Association advises you not to fly on large jets if you have certain medical conditions. Some of these maladies are more severe than others, but all of them are adversely affected by changes in air pressure or oxygen rarity at high altitudes.

You should seriously consider postponing your flight if you suffered a heart attack within the last month or a stroke within the last 2 weeks, if you have severe high blood pressure or heart disease, or if you are beset with any other condition that weakens the heart.

You should also remain on land if you have severe respiratory illnesses, such as pneumothorax (air outside the lung), cysts of the lung, or severe lung disease.

People with chronic heart and lung problems should use supplemental oxygen at all times when flying over 22,500 feet. (The average cruising altitude is 35,000 feet.) Be aware, however, that most airlines do not allow passengers to bring their own supplemental oxygen on board, as it is hazardous at high altitudes. (In fact, it was supplemental oxygen tanks that caught on fire and caused the ValuJet crash in the Everglades in 1996.) Unfortunately, most airlines charge extra for the oxygen they provide. Be aware, however, that some carriers require that you order oxygen in advance.

You should also try not to fly with the flu, a cold, allergies, acute sinusitis, or middle ear infections. Changes in air cabin pressure may produce severe, painful sinus and ear problems. Be sure to use an oral decongestant 1 hour before ascent and descent or a spray decongestant before and during takeoff and landing. This is especially true for children. You should also try the "modified Valsalva maneuver" frequently during ascent and descent. (For instructions, see "Flying with a Cold," above.)

If you underwent abdominal surgery within 2 weeks of your scheduled flight, you should postpone your trip. You should not fly if you have acute diverticulitis, ulcerative colitis, acute esophageal viruses, acute gastroenteritis, or an intestinal virus.

If you have epilepsy you should not fly, unless your condition is under sound control or you know that you will be flying at altitudes below 8,000 feet. If you are overcome by violent or unpredictable behavior, or suffered a recent skull fracture or brain tumor, you should stay on the ground.

If you have severe anemia or hemophilia with active bleeding, you shouldn't fly. If you have sickle cell anemia, you shouldn't fly over 22,500 feet.

If you underwent recent eye surgery or had your jaw wired shut, you shouldn't fly.

If you are more than 240 days pregnant (8 months) or if miscarriage is a serious threat, you shouldn't fly.

You should not fly if you went scuba diving 24 hours before departure. You may suffer from the "bends," from the rapid decrease in air pressure after time spent in a compressed air environment. Symptoms include difficulty breathing, neuralgic pains, and paralysis; and death can occur.

If you have questions regarding these guidelines, call the **American Medical Association**'s help line (☎ **312/ 464-5000**.)

BE PREPARED: GET ON BOARD WITH ALL THE INFO

Unfortunately, it's up to passengers to take precautions against midair medical emergencies. If you suffer from a chronic illness, consult your doctor before your departure. If you must fly with a condition such as epilepsy, diabetes, or heart disease, wear a **Medic Alert Identification Tag**

(☎ **800/825-3785;** www.medicalert.org), which will immediately alert doctors to your condition and give them access
to your records through Medic Alert's 24-hour hot line.
Membership is $35, plus a $15 annual fee.

If you suffer from a dental problem during a domestic flight, a nationwide referral service known as **1-800-
DENTIST** (☎ **800/336-8478**) will provide the name of a
nearby dentist or clinic when you land.

6 TRAVEL INSURANCE DEMYSTIFIED

IF YOU GET SICK OR HAVE AN ACCIDENT DURING YOUR
trip—or if you have to cancel your flight or trip due to some
other type of emergency—you may lose all or most of the
travel money you paid in advance and/or have to cover the
astronomical expense of emergency transportation home.
Travel insurance can protect you against this sort of emergency and in a few instances is worth the very high price you
pay for it—which can run you anywhere from 3% to 14%
of your trip expenses.

According to *Consumer Reports,* there are two kinds of
travel insurance worth purchasing: **Trip cancellation insurance (TCI)** and **Emergency Medical-Evacuation insurance
(EME).** Most policies are priced by the trip and provide
coverage for ordinary travelers visiting popular destinations
for a brief while. (If you travel frequently into high-risk areas
overseas, you may want to inquire about extended annual
emergency medical-evacuation insurance.) Most TCI and
EME packages also qualify you for worldwide assistance
numbers you can call for referrals to doctors, lawyers, or
other services you might need in the case of an emergency.

TRIP CANCELLATION INSURANCE (TCI)

Trip cancellation insurance will reimburse you for the
money you lose if an unforeseen emergency forces you to
cancel a trip before departure or return home earlier than

THE "SMOKING" GUN

If you're a smoker traveling in the United States, say good-bye to your rights when you set foot on a plane. The U.S. government bans smoking on all domestic scheduled-service flights, with the exception of nonstop flights over 6 hours long to or from Alaska or Hawaii—in which case smoking may be allowed if there is room for the flight crew to designate a smoking section on the plane.

If you're flying internationally, smoking is banned only on domestic portions of segmented flights—on both domestic and international carriers. For instance, if you're flying from New York to Paris with a connection in Boston, smoking is prohibited from New York to Boston. On nonstop international flights, the ban does not apply, even over U.S. airspace. For example, on a nonstop flight from New York to Paris, smoking is not prohibited by the federal government, even on an American carrier. Nevertheless, most American airlines and many foreign carriers have voluntarily banned smoking on even nonstop international flights to or from the United States. If you are taking an international flight, ask the airline about its smoking policy in advance.

Smoking is also banned on certain nonstop international scheduled-service flights by U.S. airlines when the plane seats fewer than 30 passengers. For example, smoking is prohibited on certain commuter flights from the United States to Canada, Mexico, and the Caribbean.

---

scheduled. TCI is especially advisable if you have to make a large deposit or a full payment months before the actual date of your trip, since it may be very difficult to foresee emergency schedule conflicts or health problems. If you cancel a trip soon enough, say a month in advance, you may lose just

Cigar and pipe smoking is illegal on all U.S. carrier flights (scheduled, charter, domestic, and international flights).

On domestic airline flights on which smoking is not banned, the following rules apply:

- The airline must furnish a no-smoking seat to any passenger who requests one, provided the person checked in on time. (The passenger may not necessarily choose this seat. For example, passengers cannot insist on sitting with a travel companion, or sitting in an aisle or window seat, or some other location of choice.)

- The airline is required to expand the size of the no-smoking section if there aren't enough seats to accommodate nonsmoking passengers who checked in on time.

- The flight crew must prevent passengers from smoking in the nonsmoking section. Smoke that drifts from the smoking section, however, is not a violation of the smoking ban.

- Smoking is prohibited whenever a plane is on the ground or when the ventilation system is not functioning properly.

- The government does not require carriers to have a smoking section. An airline may choose to ban smoking on any flight, on any type of aircraft, to any destination.

a pittance, but if you must back out at the last minute, the fees can be astronomical if you're uninsured. Likewise, if you purchased discounted tickets, you may lose the entire ticket value if you decide not to travel and don't have coverage. Most TCI policies will reimburse you for the following:

- Extra costs incurred by sickness (this usually applies to preexisting conditions as well, provided you weren't treated 90 to 180 days before you bought the policy), injury, or death suffered by you or a travel companion before departure or during your trip.

- Trip down payment in the event that you cancel or interrupt your journey because a close family member suffers illness, injury, or death.

- The amount of your down payment, should an airline or tour operator go bankrupt or fail to provide the purchased product (provided that you purchased coverage directly from the insurance company, not the travel provider).

- Costs of cancellation if you suffer a flood, accident, or fire at home; if you have to serve on jury duty; if you miss a flight because of an airplane hijacking, a natural disaster, an act of terrorism, or a strike.

- The costs of a single supplement, should your traveling partner have to cancel.

- The cost of rescheduling a flight if you are forced to postpone a trip.

- The cost of returning home if you must interrupt your trip.

- The cost of outside help if it is warranted by sudden sickness or an accident during your trip.

EMERGENCY MEDICAL-EVACUATION INSURANCE (EME)

Emergency medical-evacuation insurance will cover the exorbitant cost of emergency transportation if an emergency situation forces you to return home or visit a hospital far from the scene of an accident. It is often sold as part of a "bundled" coverage policy, in conjunction with trip cancellation insurance. Most EME policies will reimburse you for the following:

- The cost of emergency transportation if you fall ill or have an accident during your trip.

- The cost of special evacuation, via helicopter or emergency jet, to the nearest treatment facility.

- The cost of your trip home, if an emergency situation forces you to return early.

OTHER TYPES OF TRAVEL INSURANCE

The other types of travel-related coverage—medical/hospital insurance, baggage loss policies, trip and baggage delay insurance, or accidental death and dismemberment coverage—usually fall under other types of insurance policies. Travel insurance is the most greatly overpriced travel service, so you don't want to buy it if you unwittingly have it already.

Before you purchase any type of travel insurance, carefully read your other active policies. Your homeowner's or renter's insurance, for instance, should cover stolen luggage. Unless you absolutely must take extremely valuable personal possessions with you on your trip, additional baggage insurance is probably not worth the cost.

Your existing health insurance should cover you if you get sick while on vacation—although if you belong to an HMO, you should investigate whether you are fully covered when away from home. If you need hospital treatment, most health insurance plans and HMOs will cover out-of-country hospital visits and procedures, at least to some extent. Most make you pay the bills up front at the time of care, however, and you'll get a refund only after you've returned and filed all the paperwork. Members of **Blue Cross/Blue Shield** can now use their cards at select hospitals in most major cities worldwide (☎ **800/810-BLUE** or www.bluecares.com/blue/bluecard/wwn for a list of hospitals). You should have some type of medical coverage while you travel, though, so you may want to consider purchasing some if your home policy doesn't cover travel—or if you're altogether uninsured.

Some credit- and charge-card companies may insure you against travel accidents if you buy plane, train, or bus tickets with their cards. Some credit cards (American Express and certain gold and platinum Visa and MasterCards, for example) also offer automatic flight insurance against death or dismemberment in case of an airplane crash. Call your credit/charge-card companies if you have any questions.

If you do require additional insurance, try one of the companies listed below. Remember, however, that trip cancellation insurance costs approximately 3% to 14% of the total value of your vacation, so don't pay for more than you need. For example, if you need only trip cancellation insurance, don't purchase coverage for lost or stolen property.

RECOMMENDED AGENTS

Consumer Reports Travel Letter recommends the following issuers of travel insurance, particularly those marked with an asterisk:

> **Access America,** 6600 W. Broad St., Richmond, VA 23230 (☎ **800/284-8300**).

> * **CSA,** P.O. Box 919010, San Diego, CA 92191-9010 (☎ **800/348-9505**). Consumer Reports rated this provider a Best Buy. CSA bases its rates on a traveler's age. For travelers under 70 years of age, the rates are drastically reduced.

> **International SOS Assistance,** P.O. Box 11568, Philadelphia, PA 11916 (☎ **800/523-8930** or 215/244-1500).

> * **Travel Guard International,** 1145 Clark St., Stevens Point, WI 54481 (☎ **800/826-1300**). Travel Guard covers an especially broad range of causes.

* **Travel Insured International (The Travelers),** 52-S Oakland Ave., P.O. Box 280568, East Hartford, CT 06128-0568 (☎ **800/243-3174**). Travel Insured coverage is especially generous in regard to preexisting medical conditions.

* **Travelex Insurance Services,** P.O. Box 9408, Garden City, NY 11530-9408 (☎ **800/228-9792**). Travelex covers an especially broad range of causes.

   Worldwide Assistance, 1133 15th St. NW, Ste. 400, Washington, DC 20005 (☎ **800/821-2828**; www.worldwideassistance.com).

7 ADVICE FOR PASSENGERS WITH SPECIAL NEEDS

TRAVELERS WITH DISABILITIES

SINCE IT BECAME LAW IN 1986, THE AIR CARRIER Access Act has revolutionized domestic air travel for persons with disabilities. In essence, the law attempts to prohibit the airlines from discriminating against travelers on the basis of a physical disability by recognizing the obstacles they face, by introducing new technologies and services to accommodate them, and by training airline personnel in how best to attend to their particular needs.

It's wise to verse yourself in your rights, however, if you need to fly with a disability, as the law leaves a few points open for interpretation. Unfortunately, if you read the ombudsmen section of any travel publication or log on to **www.passengerrights.com**, a Web-based air passenger complaint service, you will still hear plenty of horror stories regarding the violation of the Air Carrier Access Act. So be sure to know your rights before you fly.

If you feel your rights as a disabled traveler have been violated, you should by all means file a complaint with the airline and the **Department of Transportation** (Aviation Consumer Protection Division, 400 Seventh St. SW C-75, Washington, DC 20590; ☎ **202/366-2220** or 202/755 to 7687). See chapter 9, "The Squeaky Wheel," for advice on how to complain effectively.

The Letter of the Law

Fundamentally, the **Air Carrier Access Act** states that:

- An airline may not refuse to transport a passenger solely on the basis of a disability.

- An airline may not limit the number of individuals with disabilities on a particular flight.

- All trip information made available to other passengers must also be made available to passengers with disabilities. This includes information regarding ticketing, scheduled departure times and gates, change of gate assignments, status of flight delays, schedule changes, flight check-in, and baggage claim and checking information.

- An airline must provide transport to a person with a disability that might affect his appearance or involuntary behavior, even if this behavior may offend, annoy, or inconvenience crew members or other passengers.

   There are a few exceptions to the rules. The premise of most of them is that the passenger with a disability may not pose a danger to other passengers. Some of the exceptions, however, leave a wide gray area open for interpretation.

- The airline may refuse to transport a person with a disability if doing so endangers the health or safety of other passengers or otherwise violate FAA safety rules.

- Airline personnel are not required to carry a special-
  needs passenger on board by hand. If the plane
  has fewer than 30 seats, the airline may refuse to
  transport the passenger if the plane has no lifts,
  boarding chairs, or other devices to help the passenger board.

- The airline may refuse to transport special-needs
  passengers if it cannot do so without seating them
  in an emergency-exit row seat. By law, these seats
  must be occupied by able-bodied adults who can
  assist other passengers in case of an emergency.

The law has its fine points as well. The airlines are also
not allowed to require advance notification of a passenger's
disabilities. They may, however, require 48-hour notice if
they will be expected to transport an electric wheelchair or
respirator. Passengers with electric wheelchairs may also be
asked to check into the airport 1 hour before departure, so
batteries can be properly packaged and stowed.

New planes with more than 29 seats—meaning aircraft
that have been in operation since April 5, 1992—must have
moveable armrests on at least half the aisle seats to accommodate passengers with disabilities. As older planes are refurbished, they must be retrofitted with movable armrests as
well. New wide-body planes must be equipped with accessible bathrooms and an onboard wheelchair. As of December
1998, ramps or mechanical lifts must be available for most
aircraft with 19 through 30 seats at larger domestic airports
and at all airports with more than 10,000 passengers annually by December 2000.

Airline personnel are required to show passengers where
to find these accommodations and how to operate them.

Airlines may not require a person with a disability to fly
with an attendant, except in limited circumstances: if a person needs to travel in a stretcher; if a person is unable to
comprehend or follow safety instructions because of a

mental disability; if a person is unable to assist in his or her own evacuation from the aircraft in case of emergency; or if a person has both severe hearing and vision impairment and would not be able to comprehend or follow safety instructions in case of an emergency.

In these situations, when the airline does have the right to insist that a disabled passenger fly with an attendant, they cannot charge for the companion's passage. If the flight in question does not have room for an attendant, the passenger is entitled to denied boarding compensation.

The airline is also under obligation to assist the disabled traveler while boarding, disembarking, and making connections. Flight attendants must help passengers move to and from seats, open and identify food, get to and from the lavatory, and load or retrieve carry-on items. This may involve assisting the passenger with a walking support or an onboard wheelchair.

Wheelchairs and other assistive devices must be given priority over other items as checked baggage if a passenger with a disability preboards. Carriers must accept battery-powered wheelchairs, including the batteries, which might

Blind Rage

A visually impaired woman from Phoenix, Arizona, recently tried to bring her Seeing Eye dog into the first-class section of an America West flight. Blind and entirely dependent on her pet, the woman was humiliated when a flight attendant asked if any other first-class passenger would agree to sit next to her and the animal. When no one stepped forward to volunteer, the attendant aggravated the insult and downgraded the woman to coach.

When the blind woman returned home, she told her story to the Arizona Center for Disability Law, which filed a complaint with the U.S. Department of Transportation. The DOT maintains that America West ignored the Air Carriers Access Act, but at press time, America West has yet to respond.

otherwise be classified as hazardous material. If necessary, the airline must also provide hazardous-materials packaging for the batteries. (If a wheelchair or assistive device is lost or damaged on a domestic flight, the airline is liable for $2,500, or twice the standard liability for mishandled luggage. On international flights, no special exceptions are made for assistive devices. (See chapter 3, "Lost in Space.")

Disabled passengers have the right to bring service animals on board, such as Seeing Eye dogs, provided they do not block aisles and emergency exits or otherwise hinder the safe and efficient passage of other travelers. Unfortunately, this caveat also leaves a vast area open for interpretation.

Usually, passengers may not bring their own oxygen on board, but the airlines must provide aircraft-approved oxygen. Disabled passengers must ask for this in advance, however, and be prepared to pay a fee. You must also ask in advance for an incubator, respirator hookup, and accommodations for a stretcher.

Disabled passengers are under no obligation to provide airlines with advance notice that they will be traveling on board. You should be aware, however, that some carriers require 48 hours notice for the following services: transportation for an electric wheelchair on an aircraft with under 60 seats; hazardous materials packaging for an electric wheelchair battery; accommodations for 10 or more passengers with disabilities flying as a group; and an onboard wheelchair, for aircraft with lavatories that would be inaccessible without the chair.

The FAA requires that aircraft personnel provide all passengers with a safety briefing before takeoff. If a traveler's disabilities necessitate that he receive individualized safety drills—in the case of passengers with, for instance, a hearing impairment—the safety briefing must be as inconspicuous and discreet as possible. For this reason, most carriers like to board disabled passengers first.

If an airline refuses to carry you because of a disability, demand an explanation in writing. The law requires the airline to provide you with one. The statement must include a rationale for why the airline thinks that transporting you would compromise the health and safety of other passengers.

If you believe your rights have been violated, consult immediately with a Complaints Resolution Official (see "Complaining 101," in chapter 9, "The Squeaky Wheel"). By law, all airlines are now required to have one immediately available, even if only by phone, to resolve disagreements on the spot. If you are still not satisfied, you may take up the case with the Department of Transportation and seek enforcement action. (See chapter 9 to investigate the proper channels for complaint.)

The airline is required to respond to a written grievance within 30 days.

Required Airport Facilities

Until recently, only airports that received federal funding were required to provide access to passengers with disabilities. Now the government is requiring that all airports be renovated or designed to accommodate the needs of disabled travelers.

While much work remains to be done, the Department of Transportation maintains that the following services should be made available to persons with disabilities at all terminals within the next few years: parking; signs that indicate accessible parking and directions to the terminal; medical aid facilities and travelers aid stations; rest rooms; drinking fountains; ticketing systems at main ticketing areas; amplified telephones and text telephones for people with hearing and speech impairments; baggage check-in and retrieval areas; jetways and mobile lounges; level entry boarding ramps; lifts and other boarding and disembarking devices; information systems using visual words, letters, or symbols with lighting and color coding; oral information systems; shuttle vehicles; people movers and walkways; and signs that indicate the location of these services.

PREGNANT WOMEN

Because sudden changes in air pressure can induce labor, most airlines allow pregnant women to fly only before they are 8 months into a pregnancy.

The American Medical Association advises against flying if you have a history of miscarriages, or if miscarriage is a serious threat otherwise.

Pregnant women should not use scopalamine ear patches, Dramamine, and other antihistamines. Studies have indicated these drugs can be passed to the child in utero and result in birth defects.

PETS

The ASPCA offers helpful safety guidelines for flying with pets. See "When Your Baggage Has a Pulse," in chapter 3, "Lost in Space."

TRAVELING WITH CHILDREN
Safe Seats for Kids

Although a child over 2 weeks old and younger than 2 years old can ride for free on a parent's lap on domestic flights, your infant will be much safer booked in a separate, discounted seat and secured in an FAA-endorsed restraining device.

All the major American airlines except Southwest now offer 50% off the parent's fare for infant seats (for children 2 years of age or younger, except on Continental, which gives children under 3 infant discounts or allows them to ride free on their parents' laps), to make it more affordable for you to reserve a separate adjacent seat for your baby and a restraining device.

If a seat adjacent to yours is available, the child can also sit there free of charge. When you check in, ask if the flight is crowded. If it isn't, explain your situation to the agent and ask if you can reserve two seats—or simply move to two empty adjacent seats once the plane is boarded. You might want to shop around before you buy your ticket and deliberately book a flight that's not very busy. Ask the reservationist which flights tend to be most full and avoid those. Only one extra child is allowed in each row, however, due to the limited number of oxygen masks.

On international journeys, children may not ride free on parents' laps. On flights overseas, a lap fare usually costs 10% of the parent's ticket (see "Minor Policies of Major Carriers," below for each carrier's policy). Children who meet the airline's age limit (which ranges from 11 to 15 years old) can purchase international fares at 50–75% of the lowest coach fare in certain markets. Some of the foreign carriers make even greater allowances for children.

In order to qualify for discounts or free seats for children, you may be asked to furnish the child's birth certificate. Children riding for free will usually not be granted any baggage allowance.

Child Seats: Should You Use Them?

The FAA highly recommends, but does not require, that children under 20 pounds ride in a rear-facing child-restraint system. Children that weigh 20 to 40 pounds should sit in a forward-facing child restraint system. Children over 40 pounds should sit in a regular seat and wear a seat belt.

Ironically, the FAA offers no specific rules regarding child-safety seats. While the government requires that carry-on bags be stowed securely during takeoff and landing, it issues no such safeguards for children. According to *Consumer Reports Travel Newsletter,* the National Transportation Safety Board says that, since 1991, the deaths of five children and injury to four could have been prevented had the children been sitting in restraint systems. Even in the event of moderate turbulence, children sitting on a parent's lap can be thrust forward and injured. When you consider that a commercial aircraft hits a significant amount of turbulence at least once a day on average, you'd do well to think about investing a few hundred dollars for a safety seat.

The airlines themselves really should carry child safety seats on board. Unfortunately, most don't. Be advised that some carriers have even given passengers a hard time for bringing their own. *Consumer Reports Travel Newsletter* recounted that a man traveling with his wife and child on US Airways was not allowed to place his child in the safety seat he brought on board—even though he had purchased a ticket for his 3-year-old son. A flight attendant confiscated the seat until after landing, despite the parents' efforts to show her paperwork that proved the seat was designed for use on aircraft.

You may have an even harder time bringing a safety seat on board an international flight. When you book a flight on a foreign aircraft, ask ahead to be sure the carrier allows child safety seats.

The FAA promotes the use of safety seats, but until they make their endorsement part of the law, *Consumer Reports Travel Newsletter* recommends that you carry a copy of the FAA policy that states that you have the right to place your child in a restraining device. If you log onto any of the major airline complaint Web sites or read a travel ombudsman column regularly, you will encounter stories from irate parents who hauled a child restraint seat on board but weren't allowed to use it—usually because a flight was too crowded. You can request a copy directly from the FAA (☎ 800/ 322-7873) or download the material from the Internet at **www.faa.gov**.

The best way to guarantee that you're able to use the seat is to book a ticket for your child in an adjacent seat and fly direct. As mentioned, major airlines now offer 50% off the parent's fare for children under 2. If you can't afford the expense, book a ticket toward the back of the plane at a time when air travel is likely to be slowest—and the seat next to you is most likely to be empty. (See chapter 2, "The Mercy Seat," for tips on picking seats with extra space in mind.) The reservationist should also be able to recommend the best (the least busy) time for you to fly.

The FAA endorses seats with labels that read "This restraint is certified for use in motor vehicles and aircraft." If the seat measures no wider than 16 inches, it should fit in most coach seats. If you own a car seat made after 1985, chances are that it is certified to double as an airplane seat. You may not use booster seats or seatless vests or harness systems. Safety seats must be placed in window seats—except in exit rows, where they are prohibited, so as not to block the passage of other travelers in the case of an emergency.

For more information, call the **FAA**'s help line at ☎ **800/322-7873.**

CHILDREN TRAVELING SOLO

Although individual airline policies differ (see "Minor Policies of Major Carriers," below for details), for the most part children aged 5 to 11 pay the regular adult fare and can travel alone as unaccompanied minors on domestic flights only with an escort from the airlines—a flight attendant who seats the child, usually near the galley, where the flight crew is stationed; watches over the child during the flight; and escorts the child to the appropriate connecting gate or to the adult who will be picking up the child. Northwest and TWA do not allow children to travel alone until they turn 15. Unaccompanied minors typically board first and disembark last.

All the airlines but Delta, Northwest, and US Airways charge $30 one way for an escort; Delta, Northwest, and US Airways charge $30 per segment—in other words, $60 one way for a connecting flight. Unaccompanied children are never left alone; escorts stay with them until turning them over to an escort on the connecting flight or to a designated guardian. Airlines require attending adults to furnish a name, address, and government-issued photo ID. The adult who drops the child off at the airport must designate then the name and address of the adult who is authorized to pick the child up. At the destination city, the airline will not release the child to anyone but the authorized adult, after receiving a signature and seeing a photo ID.

Children aged 5 to 7 may travel unaccompanied on direct and nonstop flights only; in other words, they're not allowed to change planes for connecting flights at that age. (Alaska Air is the only major carrier that allows 7-year olds to take connecting flights with an airline escort. Children aged 8 to 11 may make connecting flights with an escort, with the exception of Southwest, which does not allow any unaccompanied child under the age of 13 to take a connecting flight.)

Children over the age of 12 are considered adults and may travel without an escort on every major carrier but TWA and Northwest, which require escorts until age 15. They still qualify for assistance from the airline for the extra fee. Southwest is the only airline that does not allow children to use the escort service once they are able to fly without one, at age 12.

Because airlines want to avoid the responsibility of having to shepherd children overnight, minors are not allowed to take the last connecting flight of the day, when the risk of missed connections is greatest. Minors are usually not allowed to travel on standby, and they must have confirmed reservations.

On connecting flights, ask when you book if the child will be flying on more than one airline. (With the new airline alliances, your child may end up on a Northwest aircraft, even though you booked the flight through Continental. See "Allied Forces," in chapter 1, "Ticketing Pitfalls.") If so, make sure you know each airline's policy for unaccompanied minors. Once you receive the ticket, review it yourself to make sure the city of origin and the destination are accurate. Review the ticket carefully with your child and explain simply how it works.

If you're booking a flight for your child, the airlines will request your name, telephone number, and address—along with the name, number, and address of the guardian who will meet your child at the destination city. An adult guardian must accompany the child to the gate or plane, furnish reasonable proof that another adult will meet the child at the final destination, and remain at the airport until the plane is in the air. The accompanying adult at the destination will have to sign a release form and furnish government-issued photo identification, such as a license or passport. If a child is unusually big or small, it's wise to bring a birth certificate to the airport as proof of age.

Solo Minors on International Flights

Major carriers' policies for minors traveling alone are basically the same for both domestic and international travel, with a few exceptions: Continental, Delta, and Northwest waive the escort fee on international flights. Children may be prohibited from boarding an international flight under poor weather conditions that could require that the plane be rerouted.

If you're booking a ticket for a minor on an international flight, you should call the consulate of the destination country to find out about visas and other special entry requirements. Some countries, for instance, require a notarized letter of consent, from all parents named on the birth certificate, stating that the child is authorized to enter the country. If only one parent has custody, and the notarized letter bears only that parent's signature, documented proof of sole custody may be required. Your child may also have to furnish a birth certificate.

Minor Orientation

Even if your children are a little older, it's wise to escort them onto the plane if possible and introduce them to a flight attendant—though some airlines will require you to say good-bye at the gate. If you must leave your child at the gate, it's wise to stick around until departure to ensure that the plane is not delayed.

If your child has never flown before, it makes sense to show up at the airport a little early to wander around, watch other planes take off and land, and prepare your child in advance for how flight is going to feel. Be sure to discuss the danger of talking to strangers—even if you have had the same discussion before.

Some airlines allow unaccompanied minors to board first, so the flight crew has more time to meet the child, orient the child to the location of bathrooms and emergency exits, store carry-ons, review safety procedures, and—kids love this part—introduce the child to the cockpit crew. Make sure minors understand that they should contact an attendant in case of any type of problem—from sickness, to a malfunctioning headset, to a bothersome neighbor. If you can't make it all the way on to the plane, be sure to introduce your child to the gate attendant and ensure the child will receive help boarding if necessary.

Some airlines offer special meals for children, such as hamburgers, hot dogs, or peanut butter sandwiches, which must be ordered in advance, when you make the reservation. It's still wise to send your child off with a bagged lunch, snack, and drinks. Also pack books and other entertainment in a carry-on and make sure your child knows how to get at them on board the plane.

Make sure your child has cash and knows how to make a collect phone call. In one place, record your child's name, your own name, address, and phone number, along with the names and phone number of your child's hosts at the final destination. Review the information with your child and place it in a safe purse, pocket, or neck pouch. Be sure, however, that your child knows not to share this information with strangers—not even a friendly neighbor in the cabin.

If your child is taking medication, it may be wise to postpone the trip unless you are certain your child is responsible for self-administering dosages properly. Flight attendants are not allowed to administer drugs to minors.

MINOR POLICIES OF MAJOR CARRIERS

Alaska

- On domestic flights, children under 2 pay 50% of the parent's fare for a guaranteed reservation. Children over the age of 2 do not receive a discount.

- On international flights (Alaska travels only to Mexico and Canada), children under 2 may ride free on the parent's lap; separate seats for children under 2 are 50% off the parent's fare (provided the ticket was not purchased at discount on the Internet—in which case the child seat will cost 50% of the lowest published adult fare). Children 2 to 11 pay 67% of the lowest published adult fare on select flights to Mexico only.

- Unaccompanied children 5 to 11 must travel with escort.

- Escort is $30 each direction for connecting flights only (no fee for direct or nonstop flights).

- Children 5 to 6 may not travel on connecting flights.

- Children 7 and older may travel on connecting flights.

- Children 12 and over are no longer considered unaccompanied minors, though escorts are available to them.

- International travel: same policy, except children must furnish passport or birth certificate; in order to fly to Mexico, children must furnish notarized letter of consent from all parents named on birth certificate to fly to Mexico only. (If only one parent has custody, proof of this must be furnished.)

America West

- On domestic flights, children under 2 pay 50% of the parent's fare for a guaranteed reservation. Children over the age of 2 do not receive a discount.

- On international flights, children under 2 may ride free on parent's lap but must pay taxes; for a separate seat, an infant reservation costs 50% of the adult fare. Children 2 to 11 pay 67% of the lowest published adult fare, if child discounts are available in that market.

- Unaccompanied children 5 to 11 must travel with escort.

- Escort is $30 each direction.

- Children 5 to 7 may not travel on connecting flights.

- Children 8 to 11 may travel on connecting flights with escort.

- Children 12 and over are no longer considered unaccompanied minors, though escorts are available to them for the fee.

- International travel: Same policy, except children must furnish passport or birth certificate; in order to fly to Mexico, children must furnish notarized letter of consent from all parents named on birth certificate to fly to Mexico only. (If only one parent has custody, proof of this must be furnished.)

- Children over the age of 12 are considered adults and may travel without an escort; but they still qualify for assistance from the airline for the extra fee.

- International travel: Same policy, except children must furnish notarized letter of consent, from all parents named on birth certificate, that the child may travel out of the country named on the birth certificate. (If only one parent has custody, proof of this must be furnished.)

American

- On domestic flights, children under 2 pay 50% of the parent's fare for a guaranteed reservation. Children over the age of 2 do not receive a discount.

- On international flights, children under 2 pay 10% of the lowest published adult fare for lap seat. Children 2 to 11 pay 67% to 75% of the lowest published adult fare for a guaranteed seat, if child discounts are available in that market.

- Unaccompanied children 5 to 11 must travel with escort.

- Escort is $30 each direction for the total number of children traveling unaccompanied (if three of your children are flying, the fee is still $30).

- Children 5 to 7 may not travel on connecting flights.

- Children 8 to 11 may travel on connecting flights with escort.

- Children 12 to 17 are no longer considered unaccompanied minors, though escorts are still available to them for the fee.

- International travel: Same policy.

Continental

- On domestic flights, children under 2 pay 50% of the parent's fare for a guaranteed reservation.

Children over the age of 2 do not receive a discount.

- On international flights, children may not ride free on parent's lap in certain markets; depending on the destination, they may have to pay 10% of the parent's fare to ride on the parent's lap. For a separate seat, any child under 12 may pay anywhere from 67% to 75% of the parent's fare, if child discounts are available in that market.

- Unaccompanied children 5 to 12 must travel with escort.

- Escort is $30 each direction (connecting flights $60 each way; direct or through $30 each way).

- Children 5 to 7 may not travel on connecting flights, late flights, or redeye flights.

- Children 8 to 11 may make connecting flights.

- Children 12 to 17 are no longer considered unaccompanied minors, even on connecting flights, though escorts are still available to them for the fee.

- International travel: No charge for escort. Children aged 5 to 7 may travel unaccompanied only on nonstop flights. Children 8 to 12 may take connecting flights or direct flights with escort. All children aged 5 to 17 may not take redeyes or the last connecting flight of the day. If a connecting flight is on another airline, minors must arrive at the airport two hours before departure. Minors must also furnish notarized letter of consent, from a parent or guardian, stating that the child is permitted to leave the country. (The foreign country may require permission from both parents.)

Delta

- On domestic flights, children under 2 pay 50% of the parent's fare for a guaranteed reservation. Children over the age of 2 do not receive a discount.

- On international flights, children under 2 pay 10% of the lowest published adult fare to fly on a parent's lap. For a separate seat, children under 12 pay 25% to 75% of the lowest published adult fare, if child discounts are available in that market.

- Unaccompanied children 5 to 11 must travel with escort.

- Escort is $30 each segment (connecting flights are $60 one way).

- Children 5 to 7 may not travel on connecting flights

- Children 8 to 11 may travel on connecting flights with escort.

- Children 12 and over are no longer considered unaccompanied minors, though escorts are available to them for the fee.

- International travel: Same policy, except the escort fee only applies to domestic segment of connecting flights, if there is one (from New York to Boston to Paris, the $30 fee will apply to the New York to Boston segment). Unaccompanied minors will not be permitted to board international flights in bad weather conditions that could require the plane to be rerouted.

Northwest

- On domestic flights, children under 2 pay 50% of the parent's fare for a guaranteed reservation. Children over the age of 2 do not receive a discount.

- On international flights, children under 2 pay 10% of the parent's fare for a lap seat. For a separate seat, children under the age of 15 pay 75% of the parent's fare, if child discounts are available in that market.

- Unaccompanied children 5 to 14 must travel with escort.

- Escort is $30 each segment (connecting flights are $60 each way).

- Children 5 to 7 may not take connecting flights.

- Children 8 to 14 may travel on connecting flights but may not be on the last connecting flight of the day.

- Children 15 to 17 and over are no longer considered unaccompanied minors, though escorts are available to them for the fee.

- Any minor traveling with a child 15 or older may not request the escort service.

- International travel: Same policy, but escort service is free.

Southwest

- On domestic flights, children under 2 pay 50% of the parent's fare for a guaranteed reservation. Children over the age of 2 do not receive a discount.

- Southwest does not operate international flights.

- Unaccompanied children 5 to 11 must travel with an escort and may not take connecting flights.

- Escort service is free.

- Children 12 and over are no longer considered unaccompanied minors and may travel alone, even on connecting flights; escort service is not available to children over 12.

- International travel: Southwest does not operate international flights.

TWA

- On domestic flights, children under 2 pay 50% of the parent's fare for a guaranteed reservation. Children over the age of 2 do not receive a discount.

- On international flights, children under 2 may ride free on parent's lap but must pay taxes. Children under 12 pay 75% of the parent's fare.

- Unaccompanied children 5 to 14 must travel with escort.

- Escort is $30 each direction for nonstop or direct flights; $60 for connecting flights.

- Children 5 to 7 may take connecting flights if all travel is on TWA aircraft.

- Children 8 to 14 may take connecting flights that require a change of aircraft.

- Children 15 to 17 are no longer considered unaccompanied minors, though escorts are available to them for the fee.

- International travel: Same policy.

United

- On domestic flights, children under 2 pay 50% of the parent's fare for a guaranteed reservation. Children over the age of 2 do not receive a discount.

- On international flights, children under 2 pay 10% of the parent's fare plus taxes for a lap seat. For a separate seat reservation for a child under 12, discounts vary widely according to destination.

- Unaccompanied children 5 to 11 must travel with escort.

- Escort is $30 each direction.

- Children 5 to 7 may not travel on connecting flights.

- Children 8 to 11 may travel on connecting flights with escort.

- Children 12 and over are no longer considered unaccompanied minors, though escorts are available to them for the fee.

- International travel: Same policy, except escort service to Japan is free.

US Airways

- On domestic flights, children under 2 pay 50% of the parent's fare for a guaranteed reservation. Children over the age of 2 do not receive a discount.

- On international flights, children under 2 pay 10% of the parent's fare for a lap seat. For a separate seat, children under 12 pay 50% to 75% of the parent's fare, if child discounts are available in that market.

- Unaccompanied children 5 to 11 must travel with escort.

- Escort is $30 each segment ($60 for connecting flights).

- Children 5 to 7 may not travel on connecting flights.

- Children 8 to 11 may travel on connecting flights with escort.

- Children 12 and over are no longer considered unaccompanied minors, though escorts are available to them for the fee.

- International travel: Same policy.

8 EASING TRAVEL WITH THE TOTS IN TOW

SEVERAL BOOKS ON THE MARKET OFFER TIPS TO HELP you travel with kids. Most concentrate on the U.S., but two, *Family Travel* (Lanier Publishing International) and *How to Take Great Trips with Your Kids* (The Harvard Common Press), are full of good general advice that can apply to travel anywhere. Another reliable tome, with a worldwide focus, is *Adventuring with Children* (Foghorn Press).

Family Travel Times is published six times a year by **TWYCH** (Travel with Your Children; ☎ **888/822-4388** or 212/477-5524), and includes a weekly call-in service for subscribers. Subscriptions are $40 a year for quarterly editions. A free publication list and a sample issue are available to those who request one by phone.

If you plan carefully, you can actually make it fun to travel with kids.

- If you're traveling with children, you'll save yourself a good bit of aggravation by **reserving a seat in the bulkhead** row. You'll have more legroom, and your children will be able to spread out and play on the floor underfoot. You're also more likely to find sympathetic company in the bulkhead area, as families with children tend to be seated there.

- Be sure to **pack items for your children in your carry-on luggage.** In case you're forced to check one of your carry-ons, consolidate the children's things in one bag or in your purse. If you're forced to check a carry-on, be sure to choose the one that holds the kid's things. When you're deciding what to bring, ready yourself for the worst: long, unexpected delays without food, bathrooms without changing tables, airline meals that feature your children's least favorite dishes.

- Have **a long talk with your children** before you depart for your trip. If they've never flown before, explain to them what to expect. If they're old enough, you may even want to describe how flight works and how air travel is even safer than riding in a car. Explain to your kids the importance of good behavior in the air—how their own safety can depend upon their being quiet and staying in their seats during the trip.

- **Pay extra careful attention to the safety instructions** before takeoff. Consult the safety chart behind the seat in front of you and show it to your children. Be sure you know how to operate the oxygen masks, as you will be expected to secure yours first and then help your children with theirs. Be especially mindful of the location of emergency exits. Before takeoff, plot out an evacuation strategy for you and your children in your mind's eye.

- Ask the flight attendant **if the plane has any special safety equipment for children.** Make a member of the crew aware of any medical problems your children have that could manifest during flight.

- **Be sure you've slept sufficiently** for your trip. If you fall asleep in the air and your child manages to break away, there are all sorts of sharp objects that could cause injury. Especially during mealtimes, it's dangerous for a child to be crawling or walking around the cabin unaccompanied by an adult.

- **Be sure your child's seatbelt remains fastened properly,** and try to reserve the seat closest to the aisle for yourself. This will make it harder for your children to wander off—in case, for instance, you're taking the redeye or a long flight overseas and you do happen to nod off. You will also protect your child from jostling passersby and falling objects—in the rare but entirely possible instance that an overhead bin pops open.

  In the event of an accident, unrestrained children often don't make it—even when the parent does. Experience has shown that it's impossible for a parent to hold onto a child in the event of a crash, and children often die of impact injuries.

  For the same reason, sudden turbulence is also a danger to a child who is not buckled into his own seat belt or seat restraint. According to *Consumer Reports Travel Letter,* the most common flying injuries result when unanticipated turbulence strikes and hurtles passengers from their seats. (See "Child Seats," above, for suggestions regarding FAA-promoted child-restraint systems.)

- **Try to sit near the lavatory,** though not so close that your children are jostled by the crowds that tend to gather there. Consolidate trips there as much as possible.

- Try to **accompany children to the lavatory.** They can be easily bumped and possibly injured as they make their way down tight aisles. It's especially dangerous for children to wander while flight attendants are blocking passage with their service carts. On crowded flights, the flight crew may need as much as an hour to serve dinner. It's wise to encourage your kids to use the rest room as you see the attendants preparing to serve.

- Be sure to **bring clean, self-containing compact toys.** Leave electronic games at home. They can interfere with the aircraft navigational system, and their noisiness, however lulling to children's ears, will surely not win the favor of your adult neighbors. Magnetic checker sets, on the other hand, are a perfect distraction, and small coloring books and crayons also work well, as do card games like Go Fish.

    Visit the library before you leave home and check out children's books about flying or airplane travel. Geography-related books and coloring books that include their departure point and destination will also help engage them during air travel.

    A Walkman with a few favorite recordings will also come in handy—especially if you throw in some sleepy-time tunes. By all means, don't leave home without a favorite blanket or stuffed animal—especially if it's your kid's best friend at bedtime.

- Some airlines **serve children's meals first.** When you board, ask a flight attendant if this is possible, especially if your children are very young or seated toward the back of the plane. After all, if your kids have a happy flight experience, everyone else in the cabin is more likely to as well.

- You'll certainly be grateful to yourself for **packing tidy snacks** like rolled dried fruit, which are much less sticky and wet and more compact and packable than actual fruit. Blueberry or raisin bagels also make for a neat, healthy sweet and yield fewer crumbs than cookies or cakes. Ginger snaps, crisp and not as crumbly as softer cookies, will also help curb mild cases of motion sickness. And don't forget to stash a few resealable plastic bags in your

IN-FLIGHT FUN FOR KIDS

With one of these children's game books on board, even the longest plane ride will go faster.

Road Trip Activity Fun Pack
by DK Publishing
Retail price: $4.95
Ages 4 to 8

This book is full of travel puzzles, stickers, a travel log where your kids can record fun details about their trip, fun facts about various destinations within the United States, and a detailed map of the country.

Great Games for Kids on the Go: Over 240 Travel Games to Play on Trains, Planes, and Automobiles
by Penny Warner
Retail price: $12.95
Ages 4 to 8

This book is full of entertaining educational games to help your kids while away the miles. Each game is highly engaging and entertaining and requires few materials and very little space.

Brain Quest for the Car: 1100 Questions and Answers All About America
by Sharon Gold
Retail price: $10.95
Ages 7 to 12

This book features cards with questions about American geography, culture, and customs.

Vacation Fun Mad Libs: World's Greatest Party Game
by Roger Price
Retail price: $3.50
Ages 8 and up

As suggested by the title, this book is chock-full of Mad Libs. Your kids will want to keep playing even after you've touched down.

purse. They'll prove invaluable for storing everything from half-eaten crackers and fruit to checker
pieces and matchbox cars.

- **Juice or cookies** will not only keep them distracted
during ascent and descent, often the scariest parts
of flight for a child, they will also help their little
ears pop as cabin air pressure shifts rapidly. Juice
(paper cartons travel best) will also keep them swallowing and help them to stay properly hydrated.
Avoid giving young children gum or hard candies,
since sudden turbulence may cause them to choke.

- If your children are very young, **bring pacifiers.**
The act of sucking will keep their ears clear. By the
same logic, takeoff and landing are the perfect time
for feedings. Your kids will be distracted from the
deafening cabin noise, and their ears will pop more
easily. If your schedule won't allow this, try placing
drops of water on an infant's tongue, to facilitate
swallowing. Don't forget to pack bottles and extra
milk or formula as well, as these are unavailable on
most aircraft. Many airlines prohibit flight attendants from preparing formula, so it's best to pack
your baby's food premixed.

- **If your child has a severe cold, it's best to postpone flight.** Little ears are especially sensitive to
shifts in air cabin pressure; if your child's breathing
is blocked by stuffed sinuses, permanent eardrum
damage may result. If your kids must fly with a
cold, give them an oral child's decongestant an
hour before ascent and descent or administer a
spray decongestant before and during takeoff and
landing. (See "Flying with a Cold," above.)

6

BEAT THE CLOCK: HOW TO MINIMIZE JET LAG

Pres. Lyndon B. Johnson had an exceptionally original method for coping with jet lag. As only a U.S. president can, he simply made the world revolve around him. Johnson rarely if ever reset his watch when he crossed time zones—even when he flew to Guam, 15 hours ahead of American eastern standard time, during the Vietnam War. He would simply sleep by day (Guam time), and arrange meetings at hours that would have been reasonable on U.S. soil—even when it meant that South Vietnam Pres. Nguyen Van Thieu had to "power lunch" with LBJ at four in the morning.

The human body functions like clockwork: waking and sleeping, working and resting, eating and eliminating in a steady circadian rhythm that is typically in synch with the earth's own cycles of day, night, spring, summer, winter, and fall. When you travel by plane, however, flying faster than the speed of the earth's rotation and sometimes even against the direction of its daily turn, your own 24-hour biological schedule is going to be thwarted.

You would never think of traveling from New York to California without having to reset your watch. Imagine what such a trip does to your internal body clock, a far more finely calibrated time instrument than even a top-shelf Rolex. When you travel from east to west in a plane, your body functions fall into a sort of time warp known to chronobiologists as a *transient state of dyschronism*—more commonly known as *jet lag.* In this condition, your regular body rhythms are jostling with a new set of external cues, both natural and manufactured: The sun is not going to rise and set when it would have at home, your alarm clock is going to wail at a different hour, you won't sit sleepy over bacon and eggs, have a bowel movement, greet your friends at work, or read the newspaper on your late morning coffee break according to schedule.

1 What Is Jet Lag?

JET LAG MAKES YOU FEEL DISORIENTED, FORGETFUL, and absentminded precisely because your body *is* disoriented; your brain, nervous system, and reflexes are in part someplace else, inclined to do the things they normally would have been doing back home. The bodily functions that operate cyclically—your hormone levels, blood pressure, body temperature, digestive enzymes, kidneys, bladder, heart, and brainwaves included—all lapse into a sort of temporary state of confusion.

Let's say you fly out of New York La Guardia just after lunch at 3pm. When it would have been time for your dinner at 7 o'clock, your stomach is going to release enzymes and stomach acids in anticipation of food, but when you touch down in San Francisco, it's only going to be 4pm— too late for lunch, too early for supper. Three hours later, when you would have been curling up with a book for the evening and your bodily functions would have started shutting down in anticipation of sleep, you'll be nodding off in your gazpacho as your California business associates are plying their wits and picking at their martini olives.

JET LAG SYMPTOMS

The first stages of jet lag may include stomach upset, deep fatigue, fuzzy-headedness, absentmindedness, slow-wittedness, poor concentration, weakness, disrupted bowel movements, and changes in the frequency of urination. At more advanced stages, you may experience diarrhea or constipation, headache, loss of appetite, poor motor coordination, impaired night vision and peripheral vision, decrease in sexual appetite, muscular tremors, vertigo, and fainting.

WHAT CAUSES JET LAG?

One of the most common misperceptions regarding jet lag is that it results from flying in general—in particular, from traveling at high altitude. In fact, jet lag is caused only by long-distance, east-west travel. The crossing of time zones is the culprit. For example, if you were to fly from Montreal to Santiago, Chile—a hefty transcontinental trek of 5,434 miles, but on the same north-south axis—you might feel some of the symptoms commonly associated with jet lag: headache, fatigue, a slight dizziness. Since you didn't cross a time zone, however, your discomfort would more likely be the byproduct of dehydration, as airplane cabins are literally drier than the Sahara; shifts in air cabin pressure, which can throw off the normal function of your sinuses and lead to low-grade headaches, earaches, and sinus congestion; sitting cramped in the same position and close quarters for hours on end; and the exhausting stresses and strains that all too often accompany airplane travel, like simply getting to the airport on time, waiting on line, schlepping your carry-ons and worrying whether your checked bags are going to reach your destination when you do. With a sound night's sleep, lots of water, and a few healthy meals, you'll probably be back in fighting trim by the following day—or the one after that, at the most—if you have traveled on a north-south axis, no matter how great the distance.

Jet lag, on the other hand, may keep you from feeling your best for 2 days to 2 weeks on a trip that requires a 5- to 8-hour time change, depending on your personal disposition, age, physical fitness, and a host of other factors—most important whether you've traveled from east to west or from west to east, as west-east travel is much more difficult on your internal time clock.

Your heart rate, which is normally faster during the day than at night, may take from 5 to 6 days to return to its normal cycle; your output of urine, which usually slows at night, can take up to 10 days to function regularly; your gastrointestinal system, which governs the bowels, may not normalize for as many as 24 hours for each time zone you cross; your body's response to light and your ability to perform mathematical equations may stay out of whack for anywhere from 2 days to 2 weeks; and your physical coordination may be under par for 5 to 10 days. If you're traveling from east to west, your recovery will usually take 30% to 50% less time. You will still experience some disruption of your circadian rhythms, but the fact that you are gaining time—and therefore gaining sleep—will put you ahead of the game, so to speak, and hasten your recovery.

Alcohol, Drugs & Jet Lag

As a general rule, if a substance picks you up or brings you down, it will interfere with your body's ability to adapt to a new time frame. If you are taking prescribed medications, consult your doctor before traveling. Be sure to tell him or her where you're going, how many time zones you will be crossing, what sort of activity you have planned for your trip, and whether you anticipate other drastic changes in your diet. If you plan to use any other jet lag remedy, be sure to say so.

JET LAG WINNERS & LOSERS

Most night-owl types tend to adapt even faster to the new time frame on a trip out west. They are less prone to sleep deficiency and can extend the sleep period more easily when necessary. When traveling east, on the other hand, night owls tend to adjust far more slowly, and it's the early birds who get the worm. Likewise, "morning people" are more readily able to rise and shine at any hour, even if it means cutting short the sleep period for a few hours each day.

Several other personality factors figure into your capacity to cope with east-west travel. Gregarious types, who love to meet new people, mix among various social groups, and travel in a pack, tend to cope better with jet lag than people who reach a destination and retreat to their rooms with a book or remote control. This is because the more you expose yourself to external stimuli in your new environment, the faster the necessary chemical changes will take place in your brain to help you adapt to your new surroundings.

Surprisingly, regimented types—people who wake up, go to bed, eat breakfast, lunch, and sit down to dinner at the same time every day—will adjust more quickly to a new time and place than the sort of person who wakes and eats at whim and goes with the flow every day. The person accustomed to following the clock will have less trouble following new marching orders in a new time zone.

Calm stable types will also do better, in either direction, than neurotic types who are readily frazzled by disruptions of circumstance. Nervous types secrete hormones and neurotransmitters that unsettle body rhythms and make it even harder to establish temporary new ones.

If you are traveling under pressure—conducting business, attending many social engagements, or otherwise traveling according to a rigorous, demanding timetable—you will also do better than someone who is traveling strictly for relaxation, with no firm commitments or social and professional obligations. By having to keep up, the busy traveler will typically recover faster from jet lag—simply because he must. Like the gregarious traveler, the busy person will also encounter a greater profusion of external stimuli in the new environment, which will induce more rapid adaptation.

Age is also a factor in your ability to cope with jet lag. While even infants experience jet lag, they recover very quickly. The elderly seem to have the hardest time recovering. This is largely because 40% of men and women over age 65 already experience difficulty sleeping. When senior citizens cross time zones, they are requiring an already compromised system to work double time. The good news is that a new body rhythm, once it is finally established, may be accompanied by a new vigor, which will allow for sounder sleep.

As you might guess, healthy people cope better with jet lag than people in poor health, whose body rhythms have already been disrupted. Jet lag will make you feel even worse if you travel while ill. If you must take prescription drugs during your trip, be aware that jet lag may impair their effectiveness, as timing is usually crucial to their proper functioning. Even common or social drugs—such as coffee, cigarettes, or alcohol—alter your body rhythms enough that they usually aggravate the symptoms of jet lag and slow the recovery process.

2 How to Cope with Jet Lag

JET LAG IS ESPECIALLY VEXING BECAUSE IT LEAVES you dragging at a time when you'd like to be feeling your best. Presumably, most people trouble themselves to travel by plane either because they have to attend an important event, conduct business that's too important to handle by phone from home, or simply because they want to travel far from the stresses and strains of regular life in order to relax and enjoy themselves—not struggle with jet lag.

TOP-SECRET STRATEGIES: THE GOVERNMENT PLAN

You'd be surprised at the drastic measures people have taken in order to feel in control of their disorientation. According to Dr. Charles F. Ehret, who developed a jet lag treatment at the Argonne National Laboratory for the U.S. Army Rapid Deployment Forces, U.S. government officials—whose diplomatic responsibilities must result in especially debilitating jet lag—have concocted some of the most inventive strategies.

Henry Kissinger, for one, would attempt to acclimate himself to a new time zone a week before departure by systematically going to bed 1 hour earlier each night and rising 1 hour later. Few working people, however, have the leisure and the discipline it takes to make this system work; and even when they do, they'd still be likely to experience some minor jet lag on their trip.

In 1955, Dwight D. Eisenhower prepared himself for a crucial Monday morning summit meeting with Nikita Khruschev in Geneva by flying in the previous Friday. The idea was to reach the new time zone far enough in advance so that the symptoms of jet lag would disappear by the time of the big event. This strategy is somewhat effective but not altogether foolproof, as it can take as long as 1 day per time zone crossed to function completely free of symptoms.

GENERAL TIPS FOR COMBATING JET LAG

If you're crossing more than a few time zones or traveling to attend an important business engagement, you may want to consider one of the more intensive strategies for beating jet lag, listed below, such as melatonin or the anti–jet lag diet. For brief trips, however, you can curtail the symptoms of jet lag without having to take any drugs or follow any complicated diet regimens. Try the following tricks the next time you fly.

- **Drink lots of water before, during, and after your flight.** Experts recommend that you drink at

least two 8-ounce glasses just before departure and
1 liter for every hour you spend in the air—in
addition to beverages you drink with meals. Even if
you don't feel thirsty, drink up. Thirst doesn't necessarily precede the symptoms of dehydration,
which can set in without warning.

- The minute you step into the airplane cabin, **adopt
  the hour of the time zone you're traveling to.**
  Reset your watch and start to think according to
  the new time zone.

- **Avoid drinking alcohol** or ingesting other depres-
  sants, such as Dramamine or other motion-sickness
  drugs, before and during your flight.

- **Exercise, sleep well, and eat as healthily as you
  can** during the few days before your trip. With
  your body in peak condition you'll be better able to
  conquer jet lag.

- **Eat more lightly** than you are accustomed to
  before your flight and while you're in the air.

- If you're traveling west to east, it's to your advantage to **schedule business meetings over a late
  dinner,** during the first day or two of your trip,
  when you're likely to be the most alert member of
  the dining circle.

- Once you reach your destination, **don't sleep
  longer than you normally would** to try to "catch
  up." You'll feel much better the faster you can acclimate yourself to the new time zone.

- Travelers who have trouble sleeping on planes like
  to **fly to Europe on a morning flight,** so they
  arrive in the evening, eat supper and find a room at
  a reasonable hour, and get a good night's sleep. The
  problem with this routine is that you waste a full
  day on the plane and will still likely suffer the

effects of jet lag, at least for a few days after you arrive. You will most likely forfeit a day on the plane at the tail end your trip as well, since most U.S.-bound flights depart from Europe in the early afternoon.

MELATONIN: A MIRACLE CURE?

One of the cheapest, easiest, and most effective means of treating jet lag is through the use of synthetic **melatonin,** which has become increasingly more popular and available in recent years. You can usually buy melatonin over the counter in health food stores, nutritional pharmaceutical stores, and mail-order catalogs. Your doctor should be able to provide it as well.

Melatonin is a hormone that occurs naturally in the body, secreted by the pineal gland in the forebrain, and induces sleep. Daylight curbs the natural production of melatonin, but when night falls the pineal gland releases the hormone into the bloodstream and triggers the sleep cycle. Although the pineal gland was long thought to have out-grown any useful purpose in the human body, René Descartes called it the "seat of the soul." Though Descartes, in the 16th century, didn't need to concern himself with jet lag, he obviously understood how crucial sound sleep is to proper mental functioning. His final position was to serve as personal tutor to Queen Christina of Sweden, who required him to administer her lessons every day at 5am.

Melatonin not only induces sleep but improves sleep quality as well. Taken 2 hours before bedtime, a dose of melatonin (typically 3 to 9 milligrams) will trick your body into thinking that night has fallen earlier. Researchers say that with proper use, melatonin can help the body adjust to a new time zone at twice its normal rate. It's important that you don't nap, however, when you reach your destination. Try exercising lightly after your plane has touched down—a brisk walk around your hotel neighborhood is a perfect way to kill time and stave off slumber. Set your clock to local time and aim to stay awake until your normal bedtime—though in the new time zone, of course—and likewise set your alarm for your normal waking time the following morning. Two hours before you want to sleep, take your melatonin. Try your best to rise when the alarm sounds. Don't sleep in. Follow this routine each day until your jet lag symptoms disappear. It also helps to stay active during your trip and to expose yourself to sunlight as much as possible during the day.

Be careful not to go overboard and take too much melatonin, or you may suffer a slight hangover and feel a little addled the following day. If you're traveling to attend an important business meeting or conference, you may want to experiment with taking melatonin a few days before your departure, so you know how your body responds to it.

Some experts still warn that melatonin has not been in use long enough for its long-term side effects to be known entirely. So far, however, most clinical tests have shown synthetic melatonin to be nonaddictive, nontoxic, safe, and effective in the treatment of a range of sleep disorders.

3 THE ARGONNE NATIONAL LABORATORY THREE-STEP JET LAG PROGRAM

WHEN A TRIP ABROAD IS GOING TO HAVE FAR-REACHING effects on global politics, government officials—from White House staff members to the U.S. Army Rapid Deployment Force—use the Three-Step Jet Lag Program, developed by Dr. Charles F. Ehret at the Argonne National Laboratory. Promoted by the U.S. Olympic Committee, the program is elaborate but inexpensive and requires no drugs or special equipment. It lasts anywhere from 1 to 3 days before departure, depending on the number of time zones involved, and ends the second day of the trip.

Response to the diet is almost entirely positive, but several sources attest to the fact that it's important to follow the diet closely for maximum effectiveness. This sometimes requires air travelers to begin the regimen as many as 3 days before flight time.

The basic premise of the program is that you can hasten your body's adaptation to a new time and place by carefully manipulating your exposure to light; the amount of rigorous physical activity you undertake; environmental cues that affect sleeping habits, ranging from the buzz of your alarm clock to midmorning conversations by the water cooler at work; and the type of food and drink you ingest, as certain foods and drinks either encourage or stave off sleep. The Three-Step Jet Lag program helps you build up a resistance to jet lag before you leave and helps you lick what few symptoms you may experience soon after you reach your destination.

The program breaks down into three stages: preflight, in-flight, and postflight. The full treatment is tailored and spelled out in detail according to the number of time zones you'll be crossing. (See the time zone changes chart in the appendix.)

During the **preflight** step, you feast and fast on a special diet of foods that will either help you sleep or keep you awake. The objective of this step is to allow your body's reserves of glycogen to run low before your flight by fasting and eating sparingly for 1 to 3 days before your trip. When your body's store of glycogen is drained, you become hypersensitive to influences—light and darkness, certain foods, and methylated xanthines such as caffeine—that trick your body clock into shifting more rapidly than it normally would.

During the **in-flight** step, you simulate the time zone of your final destination by drinking coffee and tea at certain times, adhering to specific periods of light and darkness, and subjecting yourself to particular periods of rest and inactivity.

During the **postflight** step, eat foods that will provide maximum energy during the day and maximum restfulness at night. The dietary premise of the program is that feasts on high-protein foods such as red meats, eggs, and fish, activate the body. Feasts on high-carbohydrate foods, such as pastas, breads, and potatoes, induce sleep. Fasting on low-calorie, low-carbohydrate foods such as soups, salads, and fruit, depletes the body's glycogen reserves, which makes it easier to reset your body clock.

Essentially, you are fighting jet lag through the strategic use of light, nutrition, stimulants like coffee or tea, and physical and mental activity.

TOOLS OF THE THREE-STEP PROGRAM
Light

Even if you remain asleep when your bedside lamp goes on or when the sun cuts a path through your bedroom window, your body starts preparing to enter the active phase of its 24-hour cycle. When light strikes the eye, neurotransmitters send a wake-up call to the brain, which in turn alerts the rest of your body that it's time to seize the day.

Of course this pattern was much simpler before the invention of electric light, 24-hour commerce, and the alarm clock. Plenty of people also manage to work and rest routinely in the land of the midnight sun, where the sun doesn't shine in standard 12-hour shifts. These cases remain the exception, however. Humans, for the most part, are daytime animals—sensitive to light and wired to respond to it. By carefully manipulating light while you're on the plane and once you reach your final destination, you can actually trick your body into adjusting more rapidly to a new time zone.

Thus, from the moment you board a plane it's good to set your watch according to the time at your final destination and simulate light or darkness according to the hour of the day there. If you leave New York for San Francisco at 9am, for instance, set your watch for 6am and pull the shade down as soon as you board the plane. If you leave at 9pm in the summer, set your watch for 6pm and turn on the light above your seat to illuminate your section of the darkened cabin, since the sun would still be shining on the west coast.

You should continue this trickery once you touch down as well. If you leave New York at 5pm and land in San Francisco at 6pm Pacific standard time, don't retreat to your room just because night would have already fallen at home. Fight the urge to shut down and force yourself to stay exposed to the light of day in your destination. Don't wear sunglasses. Flood yourself with light during daylight hours. If you must head indoors for an appointment, turn on as much artificial light as you can.

If it's night when you arrive, avoid the light. Try to shut your eyes until dawn if possible. When day breaks, rise and shine with it. By all means fight the urge to sleep in, no matter how strong.

Food

High-protein foods such as lean meats, fish, eggs, and dairy products, will rev up your adrenal pathways—the combination of chemicals in the body, most active during the day, that give you energy and keep you active and alert. To the contrary, high-carbohydrate foods such as pastas and whole grain breads, will fuel your indoleamine pathways—the combination of chemicals in the body, most active at night, that slow down your body functions, make you drowsy, and ultimately put you to sleep.

On the anti–jet lag diet, you will generally aim to eat a high-protein breakfast and lunch, as each will supply you with a solid 5 hours' worth of energy. At dinnertime, you will aim to eat a meal high in carbohydrates, which will tire you out and signal to your body that it's time to shut down and sleep. While this is not a very complicated or difficult regimen, it does go against the standard travel diet. Most hotels serve a continental breakfast, which is very high in carbohydrates. A sticky bun, fruit, and coffee may give you a rush of energy right after you've eaten, but within an hour you'll start to drag and feel tired—and maybe even feel as though you need to take a nap. This is deadly when trying to adjust to a new time zone.

SNOOZE BOOSTERS & OTHER TOOLS
OF THE FLYING TRADE

The following products from **Magellan's** (☎ **800/962-4943;** www.
magellans.com) will help you rest more soundly on a plane, in an
unfamiliar hotel bed, or at odd hours when you're trying to adapt
to a new time zone. **Rand McNally** (☎ **800/627-2897**) and **L.L.
Bean** (☎ **800/341-4341**; www.llbean.com) are also reliable vendors of travel-related gadgets, gizmos, and gear. Shop online, or
call for a free catalog or the address of the store nearest you.

Hearos' foam ear plugs ($4.85 for a set of four; $7.85
with eye shade) shrink to half their normal size so you can slide
them deep into your ear. Then they slowly expand to fit snugly
and provide maximum, yet comfortable, insulation against environmental noise.

Magellan's **eyeshade** ($7.85 with Hearos' earplugs) spe-
cially designed for travel, features adjustable straps and a nose
bridge to keep light from filtering in underneath.

Cloud-Soft Inflatable Pillow ($9.85) wraps around your
neck in a horseshoe shape to support the back of your neck, so
you can tip back and nap, and prevents your head from bobbing
side to side. The pillow inflates as easily as it packs when it's
deflated. The soft poly-cotton cover is comfortable year-round
and zips off for easy washing.

Bucky ($24.85 or $45 with eyeshades and earplugs)
makes the **travel pillow** many frequent fliers swear by. Made
from buckwheat hulls, the pillow conforms more closely to your
neck and shoulders than an inflatable pillow. Made of soft, cozy
Polartec, the removable cover is machine washable. Bucky **eye**

The careful, strategic use of caffeine will also dramatically
help reset your body clock—especially when taken in concert
with the program of feasting and fasting (eating lightly) on

shades are made from 100% cotton blackout cloth and come with **earplugs** that fit into their own pocket.

Self-Inflating Travel Pillow ($29.85) inflates itself to provide lower back support then rolls into a 3-inch-wide tube for easy packing. With proper Lumbar support, you'll sleep more easily and be more comfortable while you're awake.

Folding Footrest ($24.85) unfolds to a 4-inch height, so you can stretch your legs to sleep, improve circulation, prevent cramping in the back of your thighs, and relieve pressure on the lower back. Folded, the footrest measures a nifty 4 by $8^1/_2$ by $3/_4$ inches for easy packing.

Light Voyager Booklight ($26.85) clips to the back cover of your book and floods the page with cool white fluorescent light, so you can maintain the active phase of the jet lag program even in a dark or insufficiently lit airplane cabin. Powered with four AA batteries, the light allows you to read for up to 10 hours without straining your eyes.

NoiseBuster Extreme ($69) counteracts the irritatingly loud, stress-inducing sound of airplane flight and helps you sleep. This high-tech device analyzes sound waves, duplicates their frequency in the opposite phase, and sends a signal to cancel out the offending noise in your headphones. NoiseBuster is very light (6 ounces) and will run for 100 hours on two AAA batteries. The headphones come with a stereo jack so you can plug them into your Walkman or CD player during the active phase of the jet lag program.

---

either high-protein or high-carbohydrate foods. When you fast as prescribed by the jet lag diet, you drain your body's reserves of glycogen, which makes you ultrasensitive to stimulants like

CAFFEINE CONTENTS OF BEVERAGES & OVER-THE-COUNTER MEDICATIONS

PRODUCT	QUANTITY	CAFFEINE LEVEL (IN MILLIGRAMS)
Coffee		
decaffeinated	5 oz.	2
instant, regular	5 oz.	53
percolated	5 oz.	110
drip	5 oz.	146
Tea		
1-minute brew	5 oz.	9 to 33
3-minute brew	5 oz.	20 to 46
5-minute brew	5 oz.	20 to 50
canned iced tea	10 oz.	22 to 36
Cocoa and Chocolate		
milk chocolate	1 oz.	6
cocoa mix (with water)	8 oz.	10
baking chocolate	1 oz.	35
Nonprescription Stimulants		
Caffedrine capsules	standard dose	200
NoDoz tablets	standard dose	200
Vivarin	standard dose	200

Source: Consumer Reports, *October 1981, p. 599.*

caffeine, food, and light. The jet lag regimen repeatedly replenishes and drains your body's supply of glycogen, allowing your internal body clock to adjust more rapidly. (The adjacent chart shows the comparative caffeine levels of various common foods, beverages, and over-the-counter stimulants.)

PHYSICAL & MENTAL ACTIVITY

You can also help psych yourself into a new time frame by staying active during daylight hours and exposing yourself to maximum social stimulation in your new environment. If you're still on a plane during what would be the active phase of the daily cycle in your new location, get up, walk around, or talk to fellow passengers. On your first day in town, don't

PRODUCT	QUANTITY	CAFFEINE LEVEL (IN MILLIGRAMS)
Nonprescription Pain Relievers		
plain aspirin	standard dose	0
Anacin	standard dose	64
Midol	standard dose	65
Excedrin	standard dose	130
Nonprescription Diuretics		
Pre-Mens Forte	standard dose	100
Aqua-Ban	standard dose	200
Permathene	standard dose	200
Nonprescription Cold Remedies		
Coryban-D	standard dose	30
Triamincin	standard dose	30
Dristan	standard dose	32
Nonprescription Weight Control Substances		
Dietac	daily dose	200
Dexatrim	daily dose	200
Prolamine	daily dose	280

linger over the newspaper in your hotel room, even if your body seems to be telling you that you need a few more hours of rest time. Get up and set out right away and stay as active as possible over the course of the day. The mere act of rubbing shoulders with other people will cause your body to secrete neurotransmitters that will help keep you alert until it's bedtime in your new locale.

4 THE ANTI–JET LAG DIET

FOR A LIST OF COUNTRIES AND THEIR TIME ZONES (relative to U.S. eastern standard time), consult the front of your local telephone book.

Get with the Jet Lag Program

You can receive a free wallet-sized version of the Argonne Three-Step Jet Lag Program if you send a self-addressed, stamped envelope to Public Affairs, **Argonne National Laboratory,** 9700 South Cass Ave., Argonne, IL 60439 (☎ **630/252-2000**). The complete program is also laid out in Dr. Ehret's book, written in conjunction with Lynne Waller Scanlon, **"Overcoming Jet Lag"** (Berkeley Publications, 1987, $10.95). A quick read, this slim volume is available in the travel section of many major bookstores.

CROSSING ONE OR TWO TIME ZONES
Traveling From West to East

STEP ONE

Two days before your flight, eliminate foods and drinks containing caffeine from your morning and evening diet. Consume caffeine only between the hours of 3 and 4:30pm. **One day** before your flight, consume high-protein meals at breakfast and lunch and a high-carbohydrate meal at dinnertime. This is a **fast** day: Keep your total caloric intake under 800 calories. At 6pm, drink two to three cups of black coffee or the caffeine equivalent.

STEP TWO

On the **day of flight,** rise earlier than usual. Set your watch according to your destination time. Do not eat breakfast until you normally would, but according to the time at your destination.

STEP THREE

On the **day of flight,** eat a high-protein breakfast at the same hour you normally would, but according to your destination time. This is a feast day. Eat a large, high-protein lunch on destination time. Eat a large, high-carbohydrate supper on destination time. Drink plenty of water. Do not drink any caffeine or alcohol. Even if you don't feel tired, try to go to bed a little earlier than you would, with a sleep mask if necessary—since 10pm at home will be midnight destination time.

Traveling From East to West

STEP ONE

Two days before your flight, eliminate foods and drinks containing caffeine from your morning and evening diet. Consume caffeine only between the hours of 3 and 4:30pm. **One day** before your flight, fast (daily caloric intake should not exceed 800 calories) on a high-protein breakfast and lunch and a high-carbohydrate dinner. You may consume caffeine only between 7 and 11am.

STEP TWO

On the day of flight, as soon as you wake up and again before 11am, drink two to three cups of black coffee or the caffeine equivalent. Do not eat breakfast yet and do not consume any more caffeine today. Set your watch to destination time.

STEP THREE

A half hour before your normal breakfast hour, destination time, activate your body and mind (see "Mind-Body Activation," below). Feast on a large, high-protein breakfast and lunch, destination time and a large, high-carbohydrate dinner. You may eat a light snack after dinner. Drink plenty of water. Do not consume alcohol or caffeine. Since midnight at home will be 10pm destination time, try to go to bed as soon as you can—with a sleep mask if necessary.

CROSSING THREE OR FOUR TIME ZONES
Traveling From West to East

STEP ONE

Beginning **3 days before flight,** eliminate foods and drinks containing caffeine from your morning and evening diet.

Consume caffeine only between the hours of 3 and 4:30pm. **One day before flight,** feast on a high-protein breakfast and lunch and high-carbohydrate dinner.

STEP TWO

On the **day of flight,** rise earlier than usual. Fast (keep your caloric intake for the day under 800 calories) on a high-protein breakfast and lunch and a high-carbohydrate dinner. Drink plenty of water. Do not drink alcohol. At 6pm sharp, drink two or three cups of black coffee or the caffeine equivalent. Reset your watch to destination time. Since 8pm at home will be midnight destination time, try to go to bed as soon as you can on destination time, even if you don't feel tired. Sleep until morning, destination time. Use a sleep mask if necessary.

STEP THREE

On the **first morning** in the new time zone, rise at your normal waking hour, destination time. Fight the urge to sleep in. One-half hour before breakfast, destination time, activate your body and mind (see "Mind-Body Activation," below). Feast on a large, high-protein breakfast and lunch and a large, high-carbohydrate dinner. Do not consume any caffeine or alcohol. Stay active throughout the day and do not nap. Go to bed by 10:30pm, destination time.

Traveling From East to West

STEP ONE

Beginning **3 days** before flight, eliminate foods and drinks containing caffeine from your morning and evening diet. Consume caffeine only between the hours of 3 and 4:30pm. **One day** before your flight, fast (daily caloric intake should not exceed 800 calories) on a high-protein breakfast and lunch and a high-carbohydrate dinner. You may consume caffeine only between 7 and 11am.

STEP TWO

On the day of flight, drink two to three cups of black coffee or the caffeine equivalent before 11:30am. Do not eat breakfast yet and do not consume any more caffeine today. Set your watch to destination time.

STEP THREE

A half hour before your normal breakfast hour, destination time, activate your body and mind (see "Mind-Body Activation," below). Feast on a large, high-protein breakfast and lunch and a large, high-carbohydrate dinner, destination time. You may eat a light snack after dinner. Drink plenty of water. Do not consume alcohol or caffeine. Since midnight at home will be 8pm destination time, try to go to bed as soon as you can—with a sleep mask if necessary.

CROSSING FIVE OR SIX TIME ZONES
Traveling From West to East

STEP ONE

Three days before flight, feast on a large, high-protein breakfast and lunch and a large, high-carbohydrate supper. Eliminate foods and drinks containing caffeine from your morning and evening diet. Consume caffeine only between the hours of 3pm and 4:30pm. **Two days before flight,** fast (keep daily caloric intake under 800 calories) on a high-protein breakfast and lunch and a high-carbohydrate supper. Do not snack after dinner. **The day before flight,** feast on a large, high-protein breakfast and lunch and a high-carbohydrate dinner. Do not snack after dinner.

STEP TWO

On the **day of flight,** rise earlier than you normally would. Fast (keep daily caloric intake under 800 calories) on a high-protein breakfast and lunch and a high-carbohydrate supper. Drink plenty of water. Do not drink alcohol. At 6pm sharp, drink two to three cups of black coffee or the caffeine equivalent. Reset your watch to destination time. Since 6pm at home will be midnight destination time, try to go to bed as soon as you can on destination time, even if you don't feel tired. Sleep until morning, destination time. Use a sleep mask if necessary.

STEP THREE

On the **first morning** in the new time zone, rise at your normal waking hour, destination time. Fight the urge to sleep in. One half-hour before breakfast, destination time, activate your body and mind (see "Mind-Body Activation," below). Feast on a large, high-protein breakfast and lunch and a large, high-carbohydrate dinner. Do not snack after dinner. Do not consume any caffeine or alcohol. Stay active throughout the day and do not nap. Go to bed by 10pm, destination time.

Traveling From East to West

STEP ONE

Three days before flight, feast on a large, high-protein breakfast and lunch and large, high-carbohydrate dinner. Eliminate foods and drinks containing caffeine from your morning and evening diet. Consume caffeine only between the hours of 3 and 4:30pm. **Two days before flight,** fast (daily caloric intake under 800 calories) on a high-protein breakfast and lunch and a high-carbohydrate dinner. Do not snack after dinner. **The day before flight,** feast on a high-protein breakfast and lunch and high-carbohydrate dinner. You may eat a light snack after dinner.

STEP TWO

On the day of flight, sleep as late as possible. As soon as you rise—but no later than 11am—drink two to three cups of black coffee or the caffeine equivalent. Do not consume any more caffeine this day. Fast (daily caloric intake under 800 calories) on a high-protein breakfast and lunch and a high-carbohydrate dinner. Do not snack after dinner. Drink plenty of water and do not consume alcohol or caffeine. Reset your watch to destination time. Since midnight at home will be 6pm destination time, get ready for a long day. Try not to rest or sleep until your normal hour on destination time.

STEP THREE

A half hour before your first breakfast, destination time, activate your body and mind (see "Mind-Body Activation," below). Feast on a large, high-protein breakfast and lunch and a large, high-carbohydrate dinner. You may snack lightly after dinner. Do not consume any caffeine today. Go to bed at a reasonable hour, destination time.

CROSSING SEVEN OR EIGHT TIME ZONES
Traveling From West to East

STEP ONE

Three days before flight, feast on a large, high-protein breakfast and lunch and a large, high-carbohydrate supper. Eliminate foods and drinks containing caffeine from your morning and evening diet. Consume caffeine only between the hours of 3pm and 4:30pm. **Two days before flight,** fast (keep daily caloric intake under 800 calories) on a high-protein breakfast and lunch and a high-carbohydrate supper. Do not snack after dinner. **The day before flight,** feast on a large, high-protein breakfast and lunch and a high-carbohydrate dinner. Do not snack after dinner.

STEP TWO

On the **day of flight,** rise earlier than you normally would. Fast (keep daily caloric intake under 800 calories) on a high-protein breakfast and lunch and a high-carbohydrate supper. You may want to skip dinner, as it falls so soon before breakfast, destination time. Drink plenty of water. Do not drink alcohol. At 6pm sharp, drink two to three cups of black coffee or the caffeine equivalent. Reset your watch to destination time. Since 4pm at home will be midnight destination time, try to go to bed as soon as you can on destination time, even if you don't feel tired. Sleep until morning, destination time. Use a sleep mask if necessary.

STEP THREE

On the **first morning** in the new time zone, rise between 6 and 7:30am, destination time. Fight the urge to sleep in. One half hour before breakfast, destination time, activate your body and mind (see "Mind-Body Activation," below). At breakfast, drink one to two cups of black coffee or the caffeine equivalent. Feast on a large, high-protein breakfast and lunch and a large, high-carbohydrate dinner. Do not snack after dinner. Do not consume caffeine at any other time but breakfast. Stay active. Do not nap. Go to bed by 10pm, destination time.

Traveling From East to West

STEP ONE

Three days before flight, feast on a large, high-protein breakfast and lunch and a large, high-carbohydrate dinner. Eliminate foods and drinks containing caffeine from your morning and evening diet. Consume caffeine only between the hours of 3 and 4:30pm. **Two days before flight,** fast (daily caloric intake under 800 calories) on a high-protein breakfast and lunch and a high-carbohydrate dinner. Do not snack after dinner. **The day before flight,** feast on a high-protein breakfast and lunch and high-carbohydrate dinner. You may eat a light snack after dinner.

STEP TWO

On the day of flight, sleep as late as possible. As soon as you rise—but no later than 11:30 am—drink two to three cups of black coffee or the caffeine equivalent. Do not consume any more caffeine this day. Eat a very late, very light (under 250 calories), high-protein breakfast. This will be your first and last meal on home time. Do not eat again until mealtime, destination time—this will be a large, high-protein breakfast only a few hours later, because of the time change. After your first, light breakfast, rest until your next meal. Drink plenty of water and do not consume alcohol. Reset your watch to destination time.

STEP THREE

A half hour before breakfast, destination time, activate your body and mind (see "Mind-Body Activation," below). Feast on a large, high-protein breakfast, destination time (this will probably take place on the plane). Feast on a large, high-protein lunch and a large, high-carbohydrate dinner. You may snack lightly after dinner. Do not consume any caffeine today. Since midnight, home time, is 4pm destination time, ready yourself for a very long day. Stay active and do not nap. Try not to sleep until your normal hour on destination time.

CROSSING NINE OR TEN TIME ZONES
Traveling From West to East

STEP ONE

Three days before flight, feast on a large, high-protein breakfast and lunch and a large, high-carbohydrate supper. Eliminate foods and drinks containing caffeine from your morning and evening diet. Consume caffeine only between the hours of 3pm and 4:30pm. **Two days before flight,** fast (keep daily caloric intake under 800 calories) on a high-protein breakfast and lunch and a high-carbohydrate supper. Do not snack after dinner. **The day before flight,** feast on a large, high-protein breakfast and lunch and a high-carbohydrate dinner. Do not snack after dinner. Go to bed earlier than usual.

STEP TWO

On the **day of flight,** rise earlier than you normally would. Fast (keep daily caloric intake under 400 calories) on a high-protein breakfast and lunch. Reset your watch to destination time. Do not eat again until breakfast, destination time. Drink plenty of water. Do not consume caffeine or alcohol.

Since 2pm at home will be midnight destination time, try to go to bed as soon as you can on destination time, even if you don't feel tired. Sleep until morning, destination time. Use a sleep mask if necessary.

STEP THREE

On the **first morning** in the new time zone, rise no later than 9am, destination time. Fight the urge to sleep in. A half hour before breakfast, destination time, activate your body and mind (see "Mind-Body Activation," below). Eat breakfast no later than 9:30am. Drink two to three cups of black coffee or the caffeine equivalent and feast on a large, high-protein breakfast and lunch and a large, high-carbohydrate dinner. Do not snack after dinner. Stay active. Do not nap. Go to bed early.

Traveling From East to West

STEP ONE

Three days before flight, feast on a large, high-protein breakfast and lunch and a large, high-carbohydrate dinner. Eliminate foods and drinks containing caffeine from your morning and evening diet. Consume caffeine only between the hours of 3 and 4:30pm. **Two days before flight,** fast (daily caloric intake under 800 calories) on a high-protein breakfast and lunch and a high-carbohydrate dinner. Do not snack after dinner. **The day before flight,** feast on a high-protein breakfast and lunch and high-carbohydrate dinner.

STEP TWO

On the day of flight, sleep as late as possible. As soon as you rise, drink two to three cups of black coffee or the caffeine equivalent. Do not consume any more caffeine this day. Eat a light (under 400 calories total), high-protein breakfast and lunch. Skip lunch if you can. Do not eat again until breakfast, destination time—just a few hours away. Rest until breakfast. Drink plenty of water and do not consume alcohol or caffeine. Reset your watch to destination time.

STEP THREE

A half hour before breakfast, destination time, activate your body and mind (see "Mind-Body Activation," below). Feast on a large, high-protein breakfast and lunch and a large, high-carbohydrate dinner on destination time. You may snack lightly after dinner. Do not consume any caffeine today. Since midnight, home time, is 2pm destination time, ready yourself for a very long day. Stay active and do not nap. Try not to sleep until your normal hour on home time.

CROSSING ELEVEN OR TWELVE TIME ZONES
Traveling From West to East

STEP ONE

Three days before flight, feast on a large, high-protein breakfast and lunch and a large, high-carbohydrate supper. Eliminate foods and drinks containing caffeine from your morning and evening diet. Consume caffeine only between the hours of 3pm and 4:30pm. **Two days before flight,** fast (keep daily caloric intake under 800 calories) on a high-protein breakfast and lunch and a high-carbohydrate supper. Do not snack after dinner. **The day before flight,** feast on a large, high-protein breakfast and lunch and a high-carbohydrate dinner. Do not snack after dinner. Consume caffeine only between 7 am and 10 am.

STEP TWO

Just before breakfast (between 7 and 11:30 am), drink two to three cups of black coffee or the caffeine equivalent. Fast (keep daily caloric intake under 400 calories) on a high-protein breakfast and lunch. Reset your watch to destination time. Do not eat again until breakfast, destination time. Drink plenty of water. Do not consume caffeine or alcohol. Since noon at home will be midnight destination time, try to go to bed as soon as you can on destination time, even if you don't feel tired. Sleep until morning, destination time. Use a sleep mask if necessary.

STEP THREE

On the first morning in the new time zone, activate your body and mind (see "Mind-Body Activation," below) a half hour before breakfast, destination time. Feast on a high-protein breakfast and lunch and a high-carbohydrate dinner. Do not consume any caffeine. Stay active. Resist the urge to nap. Go to bed by 10pm, destination time.

Traveling From East to West

See "Crossing Eleven or Twelve Time Zones," "Traveling from West to East," above.

5 Mind-Body Activation: Get Your System Jump-Started

THE IDEA HERE IS TO ROUSE YOUR WHOLE BODY ONCE you've pried open your eyes. You want your heart to speed up from its sleepy pace, your blood to circulate faster, your joints to loosen up, and your mind to clear itself from the cobwebs of sleep.

It doesn't take much to rev up your system after it has been at rest. You can do the following exercises in very little space—even within the cramped quarters of an airplane, near the lavatory, or at the back end of the aircraft.

1. Take five long, deep breaths from the diaphragm. If you're breathing properly, your abdomen should rise and fall instead of your chest.

2. Stand on your tiptoes and reach for the ceiling. Do this slowly 5 to 10 times, breathing deeply with each stretch.

3. Slowly, while breathing deeply, roll your shoulders forward and back. Roll each shoulder separately five times. Then roll each shoulder back, one by one, five times.

4. Slowly roll your head five times to the left and five times to the right.

5. Bend backward from the waist as far as you safely can. Point your chin toward the ceiling and breath deeply. Perform this five times.

6. Roll your wrists and ankles slowly five times each.

7. Pull your knees up to your waist, one by one, 5 to 10 times each.

8. Visit the lavatory. Wash your hands and face, comb your hair, and brush your teeth.

9. If possible, converse or play a quick game of cards with travel partners, newfound friends on the plane, or flight personnel. If this is not possible, play solitaire or read a book or magazine.

6   WHEN IS THE BEST DEPARTURE TIME?

AS A GENERAL RULE, YOU WANT TO SCHEDULE YOUR flight so that you arrive during the active phase of the day (between 8am and 8pm) in your destination time zone. The closer to 8am you arrive the better. You should try to avoid arriving between midnight and dawn destination time, as you will have to force yourself to be active at an hour when you should be resting. If you must take a red-eye flight, fly in a day earlier than planned so you can have at least one good night's sleep before having to attend an important meeting or event at your final destination.

WEST-TO-EAST DEPARTURE & ARRIVAL TIMES

When you're flying east, pick a flight that departs as early as possible. For short trips east, don't rise too early the morning of the flight. For medium-length trips east, don't take a flight that forces you to rise before 5:30am. For long trips east, plan to leave either as late as you can—though still before midnight—and arrive the next morning after 6am; or depart early as possible after 6am and arrive very late the same day—though before midnight, destination time.

EAST-TO-WEST DEPARTURE & ARRIVAL TIMES

When you're flying west, choose a flight that leaves as late as possible. For short trips west, sleep at least as late as usual, later if you can. For medium-length trips, try to sleep as late as the expected rising time at your destination. Pick a flight that allows you to do this. For long trips west, depart at an hour that will allow you the longest possible rest period before your destination-time breakfast feast on board the plane. If you're able to sleep on a plane, depart as early as possible after 8am.

BEST DAY OF ARRIVAL FOR MAXIMUM PERFORMANCE
On a West-to-East Flight

TIME ZONE CHANGE	WITH JET LAG PROGRAM	WITHOUT JET LAG PROGRAM
+1	same-day arrival	same-day arrival
+2	same-day arrival	same-day arrival
+3	same-day arrival	1 day early
+4	same-day arrival	2 days early
+5	1 day early	3 to 4 days early
+6	1 day early	4 to 6 days early
+7	2 days early	5 to 7 days early
+8	2 days early	6 to 7 days early
+9	2 days early	7 to 11 days early
+10	3 days early	8 to 12 days early
+11	3 days early	9 to 12 days early
+12	3 days early	10 to 12 days early

On an East-to-West Flight

TIME ZONE CHANGE	WITH JET LAG PROGRAM	WITHOUT JET LAG PROGRAM
−1	same-day arrival	same-day arrival
−2	same-day arrival	same-day arrival
−3	same-day arrival	1 day early
−4	same-day arrival	2 days early
−5	1 day early	3 days early
−6	1 day early	4 days early
−7	1 day early	5 days early
−8	1 day early	6 days early
−9	2 days early	7 days early
−10	2 days early	8 to 10 days early
−11	2 to 3 days early	9 to 11 days early
−12	3 days early	10 to 12 days early

7 SUGGESTED MENUS FOR THE JET LAG DIET

FAST DAY (UNDER 800 CALORIES)

Breakfast

1 egg, any style (82)
1/2 cup low-fat cottage cheese (86)
1/2 cup orange juice (60)
Total calories: 228

OR

2 eggs, any style (164)
1/2 slice lightly buttered toast (50)
Total calories: 214

Lunch

1/2 cup water-packed tuna with lemon juice (144)
1 slice bread, with light mayonnaise (65)

tomato slices and lettuce (20)
$^1/_4$ cup low-fat or skim milk (75)
Total calories: 304

OR

1 chicken breast, without skin (154)
1 cup bouillon (5)
$^1/_2$ cup low-fat cottage cheese (86)
Total calories: 245

Dinner

Medium-size plate of lettuce, tomato, cucumber, onion,
  green pepper, radish, celery (120)
1 tablespoon dressing (50)
1 slice bread, lightly buttered (65)
1 apple or pear (50)
Total calories 285

OR

1 small bowl of pasta, with light margarine (150)
1 slice bread, lightly buttered (65)
1 cup cooked string beans, squash, carrots,
  or broccoli (40)
Total calories 255

FEAST DAY (A FEW THOUSAND CALORIES)
Breakfast

steak and eggs or ham and cheese
plenty of milk
$^1/_2$ cup orange juice
1 slice bread, lightly buttered

OR

large omelette with cheese or vegetables
plenty of milk
1 cup orange juice
1 slice bread, lightly buttered

Lunch

 assorted cold cuts (chicken, turkey, lean meat)

 assorted cheeses

 plenty of milk

 1 slice bread, lightly buttered

 1 cup cauliflower, string beans, or carrots

 1 apple, pear, banana, or grapes

 OR

 lots of meat, fish, or poultry

 baked beans, lima beans

 cheese

 1 slice bread, lightly buttered

 1 apple, tangerine, cherries

Dinner

 pasta with meatless tomato sauce

 bread, lightly buttered

 fruit salad

 cake, cookies

 alcohol, in reasonable amount

 OR

 sautéed potatoes, corn, green beans, squash

 mixed salad

 salad dressing

 bread, lightly buttered

 cake, cookies

 alcohol, in reasonable amount

7

Sky Hounds: How to Make the Most of Your Frequent-Flier Mileage

Never get between a man and his pudding: The next time you think frequent-flyer programs don't pay off, remember the story of David Phillips. He's the 35-year-old civil engineer from California who snagged 1.25 million frequent-flyer miles—folks, that's an estimated $25,000 worth of free flights—by taking brilliant advantage of a Healthy Choice promotion. Phillips raided local grocery stores and spent $3,140 on 25¢ cups of chocolate pudding, earning 100 miles per cup. No, he's not particularly fond of the stuff (he donated the 12,000 or so containers to local charities in exchange for help removing the labels), and yes, his wife thought he was a bit kooky. But no one in the family is complaining now; a trip to Milan, Barcelona, and London is in the works. And from there, the possibilities are endless.

In this golden age for the airline industry—when profits are sky-high despite the fact that consumers feel more put down than ever—frequent-flier programs are one of the few customer-friendly traits of the business. Even the most disgruntled air travelers have to ask themselves: How many other industries systematically reward customers so generously for their loyalty—now that S&H Green Stamps have gone the way of poodle skirts and sock hops?

The next time you're sitting in cramped coach quarters, delayed indefinitely on a runway, console yourself with the fact that you are getting something extra for your hard-earned dollars. Choose your frequent-flier program wisely, and with mileage-earning opportunities at every turn, you can turn many of life's mundane, ornery-making obligations into a veritable flying machine. As you grumble about the skyrocketing cost of gasoline, you can charge your fill-ups on a mileage-earning credit card; as you haggle by phone with contrary business clients in Singapore, you can rack up miles on one of the many mileage-earning long-distance carriers. Even one of the biggest milestones of adult responsibility—buying a car—is now an opportunity to rack up frequent-flier miles.

1 How to Play the Mileage Game

IT MAKES SENSE TO HOLD INACTIVE ACCOUNTS WITH as many airlines as possible. It costs nothing, and most of the major domestic airlines allow you to maintain a card without activity for up to 3 years (see "Frequent-Flier Profiles of the Major Domestic Airlines," below, for details). Airlines cater to loyal customers and will be much more willing to go the extra mile for you if you can say you have a frequent-flier account. You'll get faster response to phone inquiries, more focused attention in the event that your luggage is lost or you need to switch your seat, and a greater chance of securing a hotel voucher if your flight is canceled and you're stranded overnight.

Nevertheless, you'll stretch your mileage by choosing only one account to accrue miles in, and flying on that airline as often as possible. Commitment no longer necessarily limits you to that carrier's route and schedules either, since

MAJOR AIRLINES' FREQUENT-FLIER SERVICE NUMBERS & WEB SITES

Alaska	☎ 800/654-5669; www.alaskaair.com
America West	☎ 800/247-5691; www.americawest.com/fltfund/default.htm
American	☎ 800/882-8880; www.aa.com
Continental	☎ 800/421-2456 or 713/952-1630*; www.onepas.com
Delta	☎ 800/325-3999; www.delta-air.com/skymile/index.html
Northwest	☎ 800/447-3757; www.nwa.com/freqfly/
Southwest	☎ 800/445-5764; www.iflyswa.com/rapid_rewards/more_rapid_rewards.html
TWA	☎ 800/325-4815; www.twa.com/frq_trav_info/index.html
United	☎ 800/421-4655; www.ual.com
US Airways	☎ 800/428-4322 or 336/661-8390*; www.usairways.com

Airlines marked with an asterisk (*) have no toll-free number designated exclusively for frequent-flier-related questions. General reservationists will be able to field most of your questions, but they may refer you to the toll number for complicated issues.

most major domestic airlines allow you to earn and spend frequent-flier miles on at least one major partner airline. You'll earn free tickets faster this way and, on most major carriers, achieve elite status if you fly 25,000 miles a year or more. Elite status affords you ample mileage bonuses for each trip you take, greater chance to upgrade (upgrades are complimentary and unlimited through some programs), and VIP benefits that range from priority boarding, seating, and baggage claim to discounts on club membership. (See "Achieving Elite Status," later this chapter, for detailed info on various elite programs.)

Some frequent-flier programs clearly offer more options and greater gains than others. Yet even some of the most frequent fliers seem to favor a particular program by default,

WHO AWARDS THE MOST SEATS?

AIRLINE	AWARD SEATS	PERCENTAGE OF ALL SEATS	PERCENT CHANGE*
American	1,084,343	8.5	+2.9
TWA	214,547	8.5	–6.1
Northwest	466,397	7.8	+8.6
Continental	551,041	7.2	–2.4
United	1,026,526	6.6	+5.2
US Airways	356,788	6.6	–17.2
Delta	646,671	5.4	–20.5
Total	**4,346,313**	**7.0**	**–3.4**

Compared with fiscal year 1996.

Source: 1997 U.S. Department of Transportation (DOT) data

rather than by educated choice: The airline's hub is near their home town, the carrier offered a great sale on flights to Europe 2 years ago and there seemed to be no point in switching accounts and losing miles. Unless you subscribe to one of the frequent-flier periodicals such as *Inside Flyer,* however, it's next to impossible to get reliable, substantive information on the various program options. Airlines agree to send detailed program information only to members once they've joined—which doesn't make frequent-flier reservationists any more willing to answer detailed questions from prospective members over the phone. (Delta and United won't even spare a brochure until a month after you've actually taken a flight on your account, and US Airways' frequent-flier literature is only available at the airport!)

In some regards, it's harder to get a frequent-flier seat these days. Although most airlines allocate 5% of their seats to travelers using free award tickets, the number of available seats dropped 4.6% industry-wide between 1996 and 1997, according to the U.S. Department of Transportation. Blackout dates make it harder to redeem mileage when you need it most, over major holidays and peak vacation-travel seasons. On the other hand, the option to earn miles is greater than ever before, and the various frequent-flier programs differ enough that you might find one that suits your most pressing travel needs just fine, if you take the time to shop around. Here are some factors to consider:

- If you travel often with companions, you may want to locate the program that offers the most generous companion upgrades.

- If you make a lot of trips overseas, you'll fly more comfortably if you seek out the program with the best upgrade options or the best elite-travel bonuses, so you profit from all those hours in the air.

- If you frequent a particular region, such as Asia, you may want to find the program that offers frequent-flier reciprocity with an Asian airline.

- If you have a bad back, or if you're too tall or too wide to fit comfortably in coach, join the program with the best upgrade features.

- If you don't fly very often, be sure you choose an account on which you don't have to actually fly to keep the account active. Some airlines keep your account active if you make charges on a mile-earning credit card or utility—even if you don't actually fly within the 3-year cut-off time. Continental and Northwest never expire your miles, even if your account remains completely inactive for more than 3 years.

- If you fly very often, choose the program that offers the best elite features.

- If you're a business traveler, find a program that offers mileage bonuses on business-class and first-class fares.

2 FREQUENT-FLIER PROFILES OF THE MAJOR DOMESTIC AIRLINES

FREQUENT-FLIER PROGRAMS CHANGE ROUTINELY. Always check the airline's customer service number or Web site for the latest rules and stipulations. See "Upgrading Policies of the Major Domestic Airlines," below, for detailed information on each airline's upgrading policies. The 500-mile minimum reward means that even flights under 500 miles earn 500 frequent-flier miles.

ALASKA AIRLINES MILEAGE PLAN; (☎ 800/654-5669); www.alaskaair.com

BASIC FF ACCOUNTS

Miles earned: mile per mile on both domestic and international flights; 500 mile-minimum.

Mile longevity: Miles do not expire.

Minimum number of miles needed for a Seattle–San Diego round trip: 20,000 (*Note:* Alaska does not fly to cities east of Phoenix).

Minimum number of miles needed for a Chicago–Paris round trip: 40,000 (*Note:* Alaska does not fly to Europe, but its partner airlines do).

When can you confirm a seat? Up to 330 days in advance of departure.

Blackout dates for 2000 (will change each year): November 22, 25–27; December 21–23, 26; other blackout dates may apply to specific routes.

Do rewards differ for economy coach, full-fare coach, business, or first-class travel? Travelers flying First Class using an upgrade or a purchased First Class ticket receive a 50% bonus of the actual/minimum miles.

Can you maintain an account without accruing miles? Yes, but if an account is inactive longer than three years, or has had no activity for nine months after opening, it may be closed.

Is literature available? The program guide is available for download from the Web site.

What are the penalties for canceling a ticket purchased with frequent-flier miles? Members are charged $40 to change the name on an unused award, extend unexpired certificates, or redeposit miles for an unused award.

Partners: American Airlines, American Eagle, British Airways, Canadian Airlines, Continental Airlines, Horizon Air, KLM Royal Dutch Airlines, Northwest Airlines, Qantas Airways, TWA.

Can you accrue miles on partner airlines? Yes.

Can you use miles on partner airlines? Yes.

Can you combine and use mileage from several programs? No.

ELITE QUALIFICATIONS AND REWARDS

All MVP members receive priority boarding, first-class check-in privileges, a priority reservations line, and priority seating. Members are entitled to purchase first-class upgrades for only 5,000 miles on Alaska Airlines.

MVP: Members must fly 15,000 miles/calendar year on Alaska or Horizon Air, or 25,000 miles (or 30 flight segments) on a combination of Alaska, American, Canadian (code-share flights), Horizon, KLM, and Northwest. Members earn a 50% bonus on actual/minimum miles, and bonuses for every 10,000 miles flown starting at 35,000 and up to 75,000 miles in one calendar year. Automatic complimentary first-class upgrades are awarded every 10,000 miles flown (see "Upgrading Policies of the Major Domestic Airlines" for more details).

MVP Gold: Members must fly 45,000 miles/calendar year (or 60 flight segments) on a combination of Alaska, American, Canadian (code-share flights only), Horizon, KLM, and Northwest. Members earn a 100% bonus for miles accrued, and a 25,000 bonus for reaching 100,000 actual miles on Alaska, Horizon, and Northwest/KLM in one calendar year. Automatic first-class upgrades are awarded every 5,000 miles flown (see "Upgrading Policies of the Major Domestic Airlines" for more details). Service charges and ticket change fees are waived for tickets issued under the Mileage Plan. The initiation fee for Board Room membership is waived.

AMERICA WEST FLIGHTFUND; (☎ 800/247-5691);
www.americawest.com/fltfund

BASIC FF ACCOUNTS

Miles earned: mile per mile on both domestic and international flights; 500 mile-minimum.

Mile longevity: will not expire if you accrue miles every 3 years.

Minimum number of miles needed for a New York–Los Angeles round trip: 20,000.

Miles needed for a Chicago–Paris round trip: 60,000 (note: America West does not fly to Europe, but its partner airlines do).

When can you confirm a seat? Up to 10 months in advance.

Blackout dates for the year 2000 (will change each year): January 2–3; April 21–30; November 22, 26; December 22–24, 26, 30–31; other blackout dates may apply on specific routes.

Do rewards differ for economy coach, full-fare coach, business, or first-class travel? First-class travelers receive a 50% mileage bonus.

Can you maintain an account without accruing miles? Yes.

Is literature available? Basic membership guide is available on the Web site; complete information is mailed upon joining.

What are the penalties for canceling a ticket purchased with frequent-flier miles? Tickets must be canceled 14 days in advance of travel. The cost is $75 to redeposit miles in your account, or to change the city pair from the original reservation. However, you can keep the original ticket and use it any time up to one year from the date of issue and pay no penalty.

Partners: British Airways, Continental Airlines, Northwest Airlines, Virgin Atlantic.

Can you accrue miles on partner airlines? Yes.

Can you use miles on partner airlines? Yes.

Can you combine and use mileage from several programs? No.

ELITE QUALIFICATIONS AND REWARDS

All elite members receive priority boarding and stand-by, first-class check-in, a priority reservations line, and preferred seating. Members also receive $75 off club membership.

Silver: Members must fly 25,000 miles/calendar year (or 30 flight segments) and receive a 50% bonus for miles accrued. Upgrades are unlimited, complimentary, and on a space-available basis (see "Upgrading Policies of the Major Domestic Airlines" for more details).

Gold: Members must fly 50,000 miles/calendar year (or 60 flight segments) and receive a 100% bonus for miles accrued. Unlimited complimentary, space-available upgrades and companion upgrades are available (see "Upgrading Policies of the Major Domestic Airlines" for details).

Platinum: Members must fly 75,000 miles/calendar year (or 90 flight segments) and receive a 125% bonus for miles accrued. Unlimited complimentary, space-available upgrades and companion upgrades are available (see "Upgrading Policies of the Major Domestic Airlines" for details).

AMERICAN AADVANTAGE PROGRAM (☎ 800/882-8880; www.aa.com)

BASIC FF ACCOUNTS

Miles earned: Mile per mile on both domestic and international flights; 500-mile minimum.

Mile longevity: Will not expire if you accrue miles every 3 years.

Minimum number of miles needed for a New York–Los Angeles round-trip: 25,000

Minimum number of miles needed for a Chicago–Paris round-trip: 40,000

When can you confirm a seat? Recommended 21 days before departure to avoid $50 fee; within 24 hours $75.

Blackout dates for the year 2000 (will change each year): January 2–3, November 26–27, December 20, 23.

Do rewards differ for economy coach, full-fare coach, business, or first-class travel? First-class and business-class travelers receive a 25% mileage bonus.

Can you maintain an account without accruing miles? Yes.

Is literature available? Members receive detailed literature after joining.

What are the penalties for canceling a ticket purchased with frequent-flier miles? You may use the ticket at a later day within a year. It costs $50 to reinstate miles. It costs $75 to change the routing.

Partners: Aer Lingus, Aerolineas Argentinas, Air Pacific, Alaska Airlines, Asiana Airlines, British Airways, British Midland Airways, Canadian Airlines International, Cathay Pacific, Crossair, El Al, Finnair, Grupo Taca, Hawaiian Airlines, Iberia, Japan Airlines, LanChile Airlines, Midway Airlines, Qantas Airways, Sabena, Swissair, TAM Airlines, Turkish Airlines, US Airways.

Can you accrue miles on partner airlines? Yes.

Can you use miles on partner airlines? Yes.

Can you combine and use mileage from several programs? No.

ELITE QUALIFICATIONS AND REWARDS

All elite members receive priority boarding, a priority reservations line, and priority seating. Members do not receive priority baggage, guaranteed reservations on sold-out flights, or free club membership.

Gold Elite: Members must fly 25,000 miles per calendar year and receive a 25% bonus for miles accrued and four

Where to Find Up-to-Date Information Online

While the information in this chapter was current at press time, the terms of an airline's frequent-flyer program can change without notice. For the latest information on special frequent-flyer offers or changes in airline policy, log on to the specific airline's Web site or try the very helpful WebFlyer (**www.webflyer.com**). The online arm of **Inside Flyer** magazine, WebFlyer is a clearinghouse for frequent-traveler information concerning flight, hotel, and car-rental programs. In addition to a continually updated list of last-minute deals and bonus award opportunities, webflyer.com is constructed so that you can establish new frequent-flyer accounts and access existing accounts from within the site.

---

one-way upgrades every 10,000 miles (see "Upgrading Policies of the Major Domestic Airlines" for details).

Platinum Elite: Members must fly 50,000 miles per calendar year and receive a 50% bonus for miles accrued and four one-way upgrades every 10,000 miles (see "Upgrading Policies of the Major Domestic Airlines" for details).

Executive Platinum: Members must fly 100,000 miles per calendar year and receive a 150% bonus for miles accrued and four one-way upgrades for every 10,000 miles (see "Upgrading Policies of the Major Domestic Airlines" for details).

CONTINENTAL ONE PASS PROGRAM (☎ 800/421-2456 or 713/952-1630; www.onepass.com)

BASIC FF ACCOUNTS

Miles earned: Mile per mile traveled on both domestic and international flights; 500-mile minimum.

Mile longevity: Miles never expire, even when account is inactive.

Minimum number of miles needed for a New York–Los Angeles round-trip: 20,000

Minimum number of miles needed for a Chicago–Paris round-trip: 40,000

When can you confirm an award seat? 320 days in advance.

Blackout dates for the year 2000: Domestic: January 2–3, April 30, June 30, November 22, 26–27, December 22–24, 29–30. International blackout dates vary by region.

Do rewards differ for economy coach, full-fare coach, business, or first-class travel? No.

Can you have an account without miles? Yes.

Is literature available? Members receive literature after joining.

What are the penalties for canceling a ticket purchased with frequent-flier miles? You must pay $35 to reinstate the miles.

Partners: Aces Airlines, Air France, Alaska Airlines, Alitalia, America West, Avant Airlines, British Midland, BWIA, China Airlines, COPA, CSA Czech Airlines, EVA, Frontier, Hawaiian Airlines, Horizon Air, KLM Royal Dutch Airlines, Northwest, Quantas Airways.

Can you accrue miles on partner airlines? Yes.

Can you use miles on partner airlines? Yes.

Can you combine and use mileage from several programs? No.

ELITE QUALIFICATIONS AND REWARDS

All elite members receive priority boarding, use of the priority reservations telephone line, priority baggage, priority seating, guaranteed reservations on sold-out flights. Member do not receive free club membership.

Silver Elite: Members must fly 25,000 miles or 30 segments per calendar year. Silver elites earn a 50% bonus and unlimited complimentary, space-available upgrades and companion upgrades (see "Upgrading Policies of the Major Domestic Airlines" for details).

Gold Elite: Members must fly 50,000 miles or 60 segments per calendar year. Gold elites earn a 100% bonus and unlimited complimentary, space-available upgrades and companion upgrades (see "Upgrading Policies of the Major Domestic Airlines" for details).

Platinum Elite: Members must fly 75,000 miles or 90 segments per calendar year. Platinum elites earn a 125% bonus and unlimited complimentary, space-available upgrades and companion upgrades (see "Upgrading Policies of the Major Domestic Airlines" for details).

DELTA SKYMILES PROGRAM (☎ 800/325-3999; www.delta-air.com/skymile/index.html)

BASIC FF ACCOUNTS

Miles earned: Mile per mile on domestic flights; 500 mile-minimum. Rewards for international travel vary widely by region.

Mile longevity: Will not expire if account is activated at least once every 3 years.

Minimum number of miles needed for a New York–Los Angeles round-trip: 25,000

Minimum number of miles needed for a Chicago–Paris round-trip: 50,000

When can you confirm a seat? 331 days before departure

Blackout dates for travel within the contiguous United States during the year 2000 (will change each year): January 2–3, November 24, 28–29, December 22–23, 26–27. Blackout dates vary widely for travel to Hawaii, Alaska, and international destinations. Call for details.

Do rewards differ for economy coach, full-fare coach, business, or first-class travel? Business-class travelers receive 125% mileage; first-class travelers receive 150% mileage.

Can you maintain an account without accruing miles? No.

Is literature available? Members receive detailed literature one month after date of first activity on the account.

What are the penalties for canceling a ticket purchased with frequent-flier miles? Members may reinstate the miles for $40, reuse the ticket for $50, or change the destination city for $50.

Partners: Aeromexico, Air France, Air Jamaica, China Southern, Finnair, Korean Air, Malaysia Airlines, Singapore Airlines, South African Airways, TAP Air Portugal, United Airlines.

Can you accrue miles on partner airlines? Yes.

Can you use miles on partner airlines? Domestically, members may use miles on United only; all international partners accept Delta miles.

Can you combine and use mileage from several programs? No.

ELITE QUALIFICATIONS AND REWARDS

All elite members receive priority boarding, use of the priority reservations telephone line, priority baggage, and priority seating. Only platinum members receive guaranteed reservations on sold-out flights (24 hours before departure). Only platinum medallions receive free club membership. Silver and gold medallions receive discounts on club membership.

Silver Medallion: Members must fly 25,000 miles or 30 segments per calendar year. Silver elites receive a 25% bonus for miles accrued and four, 800-mile-segment upgrades every 10,000 miles after achieving elite status (see "Upgrading Policies of the Major Domestic Airlines" for details).

Gold Medallion: Members must fly 50,000 miles or 60 segments per calendar year. Members receive a 100% bonus for miles accrued and four, 800-mile segment upgrades every 10,000 miles after achieving elite status (see "Upgrading Policies of the Major Domestic Airlines" for details).

Platinum Medallion: Members must fly 100,000 miles or 100 segments per calendar year. Members receive a 100% bonus for miles accrued and unlimited complimentary upgrades (see "Upgrading Policies of the Major Domestic Airlines" for details).

NORTHWEST WORLDPERKS PROGRAM (☎ 800/447-3757; www.nwa.com/freqfly/)

BASIC FF ACCOUNTS

Miles earned: Mile per mile on both domestic and international flights; 500 mile-minimum.

Mile longevity: Miles never expire.

Minimum number of miles needed for a New York–Los Angeles round-trip: 20,000

Minimum number of miles needed for a Chicago–Paris round-trip: 40,000

When can you confirm a seat? Over 30 days before departure, you can hold reservation for 14 days; 14 to 30 days before departure, you can hold reservation for 3 days; under 14 days, flight must be ticketed immediately. If seats are available, you may make a reservation 2 hours before domestic flights, and 4 hours before international flights.

Blackout dates for the year 2000 (will change each year): January 2–3; April 30; June 30; November 22, 26–27; December 22–24, 29–30.

Do rewards differ for economy coach, full-fare coach, business, or first-class travel? First- and business-class travelers receive 150% mileage.

Can you maintain an account without accruing miles? Yes.

Is literature available? Yes, after you join.

What are the penalties for canceling a ticket purchased with frequent-flier miles? Members may reinstate miles for $35.

Partners: Air China, Alaska Airlines, Aloha Airlines, America West Airlines, Big Sky Airlines, Braathens, Business Express Airlines, Continental, Eurowings, Garuda, Hawaiian Airlines, Japan Air System, Jet Airways, Kenya Airways, KLM Royal Dutch Airlines, Malaysia Airways, Midwest Express, Pacific Island Aviation.

Can you accrue miles on partner airlines? Some.

Can you use miles on partner airlines? Some.

Can you combine and use mileage from several programs? No.

ELITE QUALIFICATIONS AND REWARDS

All elite members receive priority boarding and priority seating. Gold and platinum elites receive use of the priority reservations telephone line. Full-fare gold elites and full-fare or business-class platinum elites receive guaranteed reservations on sold-out flights. Members do not receive priority baggage, but they do receive special bag tags. Elite members do not receive free club membership.

Silver Elite: Members must fly 25,000 miles per calendar year (excluding bonus miles). Gold elites receive a 50% bonus for miles accrued and four one-way domestic upgrades every 10,000 miles (see "Upgrading Policies of the Major Domestic Airlines" for details).

Gold Elite: Members must fly 50,000 miles per calendar year and receive a 100% bonus for miles accrued and unlimited complimentary upgrades. Gold members receive eight complimentary companion upgrades per year (see "Upgrading Policies of the Major Domestic Airlines" for details).

Platinum Elite: Members must fly 75,000 miles per calendar year and receive a 125% bonus for miles accrued and unlimited complimentary upgrades. Platinum elites receive twelve complimentary companion upgrades each year (see "Upgrading Policies of the Major Domestic Airlines" for details).

SOUTHWEST AIRLINES RAPID REWARDS; (☎ 800/445-5764); www.southwest.com

BASIC FF ACCOUNTS

Miles earned: Southwest counts "credits," not miles. Each one-way flight is considered one credit.

Mile/Credit longevity: Each individual credit is valid 12 months from the date of travel.

Number of credits needed for a New York–Los Angeles round trip: After 16 flight credits (or 8 round trips) within a 12-month period, travelers are awarded a free ticket. (*Note:*

Islip is the closest New York airport Southwest flies into.)

Number of credits needed for a Chicago–Paris round trip: Southwest does not fly to international destinations, and has no partner airlines.

When can you confirm a seat? No boarding passes are issued on Southwest flights, so it's first-come, first-served on the day of the flight.

Blackout dates for the year 2000 (will change each year): January 2; May 26, 29; November 21–22, 26–27; December 22–23, 26, 29–30.

Do rewards differ for economy coach, full-fare coach, business, or first-class travel? Southwest only has one cabin class, but there is the opportunity to earn "double credits" if you book your ticket online.

Can you maintain an account without accruing miles? Yes, but credits will expire 12 months from the date of travel.

Is literature available? Some information is available online. Once you achieve Freedom Reward status (meaning once you earn 16 credits), detailed membership packets are mailed to you.

What are the penalties for canceling a ticket earned with flight credits? No penalties; free ticket is valid for one year from date of issue.

Partners: No airline partners, but like other airlines, Southwest has partnerships with hotels, car rental companies, and credit cards.

Can you accrue miles on partner airlines? N/A.

Can you use miles on partner airlines? N/A.

Can you combine and use mileage from several programs? N/A.

ELITE QUALIFICATIONS AND REWARDS

A Freedom Reward Member (someone who has already reached the 16-credit level) who accumulates 100 flight credits within 12 consecutive months becomes a **Companion Reward Member** and is eligible for a Companion Pass, which entitles your designated traveling companion to fly free with you for one year. The Companion Pass is valid whenever your companion checks in and travels on the same flight in the continental U.S., whether you are traveling on a fare paid ticket or a Rapid Rewards Award Ticket. You are limited to one Companion Pass at any time, and the designated Companion can be changed three times within the 12-month period. Companion Reward Membership must be earned every 12 months.

TWA AVIATORS PROGRAM (☎ 800/325-4815; www.twa.com/frq_trav_info/index.html)

BASIC FF ACCOUNTS

Miles earned: Mile per mile on both domestic and international flights; 750-mile minimum.

Mile longevity: Will not expire if you accrue miles every 3 years.

Minimum number of miles needed for a New York–Los Angeles round-trip: 25,000

Minimum number of miles needed for a Chicago–Paris round-trip: 40,000

When can you confirm a seat? Upon ticketing, if seats are available.

Blackout dates for the year 2000 (will change each year): January 1–3, April 23, 30, November 23–24, 28–29, December 23–24, 26–27, 30.

Do rewards differ for economy coach, full-fare coach, business, or first-class travel? Business-class and first-class travelers receive 150% mileage.

Can you maintain an account without accruing miles? Yes.

Is literature available? Members receive detailed literature after joining.

What are the penalties for canceling a ticket purchased with frequent-flier miles? Reward tickets are good for 1 year from date of issue. You may reinstate the miles for $50.

Partners: Air India, Alaska Airlines, Horizon Air, Iceland Air, Royal Jordanian Airlines, Trans World Express.

Can you accrue miles on partner airlines? Yes.

Can you use miles on partner airlines? Some, though the agreements are constantly in flux; call or the airline or check its Web site for the most up-to-date rules.

Can you combine and use mileage from several programs? No.

ELITE QUALIFICATIONS AND REWARDS

All elite members receive priority boarding, use of the priority reservations telephone line, priority baggage, and priority seating. Members do not receive guaranteed reservations on sold-out flights or free club membership.

Elite: Members must fly 20,000 miles, purchase $5,000 worth of fares, or make four or more transatlantic round-trips per calendar year. Elites receive a 25% bonus for miles accrued or a $1,000 minimum, whichever is greater, and unlimited complimentary upgrades and companion upgrades (see "Upgrading Policies of the Major Domestic Airlines" for details).

Elite I: Elite I's must fly 40,000 miles, purchase $10,000 worth of fares, or make eight or more transatlantic round-trips/calendar year. Elite I's receive a 50% bonus for miles accrued or a $1,000 minimum reward, whichever is greater, and unlimited complimentary upgrades and companion upgrades (see "Upgrading Policies of the Major Domestic Airlines" for details).

Platinum Elite: Platinum Elites must fly 100,000 miles, purchase $20,000 worth of fares, or make 20 or more transatlantic round-trips/calendar year. Platinum Elites receive a 100% bonus for miles accrued or a $1,000 minimum reward, whichever is greater, a 50% class-of-service bonus, and unlimited complimentary upgrades and companion upgrades (see "Upgrading Policies of the Major Domestic Airlines" for details).

UNITED AIRLINES MILEAGE PLUS (☎ 800/421-4655; www.ual.com)

BASIC FF ACCOUNTS

Miles earned: Mile per mile on both domestic and international flights; 500-mile minimum on United Express only.

Mile longevity: will not expire if you accrue miles every 3 years.

Minimum number of miles needed for a New York–Los Angeles round-trip: 25,000

Minimum number of miles needed for a Chicago–Paris round-trip: 50,000

When can you confirm a seat? Any time.

Blackout dates for the year 2000 (will change each year): For domestic travel: January 2–3, March 10, 12, 17, 19, 24, 26, 31, April 2, November 22, 26–27, December 21–23, 26–27, 30. For international travel, dates vary widely according to region.

Do rewards differ for economy coach, full-fare coach, business, or first-class travel? Business-class travelers receive a 25% fare bonus.

Can you maintain an account without accruing miles? Yes, for up to 5 years.

Is literature available? Members receive detailed literature after making their first flight.

What are the penalties for canceling a ticket purchased with frequent-flier miles? Members may reinstate miles for $75.

Partners: Aeromar, Air ALM, Aloha Airlines, British Midland, Cayman Airways, Delta Airlines, LAPA, Mexicana, Saudi Arabian Airlines, Singapore Airlines.

Can you accrue miles on partner airlines? Yes.

Can you use miles on partner airlines? Some, though the agreements are constantly in flux; call or the airline or check its Web site for the most up-to-date rules.

Can you combine and use mileage from several programs? No.

ELITE QUALIFICATIONS AND REWARDS

All elite members receive priority boarding, use of the priority reservations telephone line, priority standby, priority waiting list, and priority seating. Members do not receive priority baggage, guaranteed reservations on sold-out flights, or free club membership.

Premier: Members must fly 25,000 or 30 segments miles per calendar year. Premiers receive a 25% bonus for miles accrued and four complimentary upgrades every 10,000 miles after reaching elite status (see "Upgrading Policies of the Major Domestic Airlines" for details).

Executive Premier: Members must fly 50,000 miles or 60 segments per calendar year and receive a 100% bonus for miles accrued and four complimentary upgrades every 10,000 miles after reaching elite status (see "Upgrading Policies of the Major Domestic Airlines" for details).

Premier 1K: Members must fly 100,000 miles or 100 segments per calendar year and receive a 100% bonus for miles accrued and four complimentary upgrades every 10,000 miles after reaching elite status (see "Upgrading Policies of the Major Domestic Airlines" for details).

US AIRWAYS DIVIDEND MILES (☎ 800/428-4322 or 336/661-8390; www.usairways.com)

BASIC FF ACCOUNTS

Miles earned: Mile per mile on both domestic and international flights; 500-mile minimum on domestic flights only.

Mile longevity: Will not expire if you make at least one flight every 3 years.

Minimum number of miles needed for a New York–Los Angeles round-trip: 20,000

Minimum number of miles needed for a Chicago–Paris round-trip: 40,000

When can you confirm a seat? Members must confirm seats at least 3 weeks in advance or they will incur a $40 charge.

Blackout dates for the year 2000 (will change each year): Domestic and Canada: January 2–3, November 21–22, 26–27, December 22–23, 26. International blackout dates vary widely by region. Call for details.

Do rewards differ for economy coach, full-fare coach, business, or first-class travel? First-class travelers receive 50% bonus for miles accrued. All other non-elites receive the same reward.

Can you maintain an account without accruing miles? Up to 3 years.

Is literature available? Literature is available at the airport; members do not receive literature by mail.

What are the penalties for canceling a ticket purchased with frequent-flier miles? Members may reinstate miles for $40 or change the destination city for $50.

Partners: Alitalia, American Airlines, American Eagle, ANA (All Nippon Airways), Austrian Airlines, LatinPass (includes Aces, Avianca, Aeropostal, Aviateca, Copa, Lasca, Nica, Saeta, and Taca), Mexicana, Metrojet, Northwest Airlines, Quantas Airways, Sabena, Swissair.

Can you accrue miles on partner airlines? No.

Can you use miles on partner airlines? American Airlines only.

Can you combine and use mileage from several programs? No.

ELITE QUALIFICATIONS AND REWARDS

All elite members receive priority boarding, use of the priority reservations telephone line, priority baggage, and priority seating. Members do not receive guaranteed reservations on sold-out flights or free club membership.

Preferred: Members must fly 25,000 miles or 30 segments per calendar year. Members receive a 50% bonus for miles accrued, four complimentary, 799-mile, one-way upgrades for every 10,000 miles flown, and two complimentary upgrades for every 20,000 miles flown (see "Upgrading Policies of the Major Domestic Airlines" for details). Blackout dates do not apply.

Preferred Plus: Members must actually fly 50,000 miles or 60 segments per calendar year. Members receive a 50% bonus for miles accrued, four complimentary, 799-mile, one-way upgrades, and two complimentary upgrades every 10,000 miles (see "Upgrading Policies of the Major Domestic Airlines" for details). Blackout dates do not apply.
Chairman's Preferred: Members must actually fly 100,000 miles or 100 segments per calendar year. Members receive a 50% bonus for miles accrued, four complimentary, 799-mile, one-way upgrades, and two complimentary upgrades every 10,000 miles (see "Upgrading Policies of the Major Domestic Airlines" for details). Blackout dates do not apply.

3 How to Manage Your Miles

ONCE YOU'VE CHOSEN A PROGRAM AND STARTED accruing points, a few general rules will help you maximize your miles.

WHEN TO REDEEM

- For domestic travel, it's best to **redeem mileage for long flights** rather than short hops. You'll pay the same amount of points for each. Unless the published fare for an east-coast hop is exorbitant—as it is on certain routes monopolized by one airline—you're better off saving your miles for a longer trip.

- **Tickets to Hawaii**—which usually require 35,000 miles but can cost as little as $300 from the west coast—are **best redeemed** with frequent-flier points **by travelers from the east coast and the Midwest.**

- On **flights to Europe, redeem your miles during summer months,** when standard fares to Europe are much higher. In the winter, it's best to snare a low fare and save your miles for a better bargain.

- **Use your credit** as soon as possible. Currently, almost all the major airlines will not expire miles if some activity takes place on an account at least once every 3 years. Southwest is the only major airline that still has no particular written policy regarding mile expiration and reserves the right to close accounts deemed "inactive"— which was fairly common industry-wide in the very recent past.

- If you're basing future travel plans on the current value of your miles, **try to get a voucher as soon as possible**—or at least stay in touch with the airline to make sure it doesn't raise the mileage requirement for your destination before you take your trip.

- **Don't buy free premium seats with your points.** If you must fly in business- or first-class, purchase cheaper fares and use (fewer) points to upgrade when possible (see "Frequent-Flier Profiles of the Major Domestic Airlines," above, for details). You'll get twice as much from your miles this way.

GET THE CREDIT

- **Keep your frequent-flier member number handy in your wallet** or purse and provide it to

---

AND THE WINNER IS...

Every year **InsideFlyer** magazine sponsors the "Freddies," awarded for excellence in frequent traveler programs. Awards are voted on by those who know the programs best—frequent travelers themselves. For more information on the winners listed below, see "Frequent-Flyer Profiles of the Major Domestic Airlines," above, and "Mile-Earning Credit Cards," below.

12TH ANNUAL FREDDIE AWARD WINNERS

Program of the Year: Continental OnePass

Best Award: Continental OnePass (a 25,000-mile award for round-trips from New York or Houston to Tokyo)

Best Bonus Promotion: Southwest Rapid Rewards (earning double credit for booking online)

Best Frequent-Flyer Web Site: Continental OnePass

Best Elite-Level Program: Continental OnePass

Best Award Redemption: Southwest Rapid Rewards

Best Customer Service: Southwest Rapid Rewards

Best Affinity Credit Card: Diners Club Club Rewards

In addition to the above awards, **InsideFlyer** publisher Randy Petersen singled out two programs for special praise: **Northwest WorldPerks,** for taking Continental's example and leading the charge to eradicate expiration dates on miles; and **Alaska Airlines' Mileage Plan,** for forging partnerships with several major airline alliances—thus allowing members to apply miles earned on other, larger airlines toward achieving elite status with Alaska's relatively small program.

---

travel and ticket agents every time you make a reservation or purchase a ticket with that airline. This will help ensure that your account is credited properly. (If you don't have your card, airline agents will look it up for you at the airport, but they won't be happy to if the check-in line is long. In this event, you're better off asking for help at a shorter line, even if it's for a different flight.)

• Get in the habit of **asking when you check in whether your mileage for that flight was credited** to your account, particularly if you made changes to your initial reservation.

- If you forget to credit a flight, a hotel stay, or a car rental, **hold onto your receipts** so you can pursue the mileage once you return home.

RACK 'EM UP

- **Make all your purchases on a credit card that earns miles** for every dollar you spend. (See "Buy to Fly," below). Change your long-distance telephone carrier every few months, for free bonus miles. You can even accrue miles with big-time expenses like new cars and home mortgages. Even if you fly only once every year or two, you can earn a free trip just about as often.

- **Stick to a single carrier** whenever possible. Make as many flights on it as you can and apply all your miles earned outside to this one account.

- **Don't forget the few tired old miles** left straggling in your account after your last big free trip. Use them for upgrades before they expire.

- **Shop smart.** If you want to buy goods through a special, mile-earning promotion, make sure you're getting a bargain. Tally up the cash value of the frequent-flier points you earn, and weigh it against the cost of the goods you're purchasing.

STAY INFORMED

- **Keep close track of the mileage you earn.** Don't lose precious points because of an error in the airline's computers, which can happen all too often. Save all your ticket receipts and boarding passes at least until you receive your next mileage statement and can verify that the airline properly credited your account. In the case that they didn't, you may need to provide documentation to correct the error.

Let "Max" Do the Work for You

If the thought of keeping track of all these Byzantine programs gives you a first-class migraine, consider joining a program like **MaxMiles** (www.maxmiles.com). Through their MileageMiner service, you'll receive one consolidated statement that updates you on all your accounts, including summaries of mileage expiration, elite status, and any missing or pending credits. Better yet, MaxMiles keeps track of special offers relevant to your specific frequent-traveler programs, and informs you of any upcoming promotions that could have you raking in double or even triple miles.

If you like to travel with e-tickets, buy them with a credit card or you'll have no other way to document the purchase.

- **Check your statement carefully** as soon as it arrives and report discrepancies immediately.

- **Look over your frequent-flier newsletter** when it arrives to see if policies have changed regarding award rates; blackout dates; deadlines for using available miles tie-ins with other airlines, car-rental companies, or consumer products and services that will help you earn additional credit—like mile-earning credit cards, utilities, and so on.

- Some airlines will **double or triple mileage for new routes.** Get in the habit of asking if your carrier has opened any new itineraries each time you make a reservation.

- If you fly often enough to have elite status (which usually means you fly over 25,000 miles each year), **you may be entitled to free upgrades** or free upgrade coupons. (See "The Politics of Upgrading," below.)

4 THE POLITICS OF UPGRADING

GIVEN THE RIGHT GATE AGENT, THE RIGHT AIRPORT, and the right configuration of the stars, a savvy, well-dressed frequent-flier can still manage to wrangle a free upgrade at the airport in the unlikely event that seats are still available. For the most part, however, airlines are getting stricter than ever about upgrades by cutting back on the number of seats allocated for reward travel, and tightening their official upgrading policies. For more specifics, see "Upgrading Policies of the Major Domestic Airlines," below.

THE PARTY LINE

At press time, no major carrier officially allows basic frequent fliers to upgrade for free. Basic frequent fliers must purchase upgrades with cash or frequent-flier miles. (On average, the cost of a round-trip upgrade on a discount coach ticket is 20,000 points—5,000 points shy of the cost of a round-trip ticket for coast to coast domestic travel.) It's much harder to upgrade on a discount economy ticket than on a full coach fare.

TWA, Continental, and United are the only airlines that allow elite frequent fliers unlimited complimentary upgrades and companion upgrades (TWA grants elite status with 20,000 miles flown per calendar year; Continental and Delta hold out until 25,000 miles).

Northwest allows only its gold and platinum elites (50,000 to 75,000 miles per year) unlimited free upgrades; Delta gives only its Platinum Elites (100,000 miles or more) this privilege. On American and US Airways, even the highest elite travelers earn only a fixed number of upgrades per miles traveled.

On all the airlines, superior elite ranking does entitle travelers to confirm award seats farther in advance. So a pecking order is established: travelers who fly 100,000 or 50,000 or even 25,000 miles per year have first dibs on the small number of seats available to frequent fliers, which doesn't leave much left for the average leisure traveler or light business flyer.

A WINNING ARGUMENT: HOW TO TALK YOURSELF UP

Whether you're confirming a free upgrade or trying to work your charm and good luck to finagle a better seat, a few rules of thumb may better your chances.

- **If you look like you mean business,** you're much more likely to receive an upgrade at the airport, even if you're just confirming an upgrade you earned as a frequent flier. Dress well—a suit is optimum—and leave your fashionably frayed dungarees in your suitcase.

- If you or your flying companion has a first-class or business-class ticket, **ask if you can sit together.**

- **Travel at off-peak times** and call the airline 48 hours before departure to ask if you can have your name placed on an upgrade wait list. At the very least, mention the fact that you're a frequent flier when you check in and see if any empty premium seats are available for you.

- If you **volunteer to be bumped** from an oversold flight or if you're flight is canceled, ask for a round-trip upgrade as part of your compensation.

- As a last resort, it's still worth **asking your travel agent for an upgrade** if you're a very frequent customer. According to Ed Perkins, consumer advocate for the American Society of Travel Agents, some travel agents are able to reward their own loyal customers with upgrades—even when the airline's reservationist says the seats are unavailable. Unfortunately, there isn't a published list of agencies with the databases and the willingness to do this—primarily because the airlines would quash the practice if they knew who was involved. Certainly you've got nothing to lose by asking, according to Perkins.

ACHIEVING ELITE STATUS

As mentioned earlier, the only way to guarantee yourself free upgrades these days is to reach elite status on the right airline (see "Frequent-Flier Profiles of the Major Domestic Airlines," above). Every airline's elite program has several tiers, defined by the number of miles flown within one calendar year. Two round-trips to Europe and one domestic round-trip flight should bring you to the first tier, which requires 25,000 miles (with the exception of TWA, which requires only 20,000). The second tier requires 50,000 miles (with the exception of TWA, which requires only 40,000). The third tier requires 100,000 miles (with the exception of Continental and Northwest, which require only 75,000). In the past, airlines did not count miles flown on partner airlines or commuter airlines to count toward elite status. Now, many of them do (see "Frequent-Flier Profiles of the Major Domestic Airlines," above). Many airlines even allow miles accrued with credit cards or public utilities to count toward elite qualifications. Short hops of under 500 miles now guarantee you a 500 frequent-flier point-minimum on all the major airlines but TWA, which awards a minimum of 750 miles per flight.

Elite frequent fliers receive a host of other perks as well. First of all, the rich get richer: Travelers who have reached the first tier receive 25% to 50% bonus miles for every flight they take. For instance, if you travel 800 miles one way, you receive 800 frequent-flier points plus an additional 200- to 400-point bonus. Second-tier elites receive a 50% to 100% bonus for miles flown. Third-tier elites receive a 100% to 150% bonus (with the exception of US Airways, which offers only 50% bonus miles to its top-grade elites). In other words that same 800-mile one-way flight earns 1,600 to 2,000 frequent-flier miles!

Elite status also entitles you to **free upgrades** and **companion upgrades**—either unlimited or a set amount of segment upgrades, depending on the airline and the level of elite status you've reached (see "Upgrading Policies of the Major Domestic Airlines," below). The highest elite travelers are allowed to confirm their upgrades either when they make their reservation, or 72 to 100 hours in advance, well before the lower elite levels. Each level is allowed to confirm at least 24 hours before the level beneath it. While this may seem to be a minor privilege, it's crucial because airlines are making fewer seats available for reward travel. Even if all the free class-upgrade seats are snapped up by gold and platinum members, basic elite flyers still get to upgrade to the front of the coach cabin, which makes for slightly greater comfort.

Elite members receive a range of additional benefits which may include priority boarding, priority seating, a designated elite reservations line, guaranteed reservations on sold-out flights, priority baggage, and discounted club membership.

5 Upgrading Policies of the Major Domestic Airlines

ALASKA

- **Non-elite:** Non-elite Mileage Plan members can purchase one-way first-class upgrades for 10,000 miles.

- **MVP members** can purchase one-way first-class upgrades for 5,000 miles. Members receive automatic first-class upgrade certificates for any "Y" class fare for every 10,000 actual air miles flown. Complimentary upgrades can be confirmed any time before departure. MVP Gold members receive automatic first-class upgrades for every 5,000 air miles traveled.

AMERICA WEST

- **Non-elite:** Non-elite FlightFund members can purchase one-way upgrades on America West and Continental flights for 5,000 miles on a full coach fare, or 10,000 miles on any other paid fare. If you're not a member of FlightFund, you can upgrade only if you've purchased a full-coach fare; in that case, the cost of the upgrade is $35 for as many 500-mile segments as that particular route encompasses. Non-elite upgrades can be confirmed as soon as the ticket is purchased.

- **Elite members** receive unlimited, one-way, space-available upgrades on America West and select Continental flights. Silver members can confirm upgrades 2 days prior to departure on full-fare tickets, and the day of departure for other paid tickets. Gold members can confirm upgrades any time after ticketing on a full-fare ticket, 2 days prior to departure for other paid tickets, and 2 hours prior to departure for companion upgrades. Platinum members may confirm any time after ticketing on a full-fare ticket, 3 days prior to departure for other paid tickets, and 2 hours prior to departure for companion upgrades.

AMERICAN

- **Non-elite:** Upgrade coupons are $45 per upgrade for one to seven one-way flights; $37.50 per upgrade for eight or more one-way flights. Confirmation available 24 hours before departure.

- **Elite members** receive four complimentary one-way upgrades, every 10,000 miles. Gold members can confirm upgrades 24 hours before departure; Platinum may confirm 72 hours before departure; Executive Platinum may confirm 100 hours before departure. All elites may use upgrades for companions traveling on the same flight.

CONTINENTAL

- **Non-elite:** Executive Pack upgrade coupons are $64.95 (valued up to $500), which includes 5,000 bonus miles; four one-segment, one-class upgrades; one $99 round-trip companion certificate; two 1-day president club passes; and discounts on select hotels and car rentals. Confirmation available at check-in 2 hours before departure.

   Prestige Pack upgrade coupons are $99.95 (valued up to $1,500), which includes 7,500 bonus miles; six one-segment, one-class upgrades; one $99 round-trip companion certificate; a discount certificate for $100 on Continental; free president's club initiation fee, two 1-day president's club passes; free Inside flyer subscription; discounts on select hotels and car rentals. Confirmation available at check-in 2 hours before departure.

- **Elite:** All Continental elite members receive unlimited, complimentary, space-available upgrades and companion upgrades.

   Silver elites may confirm their own upgrades 48 hours before departure on full fares, day of departure on discounted fares. Companion upgrades may be confirmed 2 hours before departure.

   Gold elites may confirm their own upgrades anytime after ticketing on full fares, 48 hours before departure on discounted fares. Companion upgrades may be confirmed 2 hours before departure.

   Platinum elites may confirm their own upgrades anytime after ticketing on full fares, 72 hours before departure on discounted fares. Companion upgrades may be confirmed 2 hours before departure.

DELTA

- **Non-elite** members may purchase a round-trip upgrade to first class on a full coach fare for 10,000 miles; on slightly discounted coach fares (B or M fares), a round-trip upgrade costs 20,000 miles. Confirmation is available at the airport 3 hours before departure.

- **Elite:** Systemwide upgrades are available to all medallion members who fly 20,000 miles after reaching elite status. These are good for two one-way upgrades that are valid on any Delta route, regardless of mileage (including international flights).

  Silver medallion members receive four, 800-mile segment upgrades every 10,000 miles after achieving elite status. Silver elites may confirm upgrades 24 hours in advance on all but the lowest discount fare (L fares), which can't be upgraded.

  Gold medallion members receive four, 800-mile segment upgrades every 10,000 miles after achieving elite status. Gold elites may confirm upgrades 72 hours before departure on all but the lowest discount fare (L fares), which can't be upgraded.

  Platinum medallion members receive unlimited complimentary upgrades, which may be confirmed at any time.

NORTHWEST

- **Non-elite:** On a full-fare ticket, the price of an upgrade in dollars varies by distance traveled (on a New York–to–Los Angeles flight, for instance, a one-way upgrade is $125). Confirmation is available at the airport four hours before departure. On a full-fare ticket, the price of a one-way upgrade in miles is 5,000 miles; round-trip is 10,000. On a

discounted coach ticket, a one-way upgrade is
10,000 miles; round-trip is 20,000 miles.
Confirmation is available at the time of reservation.

- **Elite: Silver Elite** members receive four complimentary one-way domestic upgrades each time they
  fly 10,000 miles. Confirmation available 48 hours
  before departure on full fares; day of departure on
  discounted fares.

    Gold Elite members receive unlimited compli-
  mentary upgrades. On full fares, confirmation
  available when the flight is booked; on discount
  fares, 48 hours before departure.

    Platinum Elites receive unlimited upgrades.
  Confirmation available at the time of booking on
  full fares; 72 hours before departure on discounted
  fares.

SOUTHWEST AIRLINES

Southwest has only one class of service, so upgrades are not
available.

TWA

- **Non-elite:** Non-elite members may purchase
  upgrades after accruing 5,000 or more actual miles
  on TWA. Cost varies widely, according to destination. Confirmation available 2 hours before
  departure.

- **Elite:** Elite members receive unlimited complimentary upgrades and companion upgrades. Confirmation is available 48 hours before departure on
  full-fare tickets and 24 hours before departure on
  economy tickets.

    Elite I members receive unlimited complimentary
  upgrades and companion upgrades. Confirmation
  is available at time of ticketing on full fares; 72

hours before departure on discounted fares.

Platinum Elite members receive unlimited complimentary upgrades and companion upgrades. Confirmation is available at time of ticketing on full-fare tickets and 100 hours before departure on economy tickets.

UNITED

- **Non-elite:** Non-elite members may purchase four 500-mile upgrades for use on full-fare tickets for $200; and eight 500-mile upgrades for use on full-fare tickets for $400. Confirmation is available 72 hours before departure.

- **Elite:** All elite members receive unlimited complimentary upgrades.

   For **Premier** and **Executive Premier elites,** confirmation is available 72 hours before departure on full fares, 24 hours before departure on discounted fares.

   For **Premier IK** members, confirmation is available 100 hours before departure on full fares, 24 hours before departure on discounted fares. Members do not receive complimentary companion upgrades.

US AIRWAYS

- **Non-elite:** Non-elite members may not purchase upgrades.

- **Elite:** All elite members receive four complimentary 799-mile, one-way upgrades, and two complimentary upgrades every 10,000 miles. All elites may also pay 10,000 miles for four one-way upgrades on full fares; 20,000 miles for four upgrades on discount fares.

   Preferred members may confirm upgrades 24 hours in advance.

Preferred Plus members may confirm upgrades
72 hours in advance on full fares; 24 hours in
advance on all other fares.

Chairman's Preferred members may confirm
upgrades anytime on full fares; 24 hours in advance
on all other fares.

6 HOW ALLIANCES AFFECT FREQUENT-FLIER MILES

AIRLINE PARTNERSHIPS AND THE PRACTICE OF CODE
sharing have amplified the number of flights and routes
available to travelers, but they've also made the frequent-flier
game trickier to play. (See "Allied Forces," in chapter 1,
"Ticketing Pitfalls.") And more than ever, it's hard to tell just
which airlines have joined forces. As mentioned in chapter 1,
as this book went to press, the Justice Department was investigating the Continental/Northwest alliance from an
antitrust standpoint; and similar proposed partnerships
between American and US Airways, and Delta and United,
were essentially limited to frequent-flier reciprocity.

ISN'T THIS A GOOD THING?

On the surface, it looks as though frequent-flier reciprocity
benefits consumers. If you have an account with
Continental, for instance, you can now use your miles to fly
on Northwest or register miles flown on Northwest in your
Continental account—and vice versa. For the most part, you
can make more from your miles this way.

When you pool miles, you are subject to the terms and
conditions of the carrier granting the award—even if you
maintain an account with the alliance partner. If you are
using American AAdvantage miles for a flight on US
Airways, for instance, your American miles are subject to US
Airways Divident Miles program rules. Your time of travel
will also be restricted according to US Airway's blackout
dates and the number of seats available for frequent fliers.

The intricate network of alliances does allow consumers to take advantage of a few loopholes. For instance, you can now use American Express's Membership Miles awards to fly American Airlines, even though American doesn't participate in the program—because US Airways, American's alliance partner, does.

SO WHAT'S THE CATCH?

The hidden disadvantage, however, is that seats available for frequent fliers are limited on each flight, and carriers are not allocating more spots to make room for customers who might want to transfer points from an account with an alliance partner. The Department of Transportation reported that in 1997, major carriers booked 152,000 fewer free round-trip tickets on the most popular routes. For instance, in 1995, US Airways made 9% of its total seats available to frequent-flier travelers. In 1997, however, it made only 5% of total seats for mileage rewards.

Consumer Reports Travel Letter predicts that alliance partnerships will make freebies even harder to procure, since alliance partners do not always offer the same number of seats to frequent fliers. You may try to cash in on a free trip and learn that no spots are left for frequent fliers on the connecting flight offered by the code share partner. For instance, Continental Airlines blocked out about 7% of its seats for awards travelers in 1997. Northwest, it's code-share partner, blocked out only 5.8% that same year. If you tried to book a frequent-flier ticket for a connecting flight on a Continental account, you could end up on a Northwestern flight, for the second leg of your trip, that didn't have sufficient frequent-flier seats left to honor your award.

Finally, alliance partners have differing blackout days—periods of time when customers can't redeem frequent-flier miles for particular destinations. While Continental, for instance, restricted frequent-flier travel to the Caribbean 11 days of the year in 1999, Northwest, its code-sharing partner, blacked out 24 days that same year. Remember, too, that carriers can also inconspicuously restrict travel to a destination by limiting the number of seats available to frequent fliers on each scheduled trip.

THE IMPACT ON INTERNATIONAL TRAVEL

When you fly segmented flights involving one of these international partners, it's even trickier to stay on top of the rules and loopholes of the frequent-flier game—which shift and change perpetually. For instance, in 1999 American Airlines shared codes with British Airways. American AAdvantage members, however, could not accrue mileage on British Airways' transoceanic flights (because American competes for the same route). Delta shared codes with Singapore Airlines, but Delta SkyMiles members could only accrue miles on Singapore if they flew in first or business class. Delta's coach travelers earned no miles on Singapore— unless, strangely enough, they were Canadian citizens, who earned full credit in coach. Qantas, Thai, Air New Zealand, and Ansett Australian Airlines only offered 50% to 70% credit to alliance partners in the United States who flew coach. On flights within Canada, Air Canada credited only 50% of coach miles flown on partner airlines. On its flights within India, Air India offered no frequent-flier credit to members of partner airlines' frequent-flier programs.

GET THE SKINNY

At the moment, few airlines offer an explicit explanation of their revised rules to help consumers make informed decisions. Programs are so much in flux that even reservations agents don't have information on hand to help you make an enlightened choice when you're booking a flight or signing up for a new frequent-flier account. Furthermore, their information sometimes conflicts with the official word from corporate headquarters.

As a general safeguard, ask some questions when you book:

- Ask if a portion of your flight involves a code-share partner's aircraft. If so, and if you have accounts with both airlines, be sure you know which account will be credited with your mileage.

- Ask how many mileage points you will earn—and compare the reward to what you would have earned on your regular frequent-flier carrier. The frequent-flier literature you receive after joining should tell you this, but the rules change so often that it's wise to double-check when you book.

- Ask about restrictions: Is mileage credit available on the route, flight, and date you plan to travel?

- Finally, check your mileage statements carefully and make sure your account was credited properly, with the same terms you agreed to when you made your reservation.

    Here are a few of the hidden perks and pitfalls of each alliance's program (as of press time).

American (Aadvantage)/US Airways (Dividend Miles)

- Miles are credited only to the airline you fly.

- You can combine miles from both accounts—draw miles from one account (a minimum of 1,000 per flight) and put them toward a free flight on the partner airline.

- You can't redeem miles for flights with international partners.

- Members of US Airways Dividend Miles program stand the most to gain, as American's program has superior features.

Continental (Onepass)/Northwest (World Perks)

- Miles are credited to either airline, even if you flew on the partner airline.

- You can't combine miles, but you can redeem miles to fly on a partner airline (though you must use a minimum of 20,000 miles).

- On international flights, you can only redeem miles on international partners of the airline you're drawing miles on (miles on a Continental account can't be used for flights on Northwest's international partner airlines, unless Continental also has a partnership with that airline).

United (Mileage Plus)/Delta (Sky Miles)

- Miles are credited to either airline, even if you flew on the partner airline.

- You can't combine miles, but you can redeem miles to fly on a partner airline on domestic flights (though you must use a minimum of 25,000 miles).

- On international flights, you can only redeem miles on international partners of the airlines you're drawing miles on. United and Delta do not share international partners.

7 BUY TO FLY: USING CREDIT CARDS TO EARN MILES

MANY CREDIT CARD COMPANIES, CAR-RENTAL AGENCIES, utilities, and other vendors also offer frequent-flier miles with a particular airline for every dollar you spend.

Consumer Reports Travel Letter recommends that you compare the price of goods that offer miles with similar merchandise from other vendors.

If you are in the habit of shopping the Internet for goods and services other than airfares, you can now convert your dollars spent into credit toward airfares. Through **www.clickrewards.com**, more than 30 merchants, in conjunction with eight major airlines, have agreed to offer sky mile points for every dollar spent online (paid for by a major credit card) on their goods and services. **Macy's** (www.macys.com) offers one point for every dollar you spend—with no minimum or maximum spending allowance. **The Gap** (www.gap.com) offers a point for every dollar and 100 bonus points for every purchase over $75. **Barnes & Noble** (www.bn.com) gives you a point for every dollar you spend over $50 and under $500. **Sky Mall** (www.skymall.com) offers one point for every dollar, with no minimum or maximum spending allowance.

You must enroll first through **www.clickrewards.com**. Once you are registered, the program will automatically keep track of your mileage. Miles never expire, and you can transfer them toward tickets with any one of eight major carriers: American, British Airways, Continental, Delta, Northwest, United, TWA, and US Airways.

MILE-EARNING CREDIT CARDS

In some respects, it's less risky to have an account with a charge card, rather than a credit card. You pay an annual fee

Cybermiles: Earn by Booking Tickets Online

Many major carriers are also rewarding bonus miles to Internet shoppers. If you buy directly from an airline Web site, you can receive free miles for booking a round-trip ticket and sometimes additional bonus miles for paperless travel if you reserve an e-ticket.

BONUS MILES FOR INTERNET SHOPPERS*

AIRLINE	BONUS FOR ROUND-TRIP BOOKING	BONUS FOR E-TICKETING
Alaska	500 miles	250 miles
American	1,000 miles	n/a
America West	1,000 miles	n/a
Continental	500 miles	500 miles
Delta	500 miles	500 miles
Midwest Express	500 miles	n/a
Northwest	1,000 miles	n/a
Southwest	double credits	n/a
TWA	1,000 miles	n/a
United	1,000 miles	n/a
US Airways	1,000 miles	n/a

* Information was current as of press time.

to maintain the account—usually a sum under $100—but you pay no interest, because you must pay off every dime you spend at the end of each month.

Many credit card companies cater to students. If you're enrolled in a college or university, be sure to call the major credit card companies and see if you are eligible for any special travel programs they may be offering.

According to *Consumer Reports Travel Letter,* **Diners Club** has the best features of all the mile-earning charge cards—though Diners Club is often not accepted where Visa, MasterCard, and American Express are welcome. Through its **Club Rewards** program (☎ **800/234-6377**), you earn one frequent-flier mile for every dollar you spend on the card. Just for joining, you receive 12,000 bonus miles—1,000 miles per month for the first year, provided you use the card at least once a month. The frequent-flier program is free with Diners Club membership, which costs $80 annually. However, you must pay the entire balance on your account when you receive your monthly statement.

Your miles never expire, and you can rack up an unlimited number of miles.

Miles are applicable on all the major domestic airlines and over 25 foreign carriers, including Air Canada, Air France, British Airways, KLM, Lufthansa, Qantas, Singapore Airlines, Swissair, and Virgin Atlantic. You'll also receive complimentary access to over 70 Diners Club lounges and business centers around the world—although these are located primarily in airports abroad.

At the other end of the scale, **American Express**' **Membership Rewards** (☎ **800/528-4800**) program costs $55 per year to maintain the charge card plus an additional $40 per year to maintain the frequent-flier account. For every dollar you spend on the card, you receive one point toward air travel on 11 major airlines: Delta, Continental, Southwest, US Airways, TWA, Hawaiian Virgin, Korean Air, Aeromexico, El Al, Mexicana, and Latin Pass. Delta offers a special credit card in conjunction with American Express that features better mileage bonuses. Depending on the airline, one domestic round-trip flight costs 25,000 points, on average; one round-trip flight to Europe costs roughly 60,000 points, on average. Points never expire.

MILEAGE-EARNING CREDIT CARD ROUNDUP

American Airlines
Citibank AAdvantage Visa and MasterCards (☎ **800/ 359-4444**; www.citibank.com)

- Earn 1 mile for every dollar spent

- Earn 3000-mile bonus for joining, when you make your first purchase with the card. One mile per dollar spent

- $50 membership fee

- Maximum of 60,000 miles per year

Citibank AAdvantage Gold Visa and MasterCards

- Annual fee $85

- Earn 1 mile per dollar spent

- Earn 4,000 bonus miles

- Maximum of 100,000 miles per year

Citibank AAdvantage Platinum Visa and MasterCards

- Annual fee $125

- One mile per dollar spent

- No bonus miles for joining

- Unlimited mileage

Points can be redeemed on American partner airlines: American, American Eagle, Aerolineas, Argentina, Alaska Air, Asiana Airlines, British Airways, British Midways, Canadian Airlines, Cathay Pacific, Finnair, Grupo Tacia, Hawaiian, Iberia, Japan, LANChile, Midway, Quantas, Reno, Singapore, South African Airways, TAM, US Airways.

Diners Club (☎ 888/923-4637; www.dinersclubus.com)

- Earn up to 12,000 AAdvantage miles for joining (1,000 miles per month for first year, provided you charge one purchase each month)

- Earn 1 mile for every dollar spent

- No preset spending limit

Continental
Continental Airlines Credit Card from Chase (☎ 800/245-9850; www.chase.com/continentalair)

- Earn 6,000 bonus miles for joining

- Earn 12 miles for every dollar spent

- Earn 1,000 mile bonus for joining

- 80,000-mile maximum per year

- Annual fee of $30

- Miles never expire

Delta
American Express SkyMiles Classic Card (☎ 877/376-1237)

- Earn 5,000-mile bonus for joining

- Earn 1 mile for every dollar spent on everyday purchases

- Earn 1.5 miles for Delta purchases and purchases with Delta's partner airlines

- Earn 2 miles for every dollar spent with Delta partners (MCI; and Olive Garden Restaurant, Red Lobster, and other restaurants)

- $60,000 annual limit

American Express SkyMiles Gold Card

- Earn 10,000-mile bonus for joining

- Earn 1 mile for every dollar spent on everyday purchases

- Earn 2 miles for every dollar spent on purchases from Delta and Delta partners

- $100,000 annual limit, excluding bonuses for Delta ticket purchases

Northwest
The WorldPerks Visa Card (☎ 800/360-2900)

- Earn 1 mile for every dollar spent

- For net purchases over $10,000, earn 1 mile for every $2 spent. (If during the calendar year, net

New Wheels, More Miles

Now it's possible to rack up the miles when you buy or lease a new car, thanks to an agency called **Automotive Dealers Market** (☎ **800/916-7232**). Call the toll-free number and an agent will refer you to one of hundreds of participating car dealerships around the country. ADM has established programs with Alaska Airlines (☎ 800/733-5877), American West (☎ 800/853-3551), Delta (☎ 888/310-3435), Northwest (☎ 800/916-7232), and TWA (☎ 888/747-9998). In general, they award 15,000 bonus miles for new vehicles over $40,000; 10,000 bonus miles for new vehicles from $20,000 to $40,000; and 5,000 bonus miles for new vehicles under $20,000.

---

purchases exceed $50,000 [Classic Card] or $60,000 [Gold Card], all miles the rest of the year are earned at the rate of 1 mile for every $2.)

- Annual Fee: $90 (Gold Visa Card), $55 (Visa Card).

The WorldPerks Visa Business Card (☎ **800/796-4650**)

(For small businesses requiring fewer than 100 cards)

- Earn 1 mile for every dollar spent

Diners Club Club Rewards (☎ **888/923-4637**)

- Earn two points for every dollar spent

TWA

MBNA Platinum Plus MasterCard and Visa (☎ **800/523-7666**)

- Earn 5,000 bonus miles for joining
- Earn 1 mile for every dollar spent

- Earn 1.5 miles for every dollar spent on TWA purchases

United
Mileage Plus Visa and MasterCard (☎ 800/472-0702)

- Earn 1 mile for every dollar spent

- Earn 5,000 bonus miles for joining

US Airways
Bank of America Visa (☎ 800/335-4318)

- Earn up to 5000 bonus miles for joining

- Earn 1.2 miles for every dollar spent

8 MILE-EARNING LONG-DISTANCE CARRIERS

OF ALL THE LONG-DISTANCE CARRIERS, **MCI WORLDCOM** (☎ 800/513-4090; www.mciworld.com) has the most extensive program. MCI offers frequent-flier miles through American, Continental, Delta, Midwest, Northwest, United, and US Airways. Members earn 5 miles for every dollar spent on MCI and a 5,000-mile bonus for joining. Frequent fliers also receive a discount on Internet service.

Sprint (☎ 800/877-4040; www.sprint.com) offers mileage on America West, Alaska, Northwest, TWA, US Airways, and Virgin Atlantic. Each airline offers its own bonus for joining, and its own mileage rate, for the Sprint plan.

AT&T does not offer frequent-flier miles for any of its long-distance plans.

MILE-EARNING CAR RENTALS

All the major car-rental companies offer frequent-flier mileage each time you rent one of their vehicles. With the

CAR-RENTAL COMPANIES & THEIR
FREQUENT-FLIER PARTNERS

CARRIER	CAR-RENTAL PARTNERS
Alamo	Aloha, America West, American Canadian, Continental, Delta, Hawaiian, Midwest Express, Northwest, Reno, Southwest, TWA, United, and US Airways
Avis	Air Canada, Alaska, Aloha, America West, American, Continental, Delta, Hawaiian, Reno
Budget	Air Canada, Alaska, Northwest, Reno, Southwest, United
Dollar	Aloha, America West, American, Continental, Delta, Northwest
Hertz	Alaska, American, Continental, Delta, Midwest Express, Southwest, United, US Airways
National	America West, American, Canadian, Continental, Delta, Midwest Express, Northwest, United, US Airways
Thrifty	Alaska, America West, American, Reno, TWA

exception of Hertz's program, awards are usually appointed per rental or days traveled, rather than per miles traveled. A few companies require you to rent a vehicle for 2 days or longer, and sometimes credit is available only when the rental is in conjunction with a flight.

In a rare instance where leisure travelers are favored over business travelers, corporate, government, or other contract rates as a general rule yield almost half as many award miles than personal rentals.

8

Cheap Fares: Easy Ways to Cut the Cost of Air Travel

A major airline recently introduced a special half-off fare for spouses who accompany their husbands and wives on business trips. Expecting valuable testimonials, the PR department sent out letters to all the spouses who had used the special rates, asking how they enjoyed their trips.

Letters are still pouring in asking, "What trip?"

Since deregulation in 1978, the average airfare has risen 39% (adjusting for inflation), and unrestricted fares have skyrocketed by 70%. Especially where coach fares are concerned, business competition among the major U.S. airlines is unlike that of any other industry. A coach seat is virtually the same from one carrier to another, yet the difference in price may run as high as $1,000 for a product with the same intrinsic value. Even within the same airline cabin, neighboring coach passengers often pay vastly different prices for the same cramped quarters, stale air, and virtually inedible food.

For instance, a cross-country coach fare from Boston to Los Angeles can range anywhere from $250 to $2,000—

even for seats on the very same flight. The price you pay depends on myriad factors, including when you book; when you travel; whether you investigated special sales; and whether you purchased your ticket through a consolidator, a travel agent, the airline's toll-free reservation number, or the airline's Web site.

With so much price fluctuation, the only general rule is: **Shop around.** Compare fares by calling several airlines or investigating their Web sites. It also helps to routinely case airline advertisements in the travel section of your newspaper for a few days before you settle on a fare.

1   HOW THE FARE GAME WORKS

RULE NUMBER ONE: TIMING IS EVERYTHING

THE MOST CRUCIAL FACTOR IN SNARING A CHEAP FARE is probably your timing. It's almost always cheaper to book an APEX fare (advance purchase excursion, also known as a supersaver fare), if your schedule allows. By booking 21 days, 14 days, or 7 days in advance, you can save drastically on a standard coach fare—up to 75%, with a 21-day advance purchase, which yields the greatest savings.

If for some reason you can't commit to travel plans in advance, you may also be able to snag a bargain by waiting until the very last minute, when airlines may drastically reduce fares for unsold tickets on flights that aren't fully booked. You might find especially plum bargains right before a major holiday, when fares are sky high until a few days before the big day, or on the day of the actual holiday itself. This trick is more of a gamble than most travelers will be able to manage, however, because last-minute tickets may end up costing two to three times the cost of an APEX fare.

Travel at off-peak times; fares are usually cheaper after 7pm. You'll also save money if you can afford to travel on a Tuesday, Wednesday, or Thursday, because most leisure travelers like to get away on weekends and therefore demand is

CAVEATS: READ THE FINE PRINT

The lowest-priced fares are often nonrefundable or carry penalties for changing dates of travel. Be sure to investigate the hidden costs before you book. Fees vary widely, depending on both the airline you're flying and the type of ticket you're purchasing.

- **APEX (advanced purchase excursion) fares** are often rigged with stiff penalties if you need to change your reservation, and you may not be entitled to any refund whatsoever if you have to cancel—though you may be able to use your ticket at a later date for a fee of roughly $50 to $75. Typically, you will also have to purchase your ticket within 24 hours of making a reservation, stay over a Saturday night, and return home within 30 days.

- **International fares** may include myriad add-on costs, such as departure taxes, customs fees, international taxes, and security surcharges. For some destinations, you may have to pay a departure tax in the local currency before you're permitted to leave.

- **Nonrefundable tickets** may become worthless if you fail to make the flight you booked. At best, you may be allowed to fly standby if you arrive within 2 hours of your scheduled departure, but this is not guaranteed. If you fall ill or suffer a death in the immediate family and can furnish proof of the fact, you may be entitled to compensation, though this may take the form of a flight at a later date. While it's always wise to show up at the airport well ahead of time, it's crucial if you are flying on a nonrefundable ticket. (See the "Airlines' Boarding Gate Deadlines" table in chapter 1.)

greatest at that time. You'll save even more if you can agree to stay over the following Saturday night. Business travelers usually want to fly during the week and return by the weekend, so you'll save money in coach if you can afford to stay over Saturday night.

All of these rules are especially true if you are traveling on a route that's popular with business travelers. Airlines cater to business travelers, because they fly so frequently and book tickets at the last minute, paying much higher prices for their seats. When a flight is carrying many business travelers, the airline doesn't need the business of economy passengers, so coach fares are much less likely to be discounted. Business travelers tend to fly just before 9am and just after 5pm, so coach seats are liable to be more expensive at these hours.

According to the same principles of supply and demand, traveling to a destination like Brazil will be more expensive from the United States in January, when it's winter here and summer there. Nantucket will be priciest in summer. New Orleans will cost the most during Mardi Gras.

RULE NUMBER TWO: SHOP ONLINE

If you have Internet access, investigate the best going rates to your destination before you book a ticket. Better yet, book your ticket online and earn bonus frequent-flyer miles, which will lower the cost of future travels. Read on to learn about the Internet's wealth of money-saving travel tools. (See "Surfing for Sales," below.)

RULE NUMBER THREE: WATCH FOR LATE-BREAKING SALES

Keep your eyes peeled for promotional rates or special sales even after you purchase your ticket. Airlines periodically lower prices on their most popular routes, which may even make it worth your while to exchange your ticket—despite the $50 to $75 charge. Check your newspaper for advertised discounts or call the airlines directly to stay on top of late-breaking discounts.

If you book your tickets from a tried-and-true, reliable travel agency, ask your representative to call you if a late-breaking sale is announced—even if you've already made a reservation. This is one of the chief advantages of working with an agent, so you should expect the courtesy. If your agent won't help, find a new one. The Internet is also a great way to keep abreast of the latest deals and discounts; for more, see "Cyberperks," below.

RULE NUMBER FOUR: DON'T OVERLOOK THE BUDGET CARRIERS

On the other hand, if even one low-budget carrier, such as Tower Air or Vanguard, operates on your route, fares will drop, even if you opt to fly a major carrier. Conversely, the biggest fare increases industry wide from 1997 to 1998 took place on routes where a low-budget carrier discontinued service, according to the Department of Transportation. The cost to fly from Denver to Wichita, for instance, rose 223% in 1998 after Vanguard dropped out—or rather, was driven out, by competition from United, whose hub is in Denver. Conversely, fares dropped by 71%, the greatest percentage decrease for the year, between Gulfport, Mississippi, and Tampa, Florida, when Reno Air set up house in Tampa. For more information on the major domestic budget carriers, see "A Look at the Budget Airlines," below.

RULE NUMBER FIVE: USE ALTERNATE HUBS

In major cities with more than one airport, subhub airports (such as Newark in the New York area, Midway in Chicago, and Oakland in the San Francisco Bay Area) tend to host more budget airlines, and fares tend to be much cheaper.

Be aware, however, that driving time into the city may take longer from a suburb, and there may be fewer options for direct flights. Booking a segmented or indirect flight, however, can also mean savings. If your schedule is flexible and you are able to make good use of your time spent in airport waiting areas or on the plane itself, you can save a significant amount of money by eschewing the luxury of flying nonstop. Note, however, that you may want to travel with carry-on luggage, because the likelihood of lost luggage increases, obviously, with each change of plane.

RULE NUMBER SIX: BIG BUSINESS MEANS BIG BUCKS

No matter how well you research the cheapest fares and prepare for your trip in advance, some routes are going to cost you more than others that cover the same distance. If a route is a hub or is popular with business travelers, for instance, fares all around are likely to be higher. Business travelers—who need to purchase tickets at the last minute or reroute their trips and fly back home by the weekend—pay costly full fares.

A handful of business passengers are enough to get a plane off the ground with profits ensured, so airlines cater to them—adding flights on popular business routes rather than venturing to new destinations, running popular business flights directly on the hour or half hour so corporate bigwigs can turn on a dime and fly off to settle a deal. Unfortunately for the budget traveler, fares all around, even in coach, are going to rise to the occasion on these popular commercial routes.

2 CYBERPERKS: HOW THE INTERNET CAN HELP YOU SAVE

WHEN YOU SHOP FOR AIRFARES ON THE INTERNET—IF you have the time and patience—you, the consumer, have direct access to the same flight information that, in the past, was solely the domain of travel agents and airline reservationists.

These days, airlines are keen on Internet shoppers, to the extent that they have even established technical support hot lines to field questions from potential Web customers. When you book a fare online—especially if you eschew paper and opt for an e-ticket—you and your computer save

AIRLINE WEB SITES

Online booking sites aren't the only places to book airline tickets—all **major airlines** have their own Web sites and often offer incentives, such as bonus frequent flyer miles or Net-only discounts, for buying online. These incentives have helped airlines capture the majority of the online booking market. According to Jupiter Communications, online agencies such as Travelocity booked about 80% of tickets purchased online in 1996, but by 1999 airline sites (such as United's www.ual.com) were projected to own about 60% of the online market, with online agencies' share of the pie dwindling each year. Here's a list of Web sites for the major domestic airlines, along with the technical support numbers, if you're having trouble accessing the site.

- **Alaska Airlines**: www.alaskaair.com; ☎ **877/502-5357**

- **America West:** www.americawest.com; no phone

- **American Airlines:** www.aa.com; ☎ **800/222-2377**

- **Continental Airlines:** www.flycontinental.com;
  ☎ **888/815-2665**

- **Delta Airlines**: www.delta-air.com; no phone

- **Northwest Airlines:** www.nwa.com; ☎ **800/692-6955**

- **Southwest Airlines**: www.iflyswa.com; no phone

- **TWA:** www.twa.com; ☎ **800/892-1911**

- **United Airlines:** www.ual.com; ☎ **800/482-2696**

- **US Airways:** www.usairways.com; ☎ **800/245-4882**

the airline money. They don't have to pay a reservationist, they don't have to pay commissions to a travel agent, and they don't have to mail you your ticket. According to

Consumer Reports Travel Newsletter, Delta's second biggest expense in 1998 was the cost of distributing tickets—over $1 billion, more than the airline spent on fuel. Internet purchases accounted for only 1% of the airlines' total sales, but in January 1999, Delta imposed a $1 surcharge per domestic segment for every ticket that was not booked online.

WHY SHOULD YOU BOOK ONLINE?

Online booking is not for everyone. If you prefer to let others handle your travel arrangements, one call to an experienced travel agent should suffice. But if you want to know as much as possible about your options, the Net is a good place to start, especially for bargain hunters.

The most compelling reason to use online booking is to take advantage of last-minute specials or other Internet-only fares that must be purchased online (see "Last-Minute Deals: E-Saver Fares," below). Another advantage is that you can cash in on incentives for booking online; you can receive bonus miles for booking a round-trip ticket and sometimes additional bonus miles for paperless travel if you reserve an e-ticket (See chapter 7, "Sky Hounds," for details). Online booking works best for trips within North America—for international tickets, it's usually cheaper and easier to use a travel agent or consolidator.

Online booking is certainly not for those with a complex international itinerary. If you require follow-up services, such as itinerary changes, use a travel agent. Though Expedia and some other online agencies employ travel agents available by phone, these sites are geared primarily for self-service.

LAST-MINUTE DEALS: E-SAVER FARES

There's nothing airlines hate more than flying with lots of empty seats. The Internet has enabled airlines to offer last-minute bargains to entice travelers to fill those seats. Most of these are announced on Tuesday or Wednesday and are valid for travel the following weekend, but some can be booked weeks or months in advance. You can sign up for weekly e-mail alerts at airlines' sites or check sites that compile lists of these bargains, such as Smarter Living or WebFlyer (see "Surfing for Sales," below, for addresses). To make it easier, visit a site that will round up all the deals and send them in one convenient weekly e-mail. But last-minute deals aren't the only online bargains; other sites can help you find value even if you haven't waited until the eleventh hour.

USING AN ELECTRONIC TRAVEL AGENT

If you don't have a favorite airline and want to survey the fare wars without consulting each carrier's Web site, try one of the travel-agent-type Web sites that scavenge the airlines' databases for you and divine the cheapest fares available at a given moment. Be warned, however, that these sites are legion. Many of them are spotty, time consuming, and sometimes even downright fraudulent. A time-tried few have been proven financially viable, easy to navigate, and more privy to the best deals. Some require registration, but all of them are free. So grab your mouse and shop around. The top online travel agencies, including **Expedia, Preview Travel,** and **Travelocity,** offer an array of tools that are valuable even if you don't book online: You can check flight schedules or even get paged if your flight is delayed.

While online agencies have come a long way over the past few years, they don't always yield the best price. Unlike a travel agent, for example, they're unlikely to tell you that you can save money by flying a day earlier or a day later. On the other hand, if you're looking for a bargain fare, you might find something online that an agent wouldn't take the time to dig up. Because airline commissions have been cut, a travel agent may not find it worthwhile to spend half an hour trying to find you the best deal. You can be your own agent on the Net, however, and take all the time you want.

3 SURFING FOR SALES: THE TOP TRAVEL-PLANNING WEB SITES

This section was written by Michael Shapiro, the author of Internet Travel 101: How to Plan Trips and Save Money Online *(Globe Pequot).*

Note: Remember this is a press-time snapshot of leading Web sites—some undoubtedly will have evolved, changed, or moved by the time you read this.

LEADING BOOKING SITES

Below are listings for the top travel booking sites. The starred selections are the most useful and best designed sites.

CHEAP TICKETS. www.cheaptickets.com

Essentials: Discounted rates on domestic and international airline tickets and hotel rooms.

Sometimes discounters such as Cheap Tickets have exclusive deals that aren't available through more mainstream channels. Registration at Cheap Tickets requires inputting a credit card number before getting started, which is one reason many people elect to call the company's toll-free number rather than booking online. One of the most frustrating things about the Cheap Tickets site is that it will offer fare quotes for a route, and later show this fare is not valid for your dates of travel—other Web sites, such as Preview Travel, consider your dates of travel before showing what fares are available. Despite its problems, Cheap Tickets can be worth the effort because its fares can be lower than those offered by its competitors.

MICROSOFT EXPEDIA. www.expedia.com

Essentials: Domestic and international flight booking; hotel and car-rental reservations; late-breaking travel news and commentary from travel experts.

You can start booking right away with the Roundtrip Fare Finder box on the home page. After selecting a flight, you can hold it until midnight the following day or purchase online. If you think you might do better through a travel agent, you'll have time to try to get a lower price. And you may do better with a travel agent because Expedia's computer reservation system does not include all airlines. Most notably absent are some leading budget carriers, such as Southwest Airlines. (**Note:** At press time, Travelocity was the only major booking service that included Southwest.)

PREVIEW TRAVEL. www.previewtravel.com
Essentials: Domestic and international flight booking; Travel Newswire lists fare sales; deals on vacation packages. Free (one-time) registration is required for booking. Preview offers express booking for members but at press time this feature was buried below the fold on Preview's reservation page.

Preview features the most inviting interface for booking trips, though the wealth of graphics involved can make the site somewhat slow to load. Use Farefinder to quickly find the lowest current fares on flights to dozens of major cities. To see the lowest fare for your itinerary, input the dates and times for your route and see what Preview comes up with.

In recent years Preview and other leading booking services have added features such as Best Fare Finder, so after Preview searches for the best deal on your itinerary, it will check flights that are a bit later or earlier to see if it might be cheaper to fly at a different time. While these searches have become quite sophisticated, they still occasionally overlook deals that might be uncovered by a top-notch travel agent. If you have the time, see what you can find online and then call an agent to see if you can get a better price.

With Preview's Fare Alert feature, you can set fares for up to three routes and you'll receive e-mail notices when the fare drops below your target amount.

Note to AOL Users: You can book flights on AOL at keyword: Travel. The booking software is provided by Preview Travel and is similar to Preview on the Web. Use the AOL "Travelers Advantage" program to earn a 5% rebate.

TRAVELOCITY. www.travelocity.com

Essentials: Domestic and international flight, hotel and rental car booking; deals on cruises and vacation packages. Travel Headlines spotlights latest bargain airfares. Free (one-time) registration is required for booking.

Travelocity's Express Booking feature enables travelers to complete the booking process more quickly than they could at Expedia or Preview. Travelocity is owned by American Airlines' parent company, AMR, and some worry that this directs bookings to American. That doesn't seem to be the case—I've booked there dozens of times and have always been directed to the cheapest listed flight—for example, on Tower or ATA. But there are rewards for choosing one of the "featured airlines." You'll get 1,500 bonus frequent-flyer miles if you book through United's site, for example, but the site doesn't tell you about other airlines that might be cheaper. If the United flight costs $150 more than the best deal on another airline, it's not worth spending the extra money for a relatively small number of bonus miles.

On the plus side, Travelocity has some leading-edge tools. Exhibit A is Fare Watcher Email, an "intelligent agent" that keeps you informed of the best fares offered for the city pairs (round-trips) of your choice. Whenever the fare changes by $25 or more, Fare Watcher will alert you by e-mail. Exhibit B is Flight Paging—if you own an alphanumeric pager with national access that can receive e-mail, Travelocity's paging system can alert you if your flight is delayed. Finally, though Travelocity doesn't include every budget airline, it does include Southwest, the leading U.S. budget carrier.

LAST-MINUTE DEALS & OTHER ONLINE BARGAINS

ARTHUR FROMMER'S BUDGET TRAVEL ONLINE.
www.frommers.com

Of course, we're a little biased, but we think this site is an excellent travel planning resource. You'll find indispensable

Staying Secure

Far more people look online than book online, partly due to fear of putting their credit cards through on the Net. Though secure encryption has made this fear less justified, there's no reason why you can't find a flight online and then book it by calling a toll-free number or contacting your travel agent. To be sure you're in secure mode when you book online, look for a little icon of a key (in Netscape) or a padlock (Internet Explorer) at the bottom of your Web browser.

---

travel tips, reviews, monthly vacation giveaways, and online booking. Subscribe to ***Arthur Frommer's Daily Newsletter*** (www.frommers.com/newsletters) to receive the latest travel bargains and inside travel secrets in your mailbox every day. You'll read daily headlines and articles from the dean of travel himself, highlighting last-minute deals on airfares and package vacations.

1TRAVEL.COM. www.1travel.com
Here you'll find deals on domestic and international flights, cruises, hotels, and all-inclusive resorts such as Club Med. 1travel.com's Saving Alert compiles last-minute air deals so you don't have to scroll through multiple e-mail alerts. A feature called "Drive a little using low-fare airlines" helps map out strategies for using alternate airports to find lower fares. And Farebeater searches a database that includes published fares, consolidator bargains and special deals exclusive to 1travel.com. **Note:** The travel agencies listed by 1travel.com have paid for placement.

BESTFARES. www.bestfares.com
Budget seeker Tom Parsons lists some great airfare bargains, but his site is poorly organized. News Desk compiles hundreds of bargains, but it's a long list, not broken down by city or even country, so it's not easy trying to find what you're

looking for. If you have time to wade through it, you might find a good deal. Some material is available only to paid subscribers.

LASTMINUTETRAVEL.COM. www.lastminutetravel.com
Suppliers with excess inventory come to this online agency to distribute unsold airline seats, hotel rooms, cruises, and vacation packages.

MOMENT'S NOTICE. www.moments-notice.com
As the name suggests, Moment's Notice specializes in last-minute vacation and cruise deals. You can browse for free, but if you want to purchase a trip you have to join Moment's Notice, which costs $25.

SMARTER LIVING. www.smarterliving.com
Best known for its e-mail dispatch of weekend deals on 20 airlines, Smarter Living also keeps you posted about last-minute bargains on everything from Windjammer Cruises to flights to Iceland.

WEBFLYER. www.webflyer.com
WebFlyer is the ultimate online resource for frequent flyers and also has an excellent listing of last-minute air deals.

Know When the Sales Start

While most people learn about last-minute weekend deals from e-mail dispatches, it can be best to find out precisely when these deals become available and check airline Web sites at this time. To find out when deals become available, check the pages devoted to these deals on airlines' Web pages. Because these deals are limited, they can vanish within hours—sometimes even minutes—so it pays to log on as soon as they're available. An example: Southwest's specials are posted at 12:01am Tuesdays (central time). So if you're looking for a cheap flight, stay up late and check Southwest's site at that time to grab the best new deals.

Click on "Deal Watch" for a round-up of weekend deals on flights, hotels and rental cars from domestic and international suppliers.

4 CONSOLIDATORS: THE PRICE CLUBS OF THE TRAVEL BIZ

LIKE DISCOUNT WAREHOUSE OUTLETS, CONSOLIDATORS, or "bucket shops," buy seats in bulk from the airlines (often major, reputable scheduled carriers) and then sell them back to the public at prices that are often cheaper than even the airlines' discounted rates. They're especially invaluable if you're flying overseas, if you can't afford to stay over a Saturday night, or if you're booking a flight at the last minute, when it's too late to get an APEX fare. Their small boxed ads usually run in the Sunday travel section at the bottom of the page.

Though the bucket shop industry is a source of deeply discounted flights, it has also attracted its share of fly-by-night operators. Some sell stolen tickets, some purchase miles from frequent fliers and sell the tickets, others may suddenly fold. If you can trust your travel agent to book your ticket from a reliable consolidator, by all means do so. Your travel agent is more likely to know a consolidator's track record, and if the company turns out to be a scam, you're more likely to get a refund.

If you're booking on your own, be sure to pay with a credit card. If the company goes under or you never receive your ticket, you can get your money back through a charge-back claim with your credit card company. Ask the consolidator for a record-locator number and then confirm your seat with the airline itself. (Be prepared to book your ticket with a different consolidator if the airline can't confirm your reservation.)

You may also want to specify the airline or airlines on which you'd like to fly. Be aware that some consolidators sell tickets on charter flights or carriers with poor safety records.

If you want to fly on a major carrier, say so when you make your reservation.

You should also know that most bucket shop tickets won't earn you frequent flier miles. Usually, they're also non-refundable or rigged with stiff cancellation penalties, often as high as 50% to 75% of the ticket price. Be sure to ask what the penalties are before you pay.

The following bucket shops have been around for a while and have a reputation for reliability:

Council Travel (☎ **800/226-8624;** www.counciltravel. com) and **STA Travel** (☎ **800/781-4040;** www.sta. travel.com) cater especially to young travelers, but their bargain-basement prices are available to people of all ages.

Travel Bargains (☎ **800/AIR-FARE;** www.1800airfare. com) was formerly owned by TWA but now offers the deepest discounts on many other airlines, with a 4-day advance purchase.

TFI Tours International (☎ **800/745-8000** or 212/736-1140) serves as a clearinghouse for unused seats. **Travel Avenue** (☎ **800/333-3335** or 312/876-1116) and the **Smart Traveller** (☎ **800/448-3338** in the U.S., or 305/448-3338), rebate part of their commissions to you. **1-800-FLY-CHEAP** (www.1800flycheap.com) has also proven to be dependable. **Unitravel** (☎ **800/325-1025** or 314/569-0900) offers discounts no matter what day of the week you fly (and sometimes you don't need a weekend stay-over, either); they also place your payment in escrow until after the flight has been completed.

Brendan Tours (☎ **800/491-9633** or 818/785-9696) sells both transpacific and transatlantic flights. **Travac Tours and Charters** (☎ **800/TRAV-800** or 212/563-3303; www.travac.com) offers often unbeatable fares to Europe, the Middle East, Africa, Asia, Australia, and South America. **New Frontiers USA** (☎ **800/366-6387** or 212/779-0600; www.newfrontiers.com) sells cut-rate tickets to all the major cities of Europe, but specializes in Paris. **Magical Holidays** (☎ **800/228-2208** or 212/486-9600) is the country's

Speaking of Price Clubs

The major warehouse club chains (Sam's Club, BJ's Wholesale Club, and Costco) now offer discounted vacation packages and other travel services to its members. Recently, **Arthur Frommer's Budget Travel Magazine** published an investigation into the merits of these respective warehouse programs. Their conclusion? That the promise of savings was only intermittently fulfilled; price comparisons showed sometimes huge discounts on cruises and package tours. But often, the prices quoted by the price clubs were significantly higher than those you'd find through a conscientious travel agent.

On the e-commerce tip, the nationwide discount chain **Wal-Mart** has inaugurated its own e-commerce site (www.walmart.com), with a travel area that allows you to book flights and reserve hotel rooms and rental cars.

The bottom line? As I've said before, no matter what kind of trip you're planning, it pays (or in this case, saves) to shop around.

---

leading specialist in reduced-price flights to Africa. **Express Holidays** (☎ **800/266-8669**, 800/223-7452, 212/223-4484, or 619/521-0549) is a major discounter of flights to Mexico, especially the resort destinations. **Fantasy Holidays** (☎ **800/645-2555** or 5I6/935-8500; www.fantasyholidays.com) specializes in discount flights to Italy, though flights to Hawaii and Tahiti are also available.

5 WORKING WITH A TRAVEL AGENT

A GOOD TRAVEL AGENT CAN PROVE AS INDISPENSABLE as a good chiropractor, hairdresser, or shoe repair shop. The **American Society of Travel Agents (ASTA)** runs a toll-free referral line (☎ **800/965-2782**) to help you find a reliable operator in your area.

OTHER SAVVY SAVING STRATEGIES

1. Do the bump

Why let the airlines be the only ones to benefit from overbooked flights? While oversold flights are by and large an inconvenience for consumers, you can work this practice to your advantage. If you are retired, if you have a flexible schedule and a laptop that will allow you to work in the airport, or if you simply have more time on your hands than money, consider traveling deliberately at peak times when airlines are most likely to ask customers to volunteer their seats in exchange for free round-trip tickets for travel at a later date.

Every airport tends to have its own periods of high-volume travel, and you should call the central number at your local airport to find out when these are. In general, however, air traffic tends to be heaviest—and flights are most likely to be overbooked—on weekday mornings between 7:30 and 9:30am and on weekday evenings between 5:30 and 7:30pm. On Monday mornings and Friday evenings, the sky is especially crowded. Congestion tends to be at its very greatest on major holidays along with the few days before and after.

It may be risky to try volunteering your seat during the holiday rush around Thanksgiving and between Christmas and New Year's Day. Travel volume tends to be so high then that you might find yourself stranded in standby for longer than you'd like. Don't give up your seat at peak travel times unless the airline confirms your seat on another flight the same day.

If you volunteer your seat early in the morning on an average business day, however, you're highly likely to secure a seat on a later flight within a few hours, if not sooner—and a voucher for a free round-trip ticket, maybe breakfast, and a few free phone calls.

If you go to the airport hoping to get bumped, be aware that there are no guarantees that a flight will sell out. You should also call the airline to make sure at least one if not several alternate flights are scheduled soon after the flight you actually book.

Also, be sure to get what you want from the airline before you give up what you've got. See "Voluntary Bumpings," in chapter 1, for tips on skillful bargaining and avoiding the hazards of bumping.

2. Book back-to-back tickets

Tickets without a Saturday night stopover cost a fortune. If you must travel during the week and need to return home before the weekend, however, you can still save money with a trick called "back-to-back ticketing." Mind you, however, that most major carriers have rules that prohibit this practice.

Here's how it works. When a Saturday-stay coach ticket costs less than half of an unrestricted round-trip flight, you simply buy two cheap round-trip coach passages—one that starts from your home, and one that begins from your destination on the day you need to fly back. You can either use the remaining portions of your tickets later or discard them altogether—and still come out ahead. This trick can be risky, but you're more likely to pull it off if you book the tickets on two separate airlines. By all means, when you present your ticket, show only one portion at a time. If the airline finds out, it has the right to confiscate your ticket and force you to buy another in order to travel.

In the past, the airlines penalized travel agents who were caught in this game. The Association of Retail Travel Agencies complained, however, because the airlines themselves were unwittingly selling back-to-back tickets directly to consumers. Continental, for one, responded by agreeing to penalize the frequent flier accounts of individual passengers caught in this game.

You want to look for an agent who not only consistently finds cheap fares for you, but who will call you if a lower fare is announced—even if you've already made a reservation. If you frequent a particular region of the country or the world, look for an agent who specializes in that area. It's always wise to ask friends and family for recommendations, too, to help you find an agent with a proven track record.

Better yet, you may want to work with more than one reliable operator. Travel agencies often specialize in certain parts of the globe and may offer better bargains in their specialty region. Agencies also sometimes buy tickets in bulk, and you may get a better a deal from an agency that purchased more tickets to the area where you're traveling. If you can shop around, you're liable to get a better bargain.

Before you book a flight through an agent, however, research available fares directly with a few airlines first, through their reservation line or Web site, or through an electronic travel agent (see "Using an Electronic Travel Agent," above) to be sure you're getting a bargain. In addition to legitimate commissions travel agents receive from airlines for each ticket sale, they often receive kickbacks, known in the business as "override commissions," from the carriers they work with most frequently. With this incentive to favor certain preferred suppliers, agents may be inclined to book you with the airline that offers them the greatest reward for your reservation—rather than the carrier that would offer you the cheapest flight. Currently, they're under no obligation to divulge preferred-supplier relationships to consumers.

Unfortunately, more agents have recently begun charging fees for their services—and the airlines are to blame. For the third time in four years, carriers have reduced the legitimate commissions they pay travel agents. Agents used to earn a standard 10% commission on each sale, but United Airlines put a $100 limit on commissions for round-trip international tickets. Nine other airlines swiftly adopted the same policy. Agents were still recovering from the pay cut when the airlines decided to cut commissions back further, to 5%, and put a $50 limit on commissions for round-trip domestic flights as well.

In turn, agents have begun trying to recoup the money from consumers. Before the first commission cuts in 1995, only 54% of travel agencies charged fees; now 64% charge an average fee of $10.35, according to a June 1998 survey of American Society of Travel Agents operators. Fees can run as high as $200 for refunds and exchanges, visa and passport services, and trip planning.

Commission reductions have also made travel agents more dependent on kickbacks for their very survival, so you want to take extra care to research fares before you book through an operator.

6 CHECKING OUT CHARTER FLIGHTS

IF YOU'RE PLANNING TO TRAVEL DURING HIGH SEASON to a popular vacation destination like Europe, the Caribbean, Mexico, or Hawaii, charter flights are solid bargains—though not without attendant risks.

Charter flights are typically sold to tour operators as part of a package vacation, but independent travelers can purchase just the airfare portion, often at rates far below the fares available on scheduled flights. They're also more convenient than APEX fares, in that you may not have to stay at your destination through Saturday night or for longer than 30 days in order to secure this rock-bottom fare. Depending on the charter, you may not have to purchase your ticket as far in advance as you would for an APEX fare either.

Charters make especially good bargains for leisure travelers who hate to ride in coach but can't afford a premium fare. In the summer, when rates to Europe are very high, you can pay as little as $1,300 from the east coast and $1,800 from the west coast for a first- or business-class seat that would typically cost you $2,400 to $6,750.

Another advantage of charters is that some of them fly nonstop on routes that scheduled carriers traverse only with segmented flights. Nonstop flights, as you may know, halve your risk of lost or mishandled baggage, delays, cancellations, missed connections, and even accidents, given that most air accidents happen during takeoff and landing.

On the other hand, keep in mind that charter flights are sometimes scheduled on smaller budget carriers, which are often criticized for operating older planes under lower safety standards. Ask when you book what company and what kind of plane you'll actually be flying. Also, charter flights and tours also tend to be laden with restrictions. Choose a charter only if the fare is significantly cheaper or the schedule is significantly more convenient than what you'd find on a scheduled flight. Otherwise, the drawbacks easily outweigh the advantages.

Charter companies are much more prone to go belly up than an airline or even most travel agencies. If something does go wrong, your contract is with the tour operator or travel agent, not the airline, so you may have a harder time securing a refund. You will not earn frequent-flier credit for miles traveled. Flights tend to be crowded, scheduled at inconvenient times, delayed for hours, or canceled suddenly. (You, on the other hand, will not be able to cancel or reschedule without paying stiff penalties.) In addition, check-in usually takes much more time—up to 3 hours, even, on international flights.

Charter operators typically don't sell seats directly to the public or advertise their fares and schedules through standard channels. Though sometimes charter fares are available from the airlines themselves, most promote trips and conduct all business through travel agents, making these local professionals your best source of information for available flights and destinations.

WHAT YOU SHOULD KNOW ABOUT CHARTER TICKETS

- **Be prepared for major changes in fare or itinerary.** Your contract does not guarantee that a charter won't raise the fare or change your itinerary. It does guarantee you a penalty-free refund if you can't accept the terms of any "major changes." "Major changes" include: a change in departure or return city (not including a change in the order in which cities are visited); a change in departure or return date, unless the date change is the result of a flight delay under 48 hours; the substitution of a hotel that was not named in your contract as an alternate hotel; a price increase of more than 10% (though in the 10-day period before departure, price increases of any kind are prohibited). If a major change is issued after your trip has begun, you can reject the change, pay for your own alternative plans, and insist on a refund.

- **One-way fares.** Charters may be sold on a one-way basis, but the Department of Transportation forbids "open returns" on charter tickets. Be sure you have a specific return date, city, and flight, so you're not stranded.

- **Remember that charter flights operate independently from scheduled airline flights.** If you need to fly to your charter's departure city on a scheduled airline, and that flight is delayed, you'll usually lose your charter flight and the money you paid for it. Likewise, if your charter flight returns late and causes you to miss a scheduled airline flight home, you'll be responsible for any expenses incurred. Be sure you allow yourself plenty of time between flights to make connections safely.

    Remember too that you can't check your baggage from a scheduled flight to a charter. Allow plenty of time to retrieve and recheck your bags before flights—especially if international flights are involved, because you'll have to clear customs as well.

QUESTIONS TO ASK BEFORE YOU BOOK A CHARTER FLIGHT

Your charter agreement will usually be called an "**operator/ participant contract,**" which you should read very carefully before signing. The Department of Transportation requires that these documents spell out certain restrictions and consumer rights. Be sure you know where you stand on these key issues before you hand over a dime.

- **What steps does the charter take to protect your money?** By law the charter is required to have a surety agreement, like a bond. The charter should also hold your money in an escrow account until your flight departs. Be sure the bank or surety company is named in your contract. If the charter goes out of business before you depart, contact the bank or surety company for a refund.

  It's best not to pay by check. If you must, you should make your check out to either your travel agent or the bank or surety company named in your contract—not the charter operator itself. Be sure to write your destination and departure date on the face of the check.

- **What is the charter's cancellation policy?** If a charter flight doesn't fill up, the operator may be able to cancel it anywhere up to 10 days before departure. Be sure to pay by credit card when you book a flight, so you're guaranteed reimbursement under federal credit regulations. During the 10-day period before departure, a charter may cancel only because physical operation is for some reason impossible.

  As a general rule, summer charters fill up more quickly than others and are more likely to fly as scheduled.

- **What are the cancellation penalties?** Once you've signed a contract with a charter, you typically pay a penalty for canceling. The penalty rates grow higher as your departure date approaches. Most discount fares on regularly scheduled airlines are also non refundable, but they do allow you to use your ticket at a later date with a fee, usually between $50 to $75; with a charter, however, once you cancel you forfeit your chance to fly on that fare. Some may allow a surrogate traveler to fly in your stead for a fee of $25.

- **How much is cancellation insurance and what does it cover?** You may be able to purchase insurance for a refund in case of a cancellation due to a death in the family or illness. Ask your travel agent or operator which health conditions the policy covers. Be aware that you may not be reimbursed for illness that results from a preexisting condition. Be sure to buy your policy from an independent provider, not the charter itself. (See "Travel Insurance Demystified," in chapter 5, "Life Preservers.")

- **If you are traveling with the charter tour and your luggage is lost, who is responsible?** While charter airlines will process claims for luggage that was lost or damaged while in their possession, both the airline and the charter operator may deny liability if it is not clear when the bag was lost. If you are traveling with the charter tour, for example, and you realize your bag is lost only after you reach your hotel, the airline may try to blame the tour operator.

- **How much delay time is the charter allowed?** Charter flights are very often delayed or rerouted. By law, however, the charter must allow you to cancel for a full refund if the flight is delayed for more than 48 hours.

7   TRAVELING AS A COURIER

COMPANIES THAT HIRE COURIERS WILL TYPICALLY USE your luggage allowance on a major airline for their business baggage and/or ask you to hand-deliver a package at the destination airport. In return, you get a deeply discounted or free ticket—usually half the going APEX coach fare—primarily for travel overseas. Flights often come up at the last minute, and typically you're allowed only one piece of carry-on luggage. Once you deliver the goods, however, you're free to go on your way.

Some courier services require you to arrange a pretrip interview, to make sure you're right for the job. At the very least, you'll probably have to meet with a courier representative at the airport or the company office before your flight departs. Most courier tickets are nontransferable and nonrefundable.

Here are a few reputable U.S.–based courier companies:

Halbart Express operates offices in New York (☎718/656-8189), Los Angeles (☎310/417-9790), and Miami (☎305/593-0260). In Europe, Halbart flies to Amsterdam, Brussels, Copenhagen, Dublin, Milan, Madrid, Paris, and Rome. In the Far East, Halbart flies to Bangkok, Hong Kong, Manila, Singapore, and Tokyo. Fares vary according to season: A round-trip to Amsterdam in the winter can cost as little as $150, while in summer the fare can be as high as $455. If you're planning summer travel around a courier flight, be sure to apply 2 or 3 months in advance.

Jupiter Air is located in San Francisco (☎ 650/697-1773), Los Angeles (☎ 310/670-5123), and New York (☎ 718/656-6050). Jupiter offers flights to Hong Kong and London. A round-trip to Hong Kong from New York in summer costs $452. For summer travel, call 1 month in advance.

Now Voyager (☎ 212/431-1616) flies from New York and Newark to Amsterdam, Bangkok, Brussels, Buenos Aires, Caracas, Copenhagen, Dublin, Hong Kong, London, Madrid, Manila, Mexico City, Milan, Paris, Rio de Janeiro,

Rome, San Francisco, São Paulo, Seoul, Singapore, and Tokyo. Now Voyager also offers rare flights from Detroit to the Far East, and to Australia from Los Angeles. The fares to South America are an especially good bargain: all year long, round-trip fares to São Paulo and Rio de Janeiro cost only $299, and flights to Mexico City cost $99. In the summer, European flights range from $500 to $700, and flights to Asia cost $700 to $800. In the winter, fares drop to $300 to Europe, and $500 to $600 to Asia. For summer travel, it's best to book your flight 2 months in advance. Now Voyager also offers noncourier discounted fares, so call the company even if you don't want to fly as a courier. When you call, a recorded message leaves detailed information about available flights. Now Voyager charges a $50 registration fee for first-time travel and a $28 airport departure tax.

8 SPECIAL DISCOUNTS FOR PEOPLE WITH SPECIAL NEEDS

"STATUS FARES" PROVIDE DISCOUNTED AIRLINE TICKETS based on who you are rather than how you're flying. Senior citizens, children, students, and bereaved persons all qualify for these discounts.

SENIOR PRIVILEGES

In general, senior citizens are entitled to a standard 10% discount on fares from all the major airlines. Several carriers

---

Join a Travel Club

A travel club such as **Moment's Notice** (☎ 718/234-6295) or **Sears Discount Travel Club** (☎ **800/433-9383,** or 800/255-1487 to join), supplies unsold tickets at discounted prices. You pay an annual membership fee to get the club's hot line number. Of course, you're limited to what's available, so you have to be flexible and prepared to take off suddenly.

also operate special programs for seniors that allow for more significant savings. Here are a few:

Senior Coupons

Consumer Reports Travel Letter deems senior coupons one of the best buys in the travel industry for older travelers who take more than two domestic round-trip flights per year. Senior coupons are available through America West, American, Continental, Delta, Northwest, TWA, United, and US Airways. In order to be eligible for most programs, you must be over the age of 62—although 65 is the minimum age for a few carriers.

Prices for coupon books vary only slightly from one airline to the next—at press time, anywhere from $540 for a book of four coupons on Northwest to $596 for four coupons on American, Delta, or United. This means you can fly anywhere in the continental United States for under $300 round-trip, provided you make four one-way flights each year. You need not fly round-trip on any one of those flights. Typically, you purchase a book of four coupons at a time, valid for one year, although Continental offers eight-coupon books for $1,079, which means you pay as little as $269 round-trip. You must usually book 14 days in advance, however, as seats are usually limited. Coupons for international itineraries are unavailable. Blackout dates may apply, so be sure to ask which days are off-limits from travel when you book your tickets.

Although almost all coupons must be used by the same individual, US Airways allows seniors to use their own coupons for one or two accompanying grandchildren aged 2 to 11. TWA sells coupon books for companions of any age as well, for $100 more than the senior fare.

Airline Discounts

Through American Airline's **AActive American Traveler Club** (☎ **800/421-5600**), senior citizens aged 62 and older can fly round-trip in coach within the Lower 48 for $98 to

AIR PASSES: A EUROPE-BASED BARGAIN

If you're flying to the United States from Europe and plan to visit several American cities, look into one of the **Visit USA** passes offered by Northwest and Delta. These fares allow you to book one-way flights from one city to the next at much lower rates than you'd pay for a standard one-way ticket. Terms and conditions can change without much notice, but through Northwest's program at press time, three coupons—for direct travel to three different American cities—cost $377 during low season and $440 during high season. Ten coupons cost $1049 during low season and $1311 during high season.

You use one coupon per flight, including connections on segmented flights. In other words, if you have to change planes in Cincinnati en route to San Francisco from New York, you have to use two coupons. Be sure to look into direct flights well in advance—as soon as you book your international trip. Unfortunately, these fares are not available domestically. You must prove that you are a foreign resident and you must purchase your coupons in conjunction with an international flight to and from the United States.

$298. Travel is cheapest from Monday to Thursday, and blackout periods apply on Thanksgiving and between Christmas and New Year's day. If you need to fly over the weekend, you'll pay an additional $20 each way. Flights to Hawaii are slightly higher: from $318 to $598, depending on whether you depart from the west or east coast.

Round-trip flights to Europe range from $358 to $538. Fares to eastern Canada will run from $218 to $358 and from $218 to $358 to western Canada. Round-trip fares to the Caribbean cost $178 to $518, $398 to $578 to Central America, and $558 to $938 to Japan. International flights to all destinations but Canada must depart between Monday and Thursday. Blackout periods apply during peak travel seasons.

All destinations require a 14-day advance purchase and a Saturday–night stay. Membership for one costs $40. A $70 membership allows you to travel with a companion of any age. The companion may differ with each flight.

Continental Airlines Freedom Flight Club (☎ 800/ 441-1135), for travelers over 62, works simply. Members receive a 15% to 20% discount on all fares, including first class, at all times. For Monday to Thursday and Saturday departures, you'll receive 20% off the ticket price; for travel on Friday and Saturday, the discount drops to 15%. You can even qualify for discounts over the holidays, as no blackout periods apply; no minimum stays are required, unless the standard fare warrants such a restriction. Itineraries are not restricted by zones, and you don't have to stay over on a Saturday night. Companion fares, however, are not part of this particular program.

Membership costs $75 per year for domestic travel in all 50 states. Membership for international travel is $125 per year and covers flights to Mexico, Canada, the Caribbean, Central and South America, and eight cities in Europe.

If you fly coach and take more than eight round-trip flights each year, **Continental's Freedom Passport** (☎ 800/ 441-1135) may be an even better deal. It allows you to travel one way as often as once a week for a full year within the Lower 48 and select Caribbean destinations. A coach pass costs $1,999, and the business/first-class pass is $3,499. You may not visit any one city (save your hometown) more than three times a year, and seats are limited.

During peak travel times, you may not make a reservation more than 7 days in advance. You may fly standby at any time during the week, but reservations are available on these fares only from noon Monday through noon Thursday and all day Saturday.

Through **Delta's SkyWise** program, seniors can travel within the Lower 48 for anywhere from $118 to $298. All travel, however, requires an advance purchase, a Saturday-night stay, and a 30-day trip maximum. Penalty for itinerary changes cost $75, and blackout rates apply. Fares to Hawaii run a little higher: from $298 to 658.

Membership costs $40 per year and $25 per person per year for up two three companions. Members must be 65 years of age or older, but companions can be of any age.

Members of **United Airlines' Silver Wings Plus** program receive a newsletter every 3 months or so with advertised discounts on airfares as well as cruises, hotels, and car rentals. The best deal in the current issue, at press time, is called **US Collection** rates. Trips are priced according to miles traveled. The first 0 to 500 miles cost $98; the next 501 to 1,000 miles cost $118; and the next 1,001 to 3,000 miles cost $178. Round-trip airfare from New York to San Francisco, for instance, is $398 for travel on Monday to Friday and $418 for travel on Friday to Sunday. Round-trip passage from New York to Atlanta is $178 from Monday to Thursday and $198 from Friday to Sunday. Bargains are often featured on international travel as well, though none figured into the current issue.

A 14-day advance purchase is usually required. Blackout dates, mandatory Saturday-night stays, and maximum or minimum stays vary according to the promotion. Companions of any age may travel at the same discounted rate. Members must be 55 and over to qualify. Membership costs $75 for 2 years and $225 for a lifetime.

Virgin Atlantic (☎ **800/862-8621**) reduces rates for travelers over 63 on international flights. Discounts range from 12% to 25% off the standard ticket price.

Association Discounts for Seniors

Members of the **Association for the Advancement of Retired Persons (AARP)** (☎ **800/424-3410**) qualify for special discounted vacation packages from **Continental** (☎ **800/634-5555**) and **Delta** (☎ **800/892-5215**). Typically, members receive $50 to $100 off for a stay of 10 nights or longer on package tours to Latin America, Mexico, Las Vegas, Florida, Europe, the Caribbean, Bermuda, Hawaii, Canada, and assorted ski packages. Call the airline for details.

Other Ways for Seniors to Save

There are several other ways for seniors to find cheap flights. For example, **The National Council of Senior Citizens,** 8403 Colesville Rd., Ste. 1200; Silver Spring, MD 20910 (☎ **301/578-8800;** www.ncscinc.org), urges its members to turn their retirement status into savings. Because most seniors do not have to report to work on a daily basis, they make perfect candidates for courier flights, where you can receive deep discounts—and sometimes even free fares—by allowing a courier operator to use your luggage allowance. (See "Traveling As a Courier," above). One minor drawback: You'll need to pack more economically to fit your belongings into carry-on bags. The chief disadvantage of this type of air travel is usually the fact that flights often come up at the last minute. But your schedule is likely to be more flexible than that of younger travelers.

By the same reasoning, seniors are much better able to take advantage of the last-minute sales that airlines offer to fill up unsold seats. By all means, sign up for E-saver programs with your favorite airlines for vastly reduced fares, even on international flights, for travel the following weekend. (See "Surfing for Sales: The Top Travel Planning Web Sites," above.) Also be sure to check the newspaper for late-breaking flight discounts.

Finally, if you've got all day and love to get away, make a habit of volunteering your seat on overbooked flights. Chances are you'll only have to wait a few more hours for the next flight out, and you'll receive free tickets for future travel to other destinations. (See "Voluntary Bumpings," in chapter 1, "Ticketing Pitfalls," and "Other Savvy Savings Strategies," above).

You can also take advantage of the myriad organizations, publications, and tour operators that cater to senior citizens. Though most won't entitle you to discounted airfares per se, many do purchase airline tickets in bulk—usually at relatively low rates—as part of package-travel programs for older travelers.

Members of the **American Association of Retired Persons (AARP)**, 601 E St. NW, Washington, DC 20049 (☎ **800/424-3410** or 202/434-2277), receive a wide range of special benefits, including *Modern Maturity* magazine, a monthly newsletter, and limited discounts on Virgin Atlantic, Delta, and Continental. In order to quality for membership, you must be 50 year of age. Membership costs $8 per year.

Mature Outlook, P.O. Box 9390, Des Moines, IA 50306 (☎ **800/336-6330**), began as a travel organization for people over 50, though it now caters to people of all ages. Members qualify for discounts on airfares and hotels and receive a bimonthly magazine. Annual membership is $19.95.

Grand Circle Travel is one of the hundreds of travel agencies specializing in package vacations for seniors, 347 Congress St., Suite 3A, Boston, MA 02210 (☎ **800/221-2610** or 617/350-7500). While you can save on airfare through many of these packages, however, be aware that they are often of the tour-bus variety, with free trips thrown in for those who organize groups of 10 or more. If you prefer more independent travel, you should probably consult a regular travel agent. **SAGA International Holidays,** 222 Berkeley St., Boston, MA 02116 (☎ **800/343-0273**), offers inclusive tours and cruises for those 50 and older, with discounted airfare rates. SAGA also sponsors the more substantial **Road Scholar Tours** (☎ **800/621-2151**), which are fun-loving but have an educational bent.

If you want fare discounts for something more than the average vacation or guided tour, try **Elderhostel,** 75 Federal St., Boston, MA 02110-1941 (☎ **877/426-8056;** www.elderhostel.org), or the University of New Hampshire's

Interhostel (☎ 800/733-9753), both variations on the same theme: educational travel for senior citizens. On these escorted tours, the days are packed with seminars, lectures, and field trips, and the sightseeing is all led by academic experts. Elderhostel arranges study programs for people 55 and over (and a spouse or companion of any age) in the United States and in 77 countries around the world, including Asia, Africa, and the South Pacific. Most courses last about 3 weeks and many include airfare, accommodations in student dormitories or modest inns, meals, and tuition. Write or call for a free catalog, which lists upcoming courses and destinations. **Interhostel** takes travelers 50 and over (with companions over 40), and offers 2- and 3-week trips, mostly international. The courses in both these programs are ungraded, involve no homework, and often focus on the liberal arts. They're not luxury vacations, but they're fun and fulfilling.

Publication Discounts for Seniors

The Mature Traveler, a monthly 12-page newsletter on senior citizen travel, is a valuable resource. It is available by subscription ($30 a year) from **GEM Publishing Group,** Box 50400, Reno, NV 89513-0400 (☎ 800/460-6676). GEM also publishes *The Book of Deals,* a collection of more than 1,000 senior discounts on airlines, lodging, tours, and attractions around the country. Another helpful publication is *101 Tips for the Mature Traveler,* available from **Grand Circle Travel,** 347 Congress St., Suite 3A, Boston, MA 02210 (☎ 800/221-2610 or 617/350-7500; fax 617/346-6700).

Although all the **specialty books** on the market focus on the United States, three do provide good general advice and contacts for the savvy senior traveler. Thumb through *The 50+ Traveler's Guidebook* (St. Martin's Press), *The Seasoned Traveler* (Country Roads Press), or *Unbelievably Good Deals and Great Adventures That You Absolutely Can't Get Unless You're Over 50* (Contemporary Books).

Also check out your newsstand for the quarterly magazine *Travel 50 & Beyond.*

STUDENT DISCOUNTS

While students don't qualify for nearly as many price breaks as senior citizens, a few airlines, travel agencies, and associations make it easier for young people to see the world on a shoestring budget.

Delta and **TWA** sell student coupon books, like those available for senior travelers. TWA's book of four coupons costs $548, so you pay under $275 for each round-trip. Delta offers even lower fares, but they're only available on Delta Shuttle flights between Boston, New York, and Washington D.C. A book of four coupons costs $229, and eight cost only $412.

Several airlines also promote special reduced student rates for certain types of travel. **Air Canada** reduces youth fare for standby travel within Canada and to select European destinations. **American Airlines** offers cut rates for college students on the Internet (www.aa.com/college). You must enroll in this program. Once you do, you'll receive email bulletins announcing special student bargains.

Students should also watch for sales on **American West, Continental,** and **Midwest,** as they periodically publish reduced junior fares on select routes.

The best resource for students is the **Council on International Educational Exchange**, or CIEE. Their travel branch, **Council Travel Service** (CTS) (☎ 800/226-8624; www.ciee.com), is the biggest student travel agency operation in the world. They can also set you up with an ID card that will entitle you to other travel discounts. Ask them for a list of CTS offices in major cities so you can keep the discounts flowing (and aid lines open) as you travel.

From CIEE you can obtain the student traveler's best friend, the $18 **International Student Identity Card** (ISIC). It's the only officially acceptable form of student identification, good for cut rates on plane tickets as well as rail passes and other discounts. It also provides you with basic health and life insurance and a 24-hour help line. If you're no longer a student but are still under 26 years of age, you can get a "GO 25" card from the same outfit, which will entitle you to insurance and some discounts, but not student admission prices in museums.

In Canada, **Travel CUTS,** 200 Ronson St., Ste. 320, Toronto, ONT M9W 5Z9 (☎ **800/667-2887** or 416/614-2887; www.travelcuts.com), offers similar services. **Campus Travel,** 52 Grosvenor Gardens, London SW1W 0AG (☎ **0171/730-3402;** www.campustravel.co.uk), opposite Victoria Station, is Britain's leading specialist in student and youth travel.

CHILDREN'S FARES

Although a child over 2 weeks old and younger than 2 years old can ride for free on a parent's lap on domestic flights, your infant will be much safer booked in a separate, discounted seat and secured in an FAA-endorsed restraining device. All major domestic airlines except Southwest now offer 50% off the parent's fare for infant seats (for children 2 years of age or younger, except on Continental, which gives children under three infant discounts or allows them to ride free on their parents' laps), to make it more affordable for you to reserve a separate adjacent seat for your baby and a restraining device.

If a seat adjacent to yours is available, the child can also sit there free of charge. When you check in, ask if the flight is crowded. If it isn't, explain your situation to the agent and ask if you can reserve two seats—or simply move to two empty adjacent seats once the plane is boarded. You might want to shop around before you buy your ticket and deliberately book a flight that's not very busy. Ask the reservationist which flights tend to be most full and avoid those.

On international journeys, children may not ride free on parents' laps. On flights overseas, a lap fare usually costs 10% of the parent's ticket (for each carrier's specific policy, see "Minor Policies of Major Carriers," in chapter 5, "Life Preservers"). Children who meet the airline's age limit (which ranges from ages 11 to 15 years) can purchase international fares at 50% to 75% of the lowest coach fare in certain markets. Some of the foreign carriers make even greater allowances for children.

If a child is traveling alone: Although individual airline policies differ, for the most part children aged five to eleven pay the regular adult fare. They can travel alone as unaccompanied minors on domestic flights only with an escort from the airlines—a flight attendant who seats the child, usually near the galley, where the flight crew is stationed; watches over the child during the flight; and escorts the child to the appropriate connecting gate or to the adult who will be picking up the child. All the domestic airlines but Delta, Northwest, and US Airways charge $30 one way for an escort; Delta, Northwest, and US Airways charge $30 per segment—in other words, $60 one way for a connecting flight. For each airline's specific policy, see "Minor Policies of Major Carriers," in chapter 5.

HELPING THE BEREAVED

Airlines try to ease the pain of death by easing the pain of having to purchase full-fare, last-minute airline tickets. If a family member is ill, you can purchase tickets for travel that day for half the price of a full coach fare. The discounted tickets are fully refundable, unlike most discounted coach fares. The airline will ask you to furnish the name and telephone number of the family doctor involved. In the case of an unexpected death in the family, the airline grants the same discount with the same freedom from restrictions—though in this case you'll be asked to furnish the name and number of the funeral home.

9   ONE-STOP SHOPPING: PURCHASING A PACKAGE TOUR

PACKAGE TOURS ARE NOT THE SAME THING AS ES-corted tours—where you're led around on a bus through activity-packed days spent with strangers. They are simply a way to buy airfare and accommodations at the same time and they can save you a lot of money without costing you your freedom. In many cases, a package that includes airfare, hotel, and transportation to and from the airport will cost you less than just the hotel alone would have, had you booked it yourself. That's because packages are sold in bulk to tour operators—who resell them to the public at a cost that drastically undercuts standard rates.

Packages, however, vary widely. Some offer a better class of hotels than others. Some offer the same hotels for lower prices. Some offer flights on scheduled airlines, while others book charters. In some packages, your choice of accommodations and travel days may be limited. Some packages let you choose between escorted vacations and independent vacations; others will allow you to add on just a few excursions or escorted day trips (also at lower prices than you could locate on your own) without booking an entirely escorted tour. Each destination usually has one or two packagers that are cheaper than the rest because they buy in even greater bulk. If you spend the time to shop around, you will save in the long run. Call the foreign government or state tourist office where you're planning to travel and request a list of tour organizers.

FINDING A PACKAGE DEAL

The best place to start your search is the travel section of your local Sunday newspaper. Also check the ads in the back of national travel magazines like *Arthur Frommer's Budget Travel Magazine* (and its companion Web site, www.frommers.com), *Travel & Leisure*, *National Geographic Traveler*, and *Condé Nast Traveller*.

Liberty Travel (☎ 888/271-1584 for the location of an agent near you; www.libertytravel.com) is one of the biggest packagers in the Northeast; they usually boast a full-page ad in the Sunday papers. You won't get much in the way of service, but you will get a good deal. And even if Liberty doesn't have an office in your area, you can still book vacation packages on its Web site.

American Express Vacations (☎ **800/241-1700;** http://travel.americanexpress.com/travel/) is another option. Check out its **Last Minute Travel Bargains** site, offered in conjunction with **Continental Airlines** (http://travel.americanexpress.com/travel/lmt/), with deeply discounted vacations packages and reduced airline fares that differ from the E-savers bargains that Continental emails weekly to subscribers. **Northwest Airlines** offers a similar service. Posted on Northwest's Web site every Wednesday, its **Cyber Saver Bargain Alerts** offer special hotel rates, package deals, and discounted airline fares.

Another good resource is the airlines themselves, which often package their flights together with accommodations. Fly-by-night packagers are uncommon, but they do exist; when you buy your package through the airline, however, you can be pretty sure that the company will still be in business when your departure date arrives. Among the airline packagers, your options include **American Airlines FlyAway Vacations** (☎ **800/321-2121;** www.aa.com), **Delta Dream Vacations** (☎ **800/872-7786;** www.deltavacation.com), and **US Airways Vacations** (☎ **800/455-0123;** www.usairways.com). Pick the airline that services your hometown most often.

The biggest hotel chains, casinos, and resorts also offer package deals. If you already know where you want to stay, call the resort itself and ask if they offer land/air packages.

10 A LOOK AT THE BUDGET AIRLINES

EVER SINCE THE FAA SHUT DOWN VALUJET, AFTER flight 592 crashed in the Everglades on May 11, 1996, the safety of some of the low-budget carriers has been debated. Often serviced by refurbished planes that major carriers retired from their fleets, these no-frills fliers nevertheless continue to win the endorsements of organizations like

FRUGAL GLOBETROTTING: SAVING ON A ROUND-THE-WORLD FARE

If you want your travels to take you from Kalamazoo to Timbuktu and back, crossing continents and cultures in one trip, purchase your airfare from a consolidator that specializes in round-the-world travel. While many airlines offer budget round-the-world fares, these discounts seldom beat the rates offered by bucket shops that cater to globetrotters—unless you're traveling in business or first class. See "Consolidators," above, to avoid the risks sometimes associated with bucket-shop tickets. One consolidator that earns high marks for its low prices and reliability is **Airtreks** (www.airtreks.com), which offers hundreds of exciting round-the-world itineraries from the West Coast and just as many from the eastern seaboard. You can also custom-design your own round-the-world route on this site. Among their sample fares:

- **$1,050:** San Francisco, London, Bombay, Bangkok, Hong Kong, San Francisco.

Consumer Reports because their very presence at an airport serves to lower fares on even major carriers there.

According to the Department of Transportation, low-fare lines save consumers $6.3 billion per year. Budget carriers are especially valuable to travelers who miss the deadlines for a 14- or 21-day APEX fare or who can't afford to stay in their destination through Saturday night. While cabin service on these flights is scant, and seating tends to be cramped, those willing to forego luxury can snag cheap tickets right up to flight time on AirTran, ATA, CityBird, Frontier, Pro Air, and Spirit. There's also no need to buy a round trip ticket to secure the cheapest fare on these particular lines, and you can stay in your destination for as long or as little time as you'd like.

- **$1,500:** Boston, San Francisco, Hong Kong, Kathmandu, London, Boston.

- **$1,950:** New York, San Francisco, Los Angeles, London, Prague, London, Amsterdam, and London, then overland on your own to Frankfurt, Delhi, Bangkok, Hong Kong, Los Angeles.

- **$2,540:** Honolulu, Tokyo, Hong Kong, Singapore, Bangkok, Kathmandu, Rome, Budapest, Paris, London, New York, San Francisco, Honolulu.

- **$3,310:** New York, Minneapolis, Los Angeles, Santa Barbara, San Francisco, Honolulu, Tokyo, Hong Kong, Bangkok, Denpasar (Bali), Bangkok, Athens, Barcelona, Athens, Tel Aviv, Istanbul, Athens, Barcelona, London, New York.

A standard round-trip fare from San Francisco to New York on ATA can cost as little as $298, with no advance purchase required—compared to $375, the lowest going APEX rate on a major carrier at press time.

The proof is in the industry's defensive reaction to the budgets. Last year, the federal government began investigating the major airlines for anticompetitive practices toward their low-cost competitors. When a budget carrier would enter an airport, it would offer the same routes as major carriers at about half the price. The major airline, in turn, would increase the number of flights on the same route and lower its price to match the competition—just long enough to drive the small line under and restore the initial high fare. In May 1999, the Justice Department sued American for monopolizing business in Dallas/Fort Worth, where the airline managed to drive Vanguard, Sun Jet, and Western Pacific airlines into the ground. American's trial will take place in October 2000, but the Justice Department is continuing its general investigation.

The Department of Transportation created new guidelines for the major carriers and has agreed to fine violators. The DOT also created space for Frontier and AirTran Airways at two of the nation's busiest airports, Dallas/Fort Worth and New York/La Guardia. Frontier now flies non-stop to La Guardia from Denver for $365 round-trip. AirTran flies from La Guardia to Miami for $226 round-trip. New York's JFK just made way for American Trans Air and Sun Country. The formula is successful enough that several major carriers are now operating their own low-budget lines.

Several of the budgets—AirTran, CityBird, Pro Air, and Tower—now offer a premium-class service at far lower rates than the majors' first-class fares. For the most part, frequent-flier miles are unavailable in conjunction with the budgets' cheap rates—though a few budget carriers do participate in a major airline's frequent-flier program (see chapter 7, "Sky Hounds," for details). Here is a sampling of some of the budget carriers that have been in operation for at least one year at press time.

AIRTRAN AIRLINES. (☎ 800/247-8726).

Base: Atlanta.

Destinations: Akron/Canton, Bloomington/Normal, Boston, Buffalo, Chicago Midway, Dallas/Fort Worth, Dayton, Flint, Fort Lauderdale, Fort Myers, Fort Walton Beach, Gulfport/Biloxi, Greensboro/High Point/Winston-Salem, Houston/Hobby, Jacksonville, Knoxville, Memphis, Miami, Mobile, Moline/Quad Cities, New Orleans, New York La Guardia, Newport News, Orlando, Philadelphia, Raleigh/Durham, Savannah, Tampa, Washington D.C. Dulles.

Sample Round-Trip Fares: New York La Guardia to Chicago $239; New York La Guardia to Miami $226.

AMERICAN TRANS AIR/ATA. (☎ 800/225-2995).

Base: Indianapolis.

Destinations: Cancún, Dallas, Dayton, Denver, Des Moines, Fort Lauderdale, Fort Myers, Grand Rapids, Honolulu, Lansing, Las Vegas, Los Angeles, Madison, Maui, Milwaukee, New York JFK, Orlando, Philadelphia, Phoenix, San Francisco, San Juan, Sarasota, Seattle, St. Petersburg.
Sample Round-Trip Fares: Chicago to New York $180; Chicago to Fort Lauderdale $280.

CITYBIRD AIRLINES. (☎ 800/637-4985).

Base: Brussels.

Destinations: Los Angeles, Miami, Oakland, Orlando.
Sample Round-Trip Fares: Brussels to Miami $344.

FRONTIER AIRLINES. (☎ 800/432-1359).

Base: Denver.

Destinations: Albuquerque, Atlanta, Baltimore/Washington, Bloomington/Normal, Boston, Chicago Midway, Dallas/Fort Worth, El Paso, Los Angeles, Minneapolis/St. Paul, New York La Guardia, Omaha, Orlando, Phoenix, Portland, Salt Lake City, San Diego, San Francisco, Seattle.
Sample Roundtrip Fares: Denver to New York $365; Denver to Los Angeles $341.

JET BLUE AIRLINES. (☎ 800/JET-BLUE).

Base: New York JFK.

Destinations: Buffalo, Fort Lauderdale, Tampa (with plans to expand to 10 cities by the end of 2000, and 30 cities thereafter).
Sample Roundtrip Fares: New York–Tampa $79; Buffalo–Fort Lauderdale $188.

NATIONAL AIRLINES. (☎ 888/757-5387).

Base: Las Vegas.

Destinations: Chicago Midway, Dallas/Fort Worth, Los Angeles, Miami, New York JFK, Philadelphia, San Francisco.
Sample Round-Trip Fares: New York to Las Vegas $289; Chicago to Los Angeles $224.

PRO AIR. (☎ 800/939-9551).

Base: Detroit City Airport.

Destinations: Atlanta, Baltimore/Washington Intl., Chicago Midway, Detroit, Indianapolis, New York La Guardia, Newark, Orlando, Philadelphia.
Sample Round-Trip Fares: New York to Chicago $217; Philadelphia to Orlando $257.

SPIRIT AIRLINES. (☎ 800/772-7117).

Base: New York (Islip, La Guardia, and Newark).

Destinations: Atlantic City, Cleveland, Detroit Metro, Fort Lauderdale, Fort Myers, Islip, Los Angeles, Melbourne, Myrtle Beach, Newark, New York La Guardia, Orlando, Tampa, West Palm Beach.
Sample Round-Trip Fares: New York La Guardia to Fort Lauderdale $169.

SUN COUNTRY. (☎ 800/752-1218).

Base: Minneapolis/St. Paul.

Destinations: Boston, Dallas/Fort Worth, Detroit, Fort Lauderdale, Fort Myers, Harlingen (Texas), Houston, Las Vegas, Laughlin (Nevada), Los Angeles, Miami, Milwaukee, New York JFK, Orlando, Phoenix, San Antonio, San Francisco, San Jose (California), Sarasota, St. Petersburg, Washington, D.C Dulles.
Sample Fares: Minneapolis to New York $309; Minneapolis to Orlando $247.

TOWER AIR. (☎ 800/348-6937).

Base: New York JFK.

Destinations: Athens (in summer), Caribbean, Fort Lauderdale, Israel, Las Vegas, Los Angeles, Miami, Paris, San Francisco, Tel Aviv
Sample Round-Trip Fares: New York to Fort Lauderdale $167; New York to Paris $366.

VANGUARD. (☎ 800/826-4827).

Base: Kansas City.

Destinations: Atlanta, Chicago Midway, Dallas/Fort Worth, Denver, Minneapolis/St. Paul, Myrtle Beach, Pittsburgh.
Sample Fares: Chicago to Myrtle Beach $185; Chicago to Denver $180.

9

THE SQUEAKY WHEEL: HOW TO COMPLAIN EFFECTIVELY

Newspapers and television stations around the world have featured scores of accounts of what appears to be an alarming increase in angry passengers who punch, kick, scratch, bite and head-butt airline workers or one another.
—THE NEW YORK TIMES

Air Rage: Anger, on the part of airline passengers, over longer lines, longer delays, and more frequent cancellations caused by increasing air traffic.
—THE NEW YORK TIMES

Employees who "go postal" in the workplace are old news, as are incidents of "road rage," when commuters in congested freeway traffic take their anger and frustration out on other drivers. The latest rage, however, is "air rage." A quick search of recent back issues of *The New York Times* yields more than 300 references to "air rage," referring to the phenomenon where airline passengers go berserk, usually midflight, and lash out at airline employees and occasionally other passengers.

When the term *air rage* was coined in 1997, passenger aggression was largely attributed to overconsumption of alcohol on long flights. In the last year, however, experts are agreeing that passengers are acting out in response to crowded flights, cancellations and delays, bad food, and other evidence of diminished airline service. The U.S. Department of Transportation's log of consumer complaints supports that travelers are more fed up than ever about the service they're receiving—or not receiving—in the air. In just the first 3 months of 1999, Americans registered more than 2,000 complaints with the Department of Transportation regarding airline performance. The rate of complaints per 100,000 passengers nearly doubled from year-end 1998 to just the first quarter of 1999.

Passengers primarily griped about delays, cancellations, and missed connections. Their grumbling extended to cover mishandled baggage, inadequate customer service, ticketing and boarding mishaps, and a host of other issues as well. The three biggest offenders for January to March 1999 were **Northwest,** with 327 complaints for 12,436,457 passengers, or 2.63 gripes per 100,000 fares; **TWA,** with 327 complaints per 5,732,792 passengers, or 2.35 gripes per 100,000 fares; and **American,** with 428 complaints for 18,368,899 passengers, or 2.33 gripes per 100,000 fares.

If you have a grievance yourself, this recent wave of passenger backlash has the industry where you want it, if not penitent, at least certainly unnerved by the realization that service is slipping, and consumers are fighting back. How though, amid the din, can you make sure that your own complaint is heard loud and clear—without losing control and head-butting the flight attendant?

COMPLAINT RANKINGS OF MAJOR AIRLINES

AIRLINE	TOTAL COMPLAINTS FOR 1998	COMPLAINTS PER 100,000 PASSENGERS	
		1998	1997
Northwest	1,117	2.21	1.39
America West	375	2.11	1.51
TWA	309	1.29	0.83
United	1,111	1.28	0.95
American	929	1.14	1.06
Continental	424	1.02	0.77
Delta	835	0.79	0.64
US Airways	490	0.84	0.78
Southwest	147	0.25	0.28
Alaska	71	0.54	0.63

Source: U.S. Department of Transportation Air Travel Consumer Report for 1997 and 1998

1 COMPLAINING 101: HOW TO SQUEAK & GET THE GREASE

1. The minute you feel you've been wronged or deprived of your hard-earned money's worth, **calm yourself.** Instead of blowing up, breathe in deeply, clear your head, and channel your ire into documenting the scene of the crime as exhaustively as possible. Note times, take down names of individuals involved (both those who aggravated and those who attempted to remedy the problem), and request the names and numbers of fellow passengers who may have experienced the same difficulty. If you approach members of the airline staff for immediate assistance and they deny you, get their names. Politely make it clear that you plan to write a letter of complaint when you get home. Hoard more details than you could possibly use in your letter. This way, when you make your case or sit

down to write your letter, the facts will speak more loudly, and far more productively, than your anger.

2. **Try to resolve your dispute before you leave the airport.** The airlines usually keep someone on duty to resolve certain problems on the spot. These employees can usually write checks for small claims or pay denied boarding compensation. If your bags are delayed, you can probably get cash right away to buy some clothes. If you are stranded, you may be able to secure a hotel voucher and have the airline research hotels that offer distressed passenger discounts. You may receive compensation on the spot for damaged luggage as well.

   First try to speak with the airline's shift supervisor or with an employee at the carrier's special services counter, which is usually located in the gate area. If you're still unsatisfied, call the airline's central customer relations number (see "Consumer Contacts for the Major Domestic Airlines," below) and ask where to locate the individual with the highest authority employed by the carrier at your particular airport.

3. **Don't exaggerate the wrongdoing.** The folks in consumer affairs have read many letters like yours and in the process have developed keen "BS" detectors. You don't want to undermine your otherwise valid argument by going overboard. Make sure minor gripes don't obscure the chief grievance you're addressing. Sit on the letter for a day after you've written it and screen for strident sarcasm or unfettered venom. You want to win their sympathy, not inspire them to chuck your letter into the loony bin or the circular file. Let the facts ring out your call for justice.

4. **Clearly state what you expect** as recompense. Again, don't shoot for the stars. Make sure your

expectations are reasonable, and your letter will be taken more seriously.

5. Before you write your letter, **call the airline.** Double check the name of the director of consumer affairs or customer relations and address the letter directly to each of them, with copies to the other. Make sure the letter is typed, brief, and professional. Since airlines hate to lose business travelers, you may want to register your grievance on your company's letterhead.

6. **Do your homework.** Call the airline or check its Web site in advance to investigate the airline's policy regarding your particular grievance. If the carrier violated its own guidelines, which sometimes happens, you may be able to invoke their own rules to make your case.

7. If your complaint regards something you can document with visuals and you have a camera, by all means **snap some photographs on the spot.** Keep copies for your files and enclose the pictures in your letter.

8. At the very least, **be sure your letter covers the basics.** Describe the problem and when, where, and how it occurred. Mention if you lost any money as a result. What have you done about the problem so far? How would you like to see the issue resolved? In other words, what do you think you deserve as recompense and from whom?

9. **Save receipts** for any out-of-pocket expenses you incur as a result of the problem.

10. **Send a copy of your letter and supporting documents** to the following agencies: Department of Transportation, Aviation Consumer Protection Division, 400 Seventh St. SW, Room 4107, Washington, DC 20590 (☎ **202/366-2220** or

202/755-7687); and the Aviation Consumer Action Project, P.O. Box 19029, 589 14th St. NW, Suite 1265, Washington, DC 20036 (☎ **202/638-4000;** www.acap1971.org/acap.html).

These agencies function as ombudsmen. While they can't represent you in court or force an airline to compensate you, they can provide leverage and additional information to help you make your case.

You may want to contact **PassengerRights.com**, a helpful advocacy Web site. Consumers use the site to file complaints, which are forwarded directly to the airline, as well as other "appropriate parties." It's also a good idea to file your complaint with your local member of Congress (☎ **202/ 225-3121**) and a few travel magazines. Be sure to tell the airline you're doing so. Many travel magazines print readers' letters, and the airlines hate bad publicity. *Condé Nast Traveller,* for instance, has a very effective ombudsman column. The ombudsman staff will investigate your claim and, if appropriate, try to use its clout to intervene on your behalf. (***Condé Nast Traveller,*** Ombudsman, 4 Times Square, New York, NY 10036; fax 212/286-2190).

2 HERE COMES THE JUDGE: GOING TO COURT

AS A LAST RESORT, YOU MAY WANT TO FILE YOUR CASE with a small-claims court. Almost all states and localities operate these as a cheap, prompt, and effective means for taxpayers to recover small sums of money without having to hire a lawyer and incur astronomical legal expenses. Be sure the airline knows you plan to follow this course of action. The very threat may prompt the carrier to negotiate to your satisfaction.

If you can demonstrate that an airline owes you money or has harmed you financially, you will have the chance to present your case in person to an impartial judge. Court

IF AT FIRST YOU DON'T SUCCEED...

Persist in your efforts if you don't hear from the airline right away. In June 1999, airlines that belong to the Air Transport Association (see "Air Transport Association Members," in chapter 1, "Ticketing Pitfalls") agreed to draft new customer service policies according to the minimum required by ATA guidelines, which require member airlines to respond to all written complaints within 60 days. The ATA guidelines are not government law, however, so only time will tell how well the airlines live up to their promise.

The Aviation Consumer Action Project says that often an airline will write a magnanimous letter of apology but then offer you less compensation than you requested. If the carrier offers you a ticket rather than cash, it might be wise to accept this payment in the form of services, as it may be worth more than the airline will pay you in cash.

The Aviation Consumer Action Project also recommends that you plead your case to a local television company if you don't receive the desired response from the airline. Consumer complaints make for lively news stories and may force the carrier to take your gripe more seriously.

procedures are usually very simple, informal, and inexpensive. If the judge rules in your favor, he or she can subpoena the carrier and demand remuneration.

WHEN SHOULD YOU SUE?

Small claims court is not an appropriate recourse for every case. The sum of money you seek must be less than the limit established by state or local law. The airline you are suing must do business in the court's jurisdiction. You must have carefully reviewed your contract of carriage with the airline, determined that the airline in fact acted in violation of the agreement, and given the carrier the opportunity and sufficient time to aright the wrongdoing. Be sure that you have communicated your grievance clearly to the appropriate consumer affairs personnel at the airline; saved records of any letters or calls you received in response or made yourself to follow up on your complaint; and allowed the carrier at least a month to respond. On the other hand, don't wait too long to respond or your case may grow too old to stand up in court.

If it seems, after careful consideration, that a judge can help you settle your dispute, check your local telephone directory for the small-claims court number under the city, county, or state listings. A local consumer affairs office, bar association, or attorney general's office should also be able to help you locate the number for the court nearest you. Call or visit the clerk of court's office to confirm that your complaint falls within the court's jurisdiction.

Even if you decide to present your own case, it may be useful to consult with a lawyer briefly beforehand. A local legal aid or legal-services office may provide brief counsel for free, or for a small fee. If you have never appeared in small-claims court, it's wise to attend a session and familiarize yourself with the proceedings before your own court date. Proceedings are open to the public.

YOU'VE GOT A GOOD CASE ON YOUR HANDS

According to the Department of Transportation, consumers received compensation from a small-claims court judge in the following situations. While this doesn't guarantee remuneration, it does suggest that it's worth taking your case one step further if the airline fails to remedy your grievance.

- An airline cancels your connecting flight and arranges to transport you to your destination by van. The van is uncomfortable and takes 4 hours to cover the distance of a 1-hour flight. The airline denies your request that they pay the difference in price between ground and air transportation.

- You purchase a first-class ticket from a consolidator, also known as a "bucket shop." In the mail, however, you receive a coach ticket. The consolidator refuses to refund the difference in fares.

- Your flight is canceled, an alternate flight is not scheduled until the following day, and you're far from home. The airline refuses to reimburse you for a hotel room.

- A carrier loses your luggage. You can prove that the contents were worth far more than the airline compensated you for their mistake.

HOW TO FILE

From state to state, small-claims court procedures vary. While you should certainly call your local court clerk for particulars, a few guidelines should be universally helpful.

- Typically, you will have to **make your complaint either in person or by mail.** In some states, you will have to fill out a standard form to complete this step.

- **Word your grievance clearly.** Name the party you are suing, explain why you are suing, and name the amount you expect to receive. You will be the "plaintiff," and the offending airline will be the "defendant." If your complaint involves a particular employee or employees of the airline, name both the individual(s) and the airline itself as the defendant. Likewise, if the carrier offended another person traveling with you, name that person along with yourself as a second plaintiff.

- When you name your defendant, you must **use the carrier's legal name.** TWA's legal name, for instance, is Trans World Airlines. You must also name the carrier's address within the court's jurisdiction. For this information, call the local Better Business Bureau or the state bureau of consumer protection, listed in the blue pages of the telephone directory, under consumer problems in the human services section.

- You may also have to **pay a small filing fee** to make your claim. These too vary from state to state. If you win your case, some jurisdictions may refund this sum in the amount of your final award.

   After you submit your claim, the court will schedule a hearing date and summon the carrier to send a representative to appear in court that day. The airline does have the right to request a different date. Scheduled court dates are often delayed by the court itself. Once the court confirms a date, you will also be obligated to make a personal appearance that day. You may not handle this stage of the process by mail, and no one may appear in court in your stead unless you have already named that person as a plaintiff in your claim. If the airline does not show up once the court date is confirmed, you will most likely win your case by default.

MAKING A CASE FOR YOURSELF

The court proceedings are usually very simple. A few guidelines will help you make your case optimally effective.

- Arrive at the court on time.

- Bring copies of any documentation that may help you to substantiate your case, such as correspondence with the airline, your ticket and contract of carriage, bills, canceled checks, baggage stubs, written estimates of damages, or photographs of damaged property or goods.

- Prepare a written list of key points you'd like to make from your written statement and rehearse them several times before you relay your story to the judge. Present them politely and briefly.

- Prepare a few key questions for the airlines regarding their actions in your grievance. The judge may ask you to question the airline official directly.

PAYBACK: WHAT HAPPENS IF YOU WIN

IF THE JUDGE DECIDES IN YOUR FAVOR, HE OR SHE will issue an order stating that you have won your case and that the airline or operator owes you money. The judge may allow the defendant to pay you in installments. If you do not receive your money by the date agreed upon, inform the court clerk. The court will not act as a collection agency on your behalf, but can advise you on how to collect.

If the judge decides against your case, you can appeal to a higher court. Ask the court clerk how to proceed. Be aware, however, that an appeal may involve the help of an attorney.

You may also want to consider suing in a higher court with the help of an attorney if: your claim involves a large sum of money; you know in advance the defendant is hiring a lawyer; you fail to collect the money owed you; or you receive notification that you are being sued.

3 CONSUMER CONTACTS FOR THE MAJOR DOMESTIC AIRLINES

THE INFORMATION BELOW WAS CORRECT AT PRESS time; as mentioned earlier, it's wise to check with the airline before sending a letter to make sure the names and addresses haven't changed.

Alaska Airlines
Ms. Valerie Svilarich
Director, Consumer Affairs
Box 68900
Seattle, WA 98168
☎ **206/431-7286;** fax 206/439-4477

America West
Ms. Jill Vicchy
Manager, Customer Relations
4000 East Sky Harbor Blvd.
Phoenix, AZ 85034
☎ **800/363-2542**

American Airlines
Ms. Mary Anne McCabe-Cipperly
Managing Director
Consumer Relations
P.O. Box 619612 M/D 2400
DFW Airport, TX 75261-9612
☎ **817/967-2000**

Continental Airlines
Ms. Judith Mensinger
Director, Customer Care
3663 North Sam Houston Parkway
Suite 500
Houston, TX 77032
☎ **800/932-2732**

Delta Airlines
Ms. Patricia J. Robinette
Director, Consumer Affairs
Hartsfield-Atlanta International Airport
Atlanta, GA 30320
☎ **404/715-1450**

Northwest Airlines
Ms. Cindy Scheer
Director, Customer and Sales Support
5101 Northwest Dr. M/S C6590
St. Paul, MN 55111
☎ **612/726-2046**

Southwest Airlines
Mr. Jim Ruppel
Director, Customer Relations
P.O. Box 36611, Love Field
Dallas, TX 75235-1611
☎ 214/792-4223

Trans World Airlines
Ms. Susan Ahl
Staff VP, Customer Relations
1415 Olive St., Suite 100
St. Louis, MO 63103
☎ 314/589-3600

United Airlines
Ms. Denise Harvill
Director, Customer Relations
P.O. Box 66100
Chicago, IL 60666
☎ 847/700-6796

US Airways
Ms. Deborah Thompson
Director, Consumer Affairs
P.O. Box 1501
Winston-Salem, NC 27102
☎ 336/661-0061

4 ADDITIONAL COMPLAINT & INFORMATION RESOURCES

Consumer Complaints

U.S. Department of Transportation (DOT)
Office of Consumer Affairs
400 7th St. SW
Washington, DC 20590
☎ 202/366-2220
www.dot.gov

Consumer Complaints & Safety Issues

Aviation Consumer Action Project
Box 19029
Washington, DC 20036
☎ 202/638-4000

Consumer Ratings Information

Consumer Reports Travel Letter
Consumer's Union of United States
101 Truman Ave.
Yonkers, NY 10703-1057
☎ 800/234-1970

Legal Action

Travel Law, by Thomas A. Dickerson
Law Journals Seminar Press
345 Park Ave. South
New York, NY 10010
☎ 212/779-9200
Cost: $118

Safety Ratings & Complaints

Federal Aviation Administration (FAA)
800 Independence Ave. SW
Washington, DC 20591
☎ 800/FAA-SURE
www.faa.gov

Consumer Hot Line: ☎ 800/322-7873
Safety Hot Line: ☎ 800/255-1111
Public Affairs: ☎ 202/267-8521

Air Traveler's Association
☎ 800/827-2755 or 202/686-2870
www.1800airsafe.com

Accident Rates

> **National Transportation Safety Board (NTSB)**
> ☎ **202/314-6551**
> www.ntsb.gov

Emergencies Abroad

> **Department of State Overseas**
>   **Citizens Services Office**
> ☎ **202/647-5225**
> http://travel.state.gov

Airline Performance Ratings

> **DOT Bureau of Transportation Statistics**
> ☎ **202/366-3282**

Plane & Estimated Arrival Time Locator

> **FLYTE TRAX**
> www.weatherconcepts.com

Airline Schedules & Seating Arrangements

> **Official Airline Guide**
> ☎ **800/342-5624**
> www.oag.com

Flying with Disabilities

> **U.S. Department of Transportation (DOT)**
> Office of Consumer Affairs
> 400 7th St. SW
> Washington, DC 20590
> ☎ **202/366-2220**
>
> **Society for the Advancement of**
>   **Travel for the Handicapped (SATH)**
> 347 Fifth Ave., Suite 610
> New York, NY 10016
> ☎ **212/447-7284**

Complaints About the Treatment of Pets

U.S. Department of Agriculture
Animal and Plant Health Inspection Service
Regulatory Enforcement and Animal Care
4700 River Rd., Unit 84
Riverdale, MD 20737
☎ **301/734-8645**

Airport Security

Department of Transportation Travel Advisory
☎ **800/221-0673**

INDEX